Lorelei Two

Lorelei Two

My Life
with Conrad Aiken

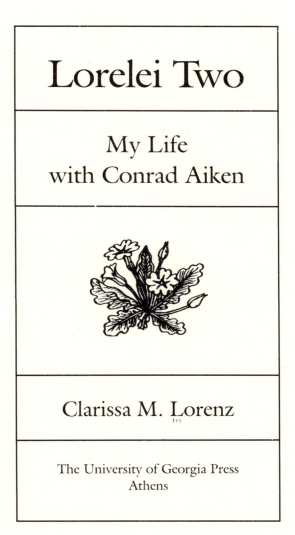

Clarissa M. Lorenz

The University of Georgia Press
Athens

Copyright © 1983 by the University of Georgia Press
Athens, Georgia 30602
All rights reserved

Designed by Sandra Strother Hudson

Set in 10 on 12 Galliard

The paper in this book meets the guidelines for
permanence and durability of the Committee on
Production Guidelines for Book Longevity of the
Council on Library Resources.

Printed in the United States of America

Library of Congress Cataloging in Publication Data

Lorenz, Clarissa M.
Lorelei Two.

1. Aiken, Conrad, 1889–1973—Biography—
Marriage. 2. Authors, American—20th century—
Biography. 3. Lorenz, Clarissa M. 4. Wives—
United States—Biography. 5. Wives—England—
Biography. I. Title.
PS3501.I5Z74 1983   818'.5209   82–17347
ISBN 0–8203–0661–4

For permission to quote from the poems of Conrad
Aiken, the author and the publisher gratefully
acknowledge Oxford University Press, publisher of the
Collected Poems (copyright © 1970 by Conrad Aiken), and
George Braziller, publisher of Thee (copyright © 1967 by
Conrad Aiken). Some of the letters quoted in this book
are from Joseph Killorin's edition of the Selected Letters of
Conrad Aiken (copyright © 1978 by Mary Hoover Aiken
and Joseph I. Killorin) published by Yale University Press.
Other letters, heretofore unpublished, are in the
Houghton Library, Harvard University.

For Katharine Sturgis Goodman

All lovely things will have an ending,
All lovely things will fade and die,
And youth, that's now so bravely spending,
Will beg a penny by and by.

from "All Lovely Things"
by Conrad Aiken

Contents

Acknowledgments

I AM GREATLY INDEBTED to Hamlen Hunt for her tireless efforts in my behalf, to Naomi Lane Babson, whose faith sustained me throughout, to the late Lucille Davis Carver for providing a summer retreat in Maine, to Edzia Weisberg for her generous guidance, and to Robert P. A. Taylor, who supplied data about the Aiken family.

Preface

THE GROUNDHOG saw its shadow today and retreated for another six weeks. I too have been hibernating, though for a longer period, in order to write the story of my marriage to the late Conrad Aiken. Four main reasons account for this memoir:

(1) Conrad left little impression of himself, though he touched the lives of many. (2) I share a sense of historical mission with wives of creative artists and feel that my ten years with Conrad, seven as his wife, belong to posterity, poetry lovers in particular. (3) Adjusting to life with a dedicated man of letters was a unique challenge worth documenting. (4) Some of his best work, as gauged by reliable opinions, was done during my tenure.

As the second of Conrad's three wives, I realize that an ex-wife's reminiscences are apt to paint an incomplete picture. I can only try to do as honest a job as possible. Diaries and letters furnish some of the material. I trust I have salvaged enough to make my saga intelligible. Let future historians judge my presentation of the delights and disasters of life with a genius.

C.M.L.
Boston, 1982

Introduction

S IXTY YEARS after he wrote "The Clerk's Journal" as a Harvard student, the poem was published along with the comments of his teacher, Dean Briggs, in a handsome numbered edition. "Unmistakably the work of a very young man," the author said wryly. Still, publication of the undergraduate poem clearly pleased him. Not long before, he had told an interviewer for the New York *Times*, "It's refreshing to be discovered, even at the age of eighty."

Conrad Aiken died at eighty-four in 1973, the year Governor Jimmy Carter named him Poet Laureate of Georgia. The Savannah-born poet-novelist-critic surpassed most of his contemporaries in prizes and honors: the Pulitzer in 1930, the Guggenheim in 1934, the Bollingen Award in 1956, the gold medal of the National Institute of Arts and Letters in 1958, and the National Medal for Literature in 1969. He was the first of his generation, in 1931, to have a book-length study of his work published, Houston Peterson's *The Melody of Chaos*. Others followed, among them *Conrad Aiken* by Frederick J. Hoffman, who considered him one of the most remarkable figures modern American literature had produced. "The extent and variety of his writings," said Hoffman, "are so impressive as to defy classification."

Conrad bore up stoically under such testimonials as "the best known unread poet of the twentieth century." Anthony Burgess called him the most underrated of American writers. His protégé Malcolm Lowry declared, "Never has such a great author been for so long recognized as such by so many and yet seemingly appreciated by so few." In the poet's own words: "At any given moment in the Pegasus Sweepstakes . . . this dubious horse has always been the last in the list of the also-ran,—he has never even placed, much less won, nor, I regret to report, have the offers to put him out to stud been either remunerative or very attractive."

Conrad's background provides some clues to his critical success and public neglect. His grandfather, Dr. William James Potter, was a radical minister who rejected the dogmas of organized religion and accepted the science of his day, Darwinism in particular. At times he shared his pulpit

in New Bedford, Massachusetts, with Emerson. Defrocked for his controversial views, he founded the Free Religious Association, his loyal congregation following him. The Unitarians caught up with him around 1890
and embraced him.

Conrad never traveled without his grandfather's sermons. His parents
were displaced New Englanders, his Quaker father an eye surgeon who
practiced in Savannah. Dr. William Ford Aiken married his cousin, Anna
Potter. They had four children, Conrad the eldest, a redhead and his
mother's favorite. This grandson of a dissenting minister ran wild with
tough playmates, making the most of freedom from school until his ninth
year. But he was determined to be a poet and nothing but a poet. The
morbid and macabre fascinated him. He explored vaults and tombstones
in an old cemetery and frightened his sister and his brothers with Poe's
horror stories.

Tragedy struck in 1901 when Dr. Aiken killed his wife in a jealous rage
and then shot himself. Conrad, eleven, found his father and mother slain
that February morning. "From then on," he wrote, "they possessed me."
He began a lifelong search for spiritual sustenance other than that provided by institutional religions and their theologies. His sister and two
brothers were adopted by Frederick Taylor, the Philadelphia efficiency
expert. Conrad decided to live with relatives in New England. Removal
there from his childhood home was a shock, but one which enriched the
stock of material the poet would later draw on.

After a year's stay with his mother's great-aunt, Jane Delano Kempton,
in New Bedford, Conrad was placed with an uncle in Cambridge, William
H. Tillinghast, and attended Middlesex School in Concord. He never
mentioned that painful period to me, but I was to learn later of the ordeal
of a sensitive boy being hazed and humiliated.

Life took on a brighter hue at Harvard. The class of 1911 abounded in
future celebrities, pupils ignited by brilliant professors. Elected to the
Harvard Advocate his freshman year, Conrad got an "A" in English 5, a
course he took twice under Dean Briggs. That genius once praised him
for a single line: "And life is paved with cobblestones." Serious study
interrupted such college capers as water-bombing passersby and muffling
the chapel bell. Conrad read Spanish and Italian poets and practiced verse
in various forms—Tuesday the sonnet, Wednesday the villanelle. Whit-
man, like Poe, impressed him deeply, and he swallowed Symons' book on
the Symbolists in one gulp. What fixed his view of poetry, however, was
Santayana's insistence on philosophical content. Poetry had to start with
understanding. Though chosen class poet, he declined the honor, partly
out of shyness. Put on probation in his senior year for cutting classes ten

days to write a poem based on Gautier's "La Morte Amoureuse," Conrad played hooky, touring Europe for six months on a bicycle. Persuaded to return, he graduated with the class of 1912 and a few days later married Jessie McDonald, a Radcliffe student.

He had a faithful friend in T. S. Eliot (Harvard M.A., 1910). Eliot had read "The Clerk's Journal" before writing "The Love Song of J. Alfred Prufrock," published after Conrad brought the manuscript to the attention of Ezra Pound, among others. Touches of Aiken have been detected in Eliot's work, parts of *The Waste Land* suggestive of *The Jig of Forslin* (1916) and *The House of Dust* (1920). "The juices went both ways," said Conrad, indebted to Eliot for his style and the verse symphonies.

They exchanged ideas, experiences, and frivolities—pundits and punsters deploring the modern world while sampling Boston's bars and burlesque shows. From 1914 on, Eliot lived in England, and Conrad moved his family there seven years later. They continued to see each other, though there was a time in the 1920s when Conrad felt that Eliot was keeping him at arm's length. "Eliot and I have always in a curious sense kept our eyes on each other . . . ," he told Houston Peterson, "something analogous to the curious relationship between Melville and Hawthorne." The occasions that brought them together were curtailed somewhat after World War II brought Conrad back to the States from England. But whenever Eliot joined him, he confided in the *Paris Review* (1968), "we invariably met to get drunk together."

In 1927 Conrad briefly returned to Harvard as a tutor. "My tutorial cup runneth over," he wrote me when Nathan Pusey, one of his students, offered him a bootlegger. He admitted having forgotten what his alma mater taught him, with the result that he picked the future university president's brains, distributing the knowledge among the other students.

"All I ever tell young people, who come to me," he said in after years, "is to become expert at the technical part of it." He advised young poets to practice forms without paying any attention to the meaning, so as to familiarize themselves with all the possibilities. "Then when you are ready to say something you have the tools to say it with." He once assigned Malcolm Lowry an exercise writing ten lines of blank verse with the *caesura* changing one step in each line, going forward and then reversing on itself. Lowry sent his mentor a batch written in a bar in Cuernavaca, where he began *Under the Volcano* in 1937. They were "very fine, and very funny," said Conrad. One line he especially liked: " 'Airplane or aeroplane, or just plain plane.' Couldn't be better."

By 1930 we were living in Rye, Sussex. My interview with Conrad for the Boston *Evening Transcript* four years earlier had brought about a change of partners. Jessie married Conrad's friend Martin Armstrong, the British novelist, and I became Conrad's second wife. Jeake's House, a haunt circa 1689, was destined to shelter all three wives.

A purist who would never split an infinitive, Conrad was often mistaken for British because of his Oxonian accent. He didn't look like the sort who wrote what he wrote. His impassiveness annoyed him. He might have passed as a robust, well-scrubbed monk—high forehead, square jaw, ruddy complexion—but no single adjective like bland, serene, innocent described his soul. To identify him as the creator of *John Deth, Forslin*, or *Punch: The Immortal Liar* was to visualize an intoxicated archangel. Malcolm Cowley pronounced him the shyest of men, but also "the best talker." His monologues, said Cowley, were a brilliant mixture of "flagrant wit and complete unself-protective candor." *Time* said he was so withdrawn that Emily Dickinson looked like a publicist by comparison. On one of his many Atlantic crossings he met a bishop who asked his name. "Aiken," said Aiken. "And what is your line, Mr. Aiken?" "Blank verse" was the answer.

Conrad favored tweeds but bought few clothes, never wore gloves, carried a stick, seldom went to tea or formal dinner, refused to dance, was a baseball and bullfight fan, and a knockout at croquet, once going through all the wickets in one turn. A former member of the Harvard tennis team, he covered the Wimbledon matches for the *New Yorker*. His London Letter as correspondent described the King's demise in January 1936. "When I reported the death of George V and Rudyard Kipling under the title, 'Kiplings and Kings depart,' the English became infuriated and I got fired. I still remember walking the two miles over Vauxhall Bridge to the House of Parliament with the mourners. But they didn't appreciate my mentioning the knitting needles that clicked as the people waited to pass the King's bier."

His working habits changed little during my tenure. He loved to sit up all night discussing profundities with cronies. It took him a long time to settle down to work. Brooding about his next book, he paced the floor to Mozart or Beethoven, smoking a pipe or cigarette. He did not subscribe to clipping services, or own a complete shelf of his works. In fact, he took violent dislikes toward some of his writings, even blasting an Aiken volume anonymously for a Chicago paper. Imaginative power and an innate critical sense spared him the drudgery of revision. He made just one rough draft of his prose. His first volume of short stories, *Bring! Bring!* (1925), went off exactly as written. Each one subsequently reached the publisher after one unrevised typing. "A great labor-saving device—with some risks," he added, "because if you lost a copy in the mails it was gone! . . . I never used a carbon because that made me self-conscious."

His poems were penciled in exercise books until the 1920s, when he switched to the typewriter for more legibility—a great boon for me, his typist. Revision might take days. Twenty versions of one poem wasn't uncommon. Some, rejected, were later restored to favor. That crumpled ball in the wastebasket might need only a twist. Then again, other poems came like lightning. "Blues for Ruby Matrix" seized him at lunch one day. He said afterwards that it wrote itself.

I admired Conrad's ability to concentrate. When carpenters invaded Jeake's House in 1930–31, he worked at the dining room table, impervious to interruptions, turning out Preludes by the dozen. Some of them appeared in the *New Yorker*. He regarded those 159 Preludes in *Memnon* (1931) and *Time in the Rock* (1936) as central, a new direction. "The time of genius," said Professor Hoffman. Yet *Memnon* sold only about seven hundred copies in three years. Reflecting on the tepid reception, I wrote in my diary: "He feels he must begin his career all over. In America he enjoyed a modest reputation and was considered an important poet. Here in England he's practically unknown, and the public indifference makes him bitter." The sweet uses of adversity were beyond his reach. Misfortune smothered the spirit, blighted creativity. His suicide attempt in 1932 was logical enough.

In prose works, Conrad evoked more response. "The gentle ironist charms in his short stories," I reported in the *Transcript* (1928). "He isn't nearly as inaccessible or doleful as his poetry paints him. He spins tales with a raconteur's verve and wide range, now dour, now teasing, now fanciful. His integrated mind is his slave. He remembers dreams vividly. They stand out like daily events, rich and alive." Pieces intended as pot-boilers emerged as finely crafted work more suitable for *The Dial* or *Criterion*. His etherealized stories tantalized readers by seeming to extract their own secrets. A few stories burgeoned into classics. "Mr. Arcularis," a macabre number, was revamped as a drama and played London and Washington. "Spider, Spider" is an autobiographical incident about a Don Juan seduced; "Silent Snow, Secret Snow," a projection of his inclination to insanity, has been televised and often reprinted.

Conrad interspersed short stories with novels—*Blue Voyage* (1927), *Great Circle* (1933), *King Coffin* (1935), *A Heart for the Gods of Mexico* (1939), *Conversation* (1940)—and *Ushant* (1952), a memoir. When *Blue Voyage* arrived at Scribner's, Maxwell Perkins was puzzled. An unfinished stream-of-consciousness novel? Even so, he thought, "it is amazing, and we'll take it at that," and he said so. A few days later Conrad's agents delivered the last segment, which had somehow been mislaid, and Scribner's published the complete novel. After reading it, Malcolm Lowry, nineteen and not yet published, crossed the Atlantic, compelled to meet the author. Twenty years later, Max Perkins dismissed rumors relayed by Malcolm's second wife that *Blue Voyage* was an imitation of *Ulysses*. "No, it was never an imitation of Joyce. . . . Conrad had been investigating the vein in which it lies long before Joyce. . . . Way back in his beginning he had been conscious of what Joyce later became conscious of, because of the events in his life and the revelations of modern psychology. He never was an imitator, nor could have been."

Blue Voyage fared better than *Great Circle*. That sold twenty-six copies in the second half year of publication, though "written with perfect taste and an astonishing verbal felicity," to quote Aldous Huxley. Freud reportedly kept a copy in his waiting room while studying the author's psyche. Hilda Doolittle, a patient of Freud in 1933, wanted Conrad to take her place in Vienna as one of the coterie practicing reciprocal analysis, but the master's illness scotched that plan. Just as Freud and Jung influenced Conrad, so he influenced numerous novelists by his technique.

His other novels suffered much the same drought. Hailed by some critics as the only major poet of the century, he did not escape fame altogether, but in the academic lottery Conrad largely drew a blank. As a rule, his work was deemed unsuitable for college students. To be sure, poets are not honored in America, as Stanley Kunitz has reminded us. At best they're given a bust in a niche—this pointed out, along with the quadratic formula and the Pragmatic Sanction, as students troop by on the yellow brick road leading to a degree.

Even so, Conrad's obscurity has puzzled many. There were, in my view, a number of factors that contributed to the paradox. He was a writer's writer, "a hellish highbrow," too difficult and serious for the average reader. There's too much analysis for his own good and the reader's. I cited Louis Untermeyer, the chief literary coroner, in my *Transcript* interview. He called Conrad one of the finest verbal musicians, but one whose poems lose their vitality in being made to conform as symphonies. And even the beauty of sound was compromised by an air of futility. "Sometimes querulous, more often resigned, this weariness . . . records itself in his very titles . . . Even a book of critical essays frightened off a yea-loving public by calling itself 'Scepticisms.' Like most introspectives, Aiken lives almost solely in the past, retreating into himself." Where few could follow him. The Freudian permitted working out a neurosis expressed in words, but only with contempt. He foresaw a decline of the arts and their eventual extinction, once man has learned to live more happily.

"Hordes of critics have turned up their noses at the lack of structure in my narrative verse," he said in rebuttal, "blind to the fact that a picture of consciousness is essentially fluid and fragmentary. I'm torn because I have to battle with the scientist in me, which is hostile to creative fiction, because I've come under the shadow of modern psychology and can't quite adjust art to a place in society. Of course the whole Freudian idea may be wrong. Art may be a permanent necessity for man, a penalty he pays for having become a social and civilized animal."

At any rate, Conrad thought Untermeyer had missed the point. "Louis is a rather simple soul," and a menace, he told a reporter decades later. "His tag has persisted for 40 years, his judgment handed down from generation to generation. This has prevented readers from coming upon me fresh and without preconceptions." His poetry wasn't difficult to understand, he said. In fact, it was quite easy. Young people had begun to discover him. "These young people, I think, are interested in my freewheeling attitude to life, my skepticism, my belief that there are no final solutions, that things may have no meaning and that we've got to face that possibility all the time. Everything is in a sense reversible."

Including his life style, and this is reflected in his work. New England served as one spiritual pole, the South the other, forcing a life of uneasy perpetual motion on him. Admittedly it allowed him to stay forever on the floor of his nursery in Savannah's historic Marshall Row, reading poetry. But a transient searching for his roots hardly satisfies the woman who dreams of a home with "roses peeping in and babies peeping out." He pined for America when in England and for England when in America, delighted by the British flair for conversation and other attractions. He couldn't resist the pretty girl who described herself as a "pièce de non-résistance."

An undoubted Anglophile, Conrad, but "the history and landscape of Puritan America in his bones created his most distinguished poetry," observed Julian Symons in a BBC program called "The Poetry of Conrad Aiken," a transcription of which appeared in a special Conrad Aiken number of *Wake* in 1952. "Yet the other side of his writing is more important, and developed first—the side that made him brood over Poe's tales of horror among the Savannah tombstones, that is profoundly aware of change, decay, and the vanity of human wishes, that explores the violence of dreams through appropriate psychoanalytic symbols."

Unquestionably more important, but still unpalatable to the public at large. He who travels with a death's-head as companion travels alone. Conrad wavered between the sensuous and the intellectual, between a romantic's upbeat and a realist's downbeat. " . . . Take the sun / Between your hands like a ball of flaming crystal, / Poise it to let it fall, but hold it still, / And meditate on the beauty of your existence; / The beauty of this, that you exist at all."—*Chiaroscuro: Rose.* " . . . Cry death cry death / we come into the world / kicking and screaming / we go out of the world / kicking and screaming / and all between / is but / scheming / and / dreaming / and / seeming."—*Thee.*

The human scene is mostly a theme for somber reflection to Aiken. Few authors have written more poetry devoted to soul-searching, said the late John Holmes, his former pupil. "The poetry is a sensuous catalogue that celebrates and laments as it itemizes. Time itself, and our lives in time floating and turning, is the subject." He descends into passionate mysticism, into a fantastic key that knows no signature. Houston Peterson's book *The Melody of Chaos* traces the poet's obsession with death and decay. In *The Charnel Rose* (1918) he aspires to the stars, but in *Senlin* (1925) he hammers away at the destruction of beauty, illusion, love; death ever approaching. In *The Pilgrimage of Festus* (1923) his hero dances a tarantella with madness on the brink of the abyss, deriving ultimate satisfaction from the dissection of a beautiful girl.

As for "Voyage to Spring," a poem blending idealism and cynicism, I wouldn't recommend it to honeymooners:

> . . . Useless to remind the lovers
> while still they are locked in undivided delight
> in their self-woven chrysalis of night
> that this is not an end or a beginning
> nor a single birth nor a single death nor climax
> nor an exploration nor a discovery nor a voyage
> but the gross usufruct, indifferent and mechanical,
> automatic as the bursting of a seed-pod,
> of life itself, the source and sink of all.
> Useless, too, to tell oneself. One looks and envies,
> one listens and envies, longing only again to know
> the accelerated heartbeat, the blind passion to touch,
> the inexhaustible need for surrender, the suffocation
> of anguish that one feels in separation,
> and the unappeasable suffocation of desire
> of each to be incorporated in the other.
> False, false, false, all of it false,
> the necessary inevitable illusion, chromatic deception
> of the vernal and venereal equinox: the mere rubescence
> of old whore earth in the spring.
>
> *Collected Poems*

Aiken shrank from promoting himself. His whole life was devoted to his own genius, as one critic noted. He made no effort to polish his image; he forbade the reprinting of one of his most popular early poems because he detested it. He was known to pay a price for sticking to writing, and writing only what he believed in. His only profession of being a poet was a rarity. "He is one of the few genuine men of letters left in our world today," Allen Tate said in 1952. Robert Frost was allegedly a farmer, Wallace Stevens had a job in an insurance office, L.E. Sissman wrote advertisements. Conrad held four jobs briefly: tutor at Harvard, London correspondent for the *New Yorker* (he wrote under the name Samuel Jeake, Jr.) contributor to the Federal Writers' Project, and Consultant in Poetry at the Library of Congress.

Lest his father's insanity doom him, too, he lived his life offstage, behind the scenes, remote whether in Savannah, Boston, Cambridge, Rye, Cape Cod, or Manhattan. He never lifted a finger (except at the typewriter) to advance his own reputation. Throughout the Depression we lived on gifts and loans and paying guests like Malcolm Lowry. Conrad submitted to interviews but confessed relief when they were over. He let his books speak for themselves; no autograph parties, TV appearances, lecture tours, or readings (only on tape), no plugging his name—just once, I believe, endorsing an opera singer in the *New Yorker*. In the 1960s he turned down a generous offer to advertise a commercial product.

All this exclusiveness frustrated publishers. Women's clubs and similar groups of bookbuyers wanted to see and hear their author. But sneers and jeers came from several sources. When Conrad began wintering in Savannah, the late Flannery O'Connor wrote her friends Sally and Robert Fitzgerald, "Apparently he serves the interviewers martinis in frosted silver goblets, and I guess this encourages the trade." With the publication of *Ushant* she exulted to a reviewer, "I think you have nailed the lid on his box. He makes me sick just to read about . . . " Had the antifeminist got under her skin?

While Conrad longed for success but sought obscurity, the literary critic stood firm, thereby jeopardizing his career by his uncompromising integrity. "He was the perfect reviewer," Marianne Moore recalled in *Wake*, "Diogenes' one honest man, fearing only to displease himself; determined before pronouncing, to have read everything pertaining to the subject in question, and by the subject . . . " With unerring judgment he exposed flaws such as meager intellectual or subconscious substance. His waspish pen once defined Alfred Kreymborg's verse in *Mushrooms* as "the poetic paraphrase of the lisp and coo." Examined in the harsh light of a perfectionist, offended authors panned him in turn as "decadent, derivative, and fabricating enervated music," the poeticizing "too damned beautiful." *Blue Voyage* was termed the Harvard Square *Hamlet*. Close friends, including John Gould Fletcher and T. S. Eliot, had their innings. One day while Conrad was lunching with Eliot in London, Eliot remarked gravely, after the duo voiced their dislike of certain poets and others in the arts, "Literary people are shits!" Conrad, recalling the scene in a letter, added, "He said a mouthful. I recognized myself instantly."

Louise Bogan, his sparring partner for a time, never forgave him for describing her in his novel *Conversation* as an unseen but audible character playing the piano, now "ploughing through a Chopin Etude," now tackling Gershwin's *Rhapsody in Blue*, which she "played languishingly, sentimentally, heavily." Louise had her revenge in the *New Yorker*, reviewing his novel about her young friend John Coffey, an Irish Robin Hood who stole and gave to the poor. Malcolm Cowley chided her for malice, and she admitted mentioning the horrid things Conrad did just to show he wasn't above a little envy and malice himself. "Actually, what has Aiken got to kick about?" she wrote Cowley. "He was off in Deakes [Jeake's] House, Rye, Sussex, for *almost 20 years*, meanwhile getting all the American honors: Pulitzer, Guggenheim, etc.—I have been sitting right here in New York, and did anyone ever invite *me* to join the A. Academy of Arts and Letts?" Of the likes of this, Cowley commented sadly, "Maybe she thought all passion was spent before she wrote reviews of his works, but not quite, not quite."

Other critics became upset whenever a new Aiken volume appeared for the public to ignore. Winfield Townley Scott was grieved that so prestigious a writer was still less honored, and above all less read than he deserved to be. Malcolm Lowry once said (tongue in cheek?) that Conrad never intended being other than unhelpful. The first to commend Faulkner's sense of character, style, and humor, Conrad also helped put Emily Dickinson before the public, it is thought, with the edition of her poems that he edited in 1924. Many young aspirants are today beholden to him. He answered all appeals, though once duped by a prankish friend into sending a "poor farmer lad" advice. Conrad even threw in a copy of the *Golden Treasury*.

Ushant gave snipers a field day. Lewis Gannett took a high moral tone in the *Herald Tribune*: "Mr. Aiken cannot bring himself to say 'I'. He is a third-person 'D' throughout. His three wives appear as Lorelei One, Lorelei Two, and Lorelei Three, but he is less explicit about them than about the 'Loreliebchen' of whom he boasts." The New York *Times* reviewer said, "It would have been better for Mr. Aiken, a Conrad in quest of his youth, to have followed Gertrude Stein's lead . . . and speak out in plain English. If he had done that . . . he would have done a greater service to the cause of the poet in America."

Conrad began *Ushant* in 1934, though he wrote half of it later, while at the Library of Congress. The title is a pun on Isle d'Ouessant off Brittany, a notorious hazard to navigation; he made it a symbol of danger to the spiritual-physical voyager. I found his literary odyssey heavy going without a dictionary. "Identifications are not made explicit," one critic objected, "because of reticence about specific events like his parents' violent death." There are both amusing and painful vignettes of celebrities, among others Eliot, John Gould Fletcher, Phyllis Bottome, Malcolm Lowry, Rupert Brooke, Virginia Woolf, and Katherine Mansfield. The latter two exchanged superficial pleasantries at a luncheon of the Bloomsbury set while harboring murder in their hearts, as Conrad discovered later.

The 1950s, 1960s, and 1970s were kinder to him. A character in Paddy Chayefsky's *Marty* remarked, "Boy, that Conrad Aiken, he sure could write!" As the poet himself put it, "It is the answer that no question asked." His brother Rob once visited him when the postman brought a handsome royalty check from a paperback publisher. Conrad tossed it on the desk after a cursory glance, without comment.

At age eighty he gave the New York *Times* a gloomy picture of the American literary scene. The state of poetry? "It has come to a temporary pause." Wallace Stevens was our last great poet, and he died in 1955. He thought Robert Lowell "greatly overestimated." As for Allen Ginsberg, "I don't care for him at all." He had no better word for the fiction writers. "I think we're going through a very depressing decline in taste, which is on all levels everywhere. I don't think there is any first-rate fiction, and I mean to include everybody in that—Nabokov, Bellow and so on . . . nor are any of the current novelists as good as they think they are."

Conrad had formulated a view of poetry as the one tenable or viable religion. "Evolving human consciousness gives all that man could possibly require in the way of a religious credo. When the half gods go, the gods arrive: man can, if only he will, become divine." He regarded himself as an extension of his grandfather, a teacher-preacher distributing knowledge in poetic terms, the news of the world. His cherished friend and admirer Dr. Henry A. Murray said Amen to that. "What the profound poet feels and perceives today, Everyman will feel and perceive tomorrow or several generations hence."

Acclaim if not fame made a delayed appearance though marred by Conrad's illness. The last major poem, *Thee*, summarized his beliefs in a deity, "The Supreme Consciousness," a philosophy akin to Emerson's Transcendentalism. Total awareness meant suffering and offering oneself as a secular Christ in an anxiety-burdened crucifixion. "Poets are the indispensable evolutionary fuglemen of mankind, the extenders of awareness, and therefore of control, and therefore of wisdom." He elaborated on that in a letter to Fletcher: " . . . I see him [the poet] as the advancing consciousness and conscience and genius of mankind, the forerunner, firebringer, orderer and releaser; the one who by finding the word for life makes life possible and coherent, and puts it within the reach of all. The

scientist and philosopher and mathematician do not make *whole* state-
ments, because they leave out the feelings; it is only the poet who, by
adding the feelings, or rather by transmuting his knowledge *through* the
feelings, makes, at each stage of man's development, the *whole* statement;
he always has the last word, because it is always the first—the poet was
and is the one who invents language. Which is tantamount to inventing
experience, or awareness."

A poet's real importance lies in the rhythms he creates, said the late
Marshall MacLuhan, rather than the ideas or opinions he propounds. The
rhythms exert a terrific impact on people. Malcolm Cowley's "buried giant
of American writing" may yet be heard from. Conrad Aiken knew terror,
guilt, and despair, and he struck out forcefully when ignored. His ideas
are no rehash of old myths catering to weakness and superstition. I found
his *Selected Letters*, posthumously published, rich in drama, wit, and wisdom. He "bangs out letters . . . in such fresh, delicious, and clairvoyant
words and phrases," said Harry Murray, "that the effect is hardly distin-
guishable from that of verse." They revealed the Conrad I knew far more
vividly than any of his books—and also a Conrad I had overlooked. They
should be required reading for all generations.

Part One

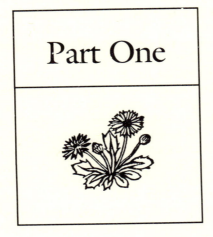

MY HEART still skips a beat, after more than half a century, whenever I pass his uncle's house in Cambridge. What Conrad called "the fatal interview" took place in 1926. He was thirty-seven, ten years my senior. A major American poet grossly neglected, said Dr. Henry A. Murray, my number two boss at the Harvard Psychological Laboratory. Harry suggested I do a profile of Aiken for the Boston *Evening Transcript*, but I'd have to hurry, he was soon returning home to England.

The night after Halloween I set out from my lodgings in a drizzle. Just another assignment, I thought, having interviewed several authors. But this was my first poet, and he just a name to me. Bards were beyond my ken. I lumped them together as exalted beings, libertines, topers, and lunatics (Swinburne dancing naked before the mirror). Oh well, we could always play tiddledywinks! At the red brick house on Fayerweather Street I passed through a high iron fence, furled my umbrella, and pressed the bell. My life took an unexpected turn as the door opened on a robust figure in brown tweeds. "Good of you to come, Miss Lorenz, in this murky weather," he said, taking my raincoat and umbrella.

The faint tremor and British accent in the resonant voice paralyzed my reflexes. I sat opposite him in the living room, hoping that my blue serge with the white piqué collar and cuffs looked professional enough. ("I see you again," he was to write later, "sitting rather primly on my Aunt Edith's red leather sofa, notebook in hand, punctuating every other sentence with a 'sir'! Heavens heavens heavens heavens. Every night I dream things more rational.")

We exchanged surreptitious glances. Was he here on business? That's right. To sell his first novel, *Blue Voyage*, a four-year stint, the action compressed into four days on an Atlantic liner, an analysis of love and the self with Oedipal overtones, death as a condition of life, but all of life revolving around the business of falling in love. That phrase shattered me. I scanned my shorthand notes: "Born 1889, Savannah; educ. N.E., Middlesex and Harvard; President Hvd. Advocate; grad. 1911, class poet; author nine vols., poetry incl. Senlin, Festus, Nocturne."

"What brought you North for your education?" I asked. He dodged the question. His Uncle Alfred, librarian at the Widener, would give me personal data. What lay behind that mask? Shy, austere, more like a parson than poet, he sat smoking a cigarette, his reddish hair catching the glow of the open fire. He had great presence, said much without speaking. I recognized an aristocrat and genius.

My flounderings amused him. What I knew about poetry would fill a thimble. Some childhood episode must have conditioned me against the metrical form. I caught the imagery but missed the concept and meaning. At least I no longer believed poems were something you wrote in adolescence or outgrew with the measles. During the First World War Conrad, a pacifist, had convinced his draft board that poetry was an essential profession.

He had an evocative way of talking, and I, spellbound, could never get the words, ideas, and delicately balanced phrases down on paper. From my scribbled notes I must have asked fairly sensible questions at first. When had he begun writing poetry? Around age nine, he replied, inspired by an epigraph in *Tom Brown's School Days*: "I'm the Poet of White Horse Vale, Sir,/ With liberal notions under my cap." He wrote the poems in lined exercise books, in pencil, working them over twenty times if need be. Prose was done directly on the typewriter after mental revision. Once on paper, the words couldn't be examined critically. He was apt to revise out essentials and lose his sense of values. With few exceptions, the first draft was the last. No corrections? I asked. None. He did those in his head while ideas were still fluid.

What magic! My heart swelled. I had an elaborate set of defenses against poetry, but none against poets. We gazed at each other during eloquent silences, his blue eyes behind black-rimmed glasses probing like klieg lights. Everything he said seemed an invitation, everything on my part acceptance. I then touched a raw nerve, quoting from his popular poem from "Discordants": "Music I heard with you was more than music/ And bread I broke with you was more than bread." Had his wife or a lady love inspired that? He detested it, he said. Trite stuff. "I'll never live it down," and he tossed his cigarette in the fire to light another. (The poem was reprinted so often that he finally stopped giving permission.)

"Some of my work I dislike intensely," he said. "I once wrote a scathing review of *Nocturne* for a Chicago paper. Louis Untermeyer criticizes my work for its air of futility—'the cult of chaos,' but the human psyche *is* chaos. Sorrow cancels out joy."

That philosophy contradicted my grandparents' *"Durch Leiden, Freude."* Furthermore, "Through sorrow, joy" suited my present dilemma. "Only a simpleton portrays life in depth with any optimism," he was saying. "A

poet is defeated by his very nature, recording human emotions honestly. There's little demand for a psychoanalytic bard in our culture, but since I believe a poet should unmask I keep on writing about my inner world, hoping to produce a complete portrait of a mind." He was to create a brilliant literature of *memento mori*, human awareness mediating between living and dead matter, a belief in the evolving consciousness as the only philosophical order.

I remember fielding personal questions, except for one or two. "I hope I haven't bored you," he said, pacing the room, hands in trouser pockets and studying me intently. "Sometimes I allow rhetoric to run off with me, like Sergius, who discovered he was six people, in *Arms and the Man*, and never knew which one was on duty. Suppose I hear from you for a change." He asked about Milwaukee, why I came to Boston, why Harry Murray called me Jerry, a nickname I never outgrew. I told him that it originated with a wild, skittish pony in our neighborhood. *How* wild was I? "Oh, I used to shin up trees, hitch rides on wagons and pungs, mimic Papa's walk, break his mustache cup, rollerskate in the attic on rainy days." Terrible, terrible, he grinned. "I always hated my given name. So German." "German?" he echoed, cocking an eyebrow. "On the contrary, it's English. Haven't you read Richardson's *Clarissa Harlowe*?" No, I said, we spoke German at home until I rebelled. English was a second language.

He never cracked a smile when I asked whether poets ever thought in rhyme, merely said, "You must be pulling my leg. Probably bored? I'm easily bored. I once unhinged my jaw while yawning. Very painful. Would you like some claret?" No, it was late and I must be going, I murmured, making no move. But he had much more to tell me about his work. "Besides, I'd like to know you better, if you don't mind." Mind? "Far from it. I do need more copy." And after all I had come as a reporter, not a fan.

"Shall we *dis*continue the interview tomorrow over dinner at the Greek's?" He helped me into my raincoat. "We could meet around six at the Touraine." I nodded and shook his hand. He held mine until reminded that I needed it for typing and piano practice. "Oh, you play, too?" In a way.

Dazzled, I walked out into the foggy night, restraining a mad impulse to shout "I'm in love" from the housetops. What G. B. Shaw called lunacy. Please don't let him be married, please, God. One minute I felt like a balloon about to burst; the next minute I began crying.

Pumpkins grinned mockingly from the doorsteps on my way to Avon Hill Street; soaped windows proclaimed yesterday's hallowed eve. The lights in Harvard's observatory on Concord Avenue brought twinges. Was my Russian beau, Paul, there, searching the heavens for the asteroid he promised to name after me, while I, fickle one, wondered if a certain red-haired poet was conceivably falling for me?

2

MORNING DAWNED newly minted; people, trees, houses were touched with Halloween magic, even that mad whirligig, Harvard Square. The sight of Conrad's name in the card catalogue at Widener gave me a *frisson*. I left with several Aiken volumes.

Climbing to the third floor of Emerson Hall, that ivy-clad haven of philosophers, I sat down at the typewriter and began transcribing last night's shorthand notes, when Harry Murray's vibrant voice broke in. "Well, Jerry, how did it go?" He beamed at me from the doorway. "You look absolutely transfigured. Nothing in the world like it, is there!" Like what?

He vanished with a wink before I could ask. Had he *expected* a romance? My imagination took flight. What more sublime mission than to serve the muse, become another Beatrice or a second Dark Lady? Meanwhile, how live until six? Dr. Morton Prince's lecture awaited typing. It described a woman with a triple personality he had hypnotized and demonstrated in class—housewife, prostitute, and opera singer, her case history probably to be published in his *Journal of Abnormal Psychology.*

I sailed through my duties with blithe disregard of the memo on my Underwood: "Stop, Look, Listen!" Whenever the eminent neurologist lost his temper, he became my father blasting me for a *Schwindelkopf.* The resemblance between the two men was chilling. At five-thirty I flew to the subway, previewing a romantic idyll while telling myself this was business.

Fantasy took over in the subway, I applying for a lifelong job: "Can you cook?" Well, I'm a short-order cook. "How about housekeeping?" There I get around fast. "Do you go into a funk in emergencies?" Try not to. "Do you like children?" Yes, yours definitely. "Are you good in bed?" That remains to be seen.

The Touraine's carpets, springy and mosslike, reinforced the illusion of walking on air. I waited in the lobby, fussing with gloves, veil, mesh bag, notebook. I wore my best hat, a brown velour with an orange feather. A touch of lemon verbena on my coppery satin-back dress counteracted the camphor smell from the muskrat jacket. Rice-powder, lipstick, nail polish; everything but mascara.

Nonchalance forsook me when Conrad appeared in a Burberry and fedora. How *dégagé*, I thought, when he drummed shyly on his hat brim by way of salutation. Walking to Stuart Street, he shortened his stride to suit mine. What were my thoughts last night going home? I wondered aloud if he could be falling for me. His lopsided smile melted my heart, causing that well-known flutter.

At the Greek's I caught sight of us in the mirror at the head of the high marble staircase—a weird sensation, I radiant, glowing like a 100-watt light bulb. The Athens-Olympia is still a favorite haunt of Harvard men. It has survived the incursions of progress, though chairs replace those high-backed wooden booths unyielding as church pews.

Conrad ordered shish kebab for two, a retsina, and milk for me. A poet should always be hungry, I read somewhere, or have a lost love. He, being well fed, wouldn't qualify for the first test; as for the second, I couldn't say. "I miss my dry martinis," he remarked after the waiter brought our drinks. "Damn Prohibition."

"Try milk for a change." I raised my glass. "Here's cow!"

He grinned. "You make me feel clumsy and stupid, and I want desperately to please you."

"Now you're pulling my leg," I said. "*I'm* the inarticulate one, stammering and wallowing in ignorance. What little I read of *The Charnel Rose* was way over my head, for instance."

"Oh don't give up," he said. "Keep exposing yourself to all kinds of poetry." Unskewering the lamb brochette with fastidious fingers, he asked about my history, the blue eyes quizzical. I said I was just an ear, and plied him with questions. He parried some, feeding me only morsels such as having two younger brothers and a sister, playing with tough kids in Savannah, and once rescuing a stranded cat from a telegraph pole.

"Evidently you're a cat lover," I said. "I'm a dog lover. The bottom dropped out of my world when I lost my collie in Boston. How about your experiences at Harvard? I understand the class of 1911 included several authors—Eliot, Lippmann, Broun, Benchley, Cummings."

Visibly relieved, he described meeting Eliot in his freshman year, dining at the same table in Memorial Hall. Actually, he said, they weren't in the same class—Tom Eliot was ahead of him. What was he like? "A wonderful fellow. Marvelous sense of humor. We were both addicts of the comic strips, made the rounds of bars and burlesque shows, talked about everything from free verse to love and human folly. After I moved to England we met less often."

In his senior year, Conrad said, he was put on probation for cutting classes ten days in order to write a poem based on Gautier's "La Morte Amoureuse." "That angered me so much that I quit college and went abroad for six months, bicycling through Italy and Switzerland. Fortunately Uncle Alfred persuaded me to return and graduate. Harvard had outstanding teachers—Briggs, Kittredge, Santayana, Copeland. When Copey asked what I got out of the course, I said, 'Well, it made me write regularly.' He called me a very dry young man. Santayana was a far greater teacher. He had me write a poem a day, each one a different form."

With the baklava and Turkish coffee we had poetic dreams. Conrad said he once dreamt a couplet: "Choose distant objects for your adoration / For near things move, but far things know their station." He asked if it didn't sound like Shakespeare, and I said, "Yes, *isn't* it?" switching from fork and spoon to pencil throughout the meal. His reserve intrigued and maddened me. Again he referred me to his uncle for biographical material, then begged me to throw him a bone. "Harry Murray tells me you're quite versatile—pianist, journalist, athlete."

I sketched my inglorious past. "Father and I got along like flint and tinder. One day on a wager I masqueraded in my brother's suit and asked for myself, ringing the front doorbell. Father went through the house calling 'Clarissa,' then returned saying she wasn't at home. 'Isn't she?' He was dumbfounded when I whipped off my cap and shook my hair loose. 'What kind of a woman will you turn out to be, parading around town in knickers?' Mother assured him that the worst hoydens sometimes became the best housewives."

"What would she say now?" he asked. When I said she had died early— I eleven at the time—a profound change came over Conrad. "How odd," he said. "I, too, lost my mother at eleven." Then he changed the subject. How did I like being Dr. Prince's secretary?

"He's a tyrant." I made a face. "But then I'm a great trial to him. I mis-hear, mis-file, misunderstand everything. Office jobs have always bored me. Still I shouldn't gripe, earning twenty dollars a week and getting a liberal education. The Psychological Laboratory is supposed to be unique in the country. We have a lie detector, ESP tests, crystal-gazing, hypnosis, and I once bet Don—he's an instructor and my sister-in-law's cousin—that he couldn't hypnotize me. He had a Radcliffe student in the room, a good subject, and told her to stay awake, reading a timetable. She fell asleep the minute he began his abracadabra over me. So I won the bet. But I'm sure *you* could weave a spell over me."

"I'm no Svengali," he said, looking pleased and lighting a cigarette. "Everything you tell me makes me want to hear more about you."

We were doing our utmost to charm one another when I braced myself to ask the burning question. Was he married? He flushed and confessed having a wife and three children. I said, "How interesting." I might have known, though he didn't look married somehow. After murmuring some-thing about the tragic ironies in life, he said, "You would adore my three J's. John and Jane were born here, Joan in England. We moved there four years ago because Jessie and I agreed that British culture and schools were superior to American."

The raucous bohemian atmosphere no longer appealed to me. Served me right for chasing rainbows. "Spend all for love" sounds splendidly romantic, but where would it get me?

"A penny . . ."

"No sale." I wrenched my eyes from the golden fuzz on his hands. "You promised me more notes about your work, Mr. Aiken." Back to business, the light tone safest.

"So I did. But why so formal?" He described the phantasmagoria of his private world at some length, then asked if he could see me every night for the next three. "Unfortunately, Thursday is preempted. I'm returning on Sunday, you know. Please?" He tilted his head. "We must make every moment count."

Count for what? I temporized, nursing a finely honed pride. "It depends on the interview," I said, doodling in my notebook, that boring conscience nagging. "We've still only scratched the surface. In any case, nothing after you sail. If that's understood . . ."

"If you insist." With an inscrutable smile, he signaled the waiter.

3

I BECAME increasingly entangled and bewitched in the short time left, caught in a silken net of eloquence. The poet's eye enriched the most prosaic object, his charm mostly verbal, an amalgam of intellect, imagination, and sex appeal. Every sentence was balanced and rhythmical, a joy to musically trained ears. We shared a love of words, nonsense jingles, malapropisms, risqué stories, puns.

If lightning were to strike nearby I would run for my life. Why did I then hesitate and dismiss the perils of falling in love with a married man? How pathetic that starry-eyed, muddle-headed creature must have struck Conrad, coquetting while posing as an impersonal reporter, trying to match his savoir-faire.

After dinner on Wednesday he shied away from my idea of a nightclub, suggesting vaudeville instead. "I never got over being pushed into dancing school," he explained, then jolted me by his view of dancing as a dishonest form of copulation. A puritanical streak in a vaudeville addict? While we watched a striptease act at the Old Howard, he whispered, "I suspect you of having a wicked past. No one can possibly be as innocent and guileless as you look."

"You're so right," I replied glibly. "I have illegitimate twins in every state of the Union." My one affair was my own affair. My guilt, too. "Swift, demure, impossible, is how my friends see me."

"And secretive to boot," he said crisply, strolling to Park Street from Scollay Square. The pot calling the kettle black. "You must have a swarm of beaux, an attractive brunette like you."

"And you must attract a swarm of women, a fascinating man like you."

"How many scalps *have* you collected?"

"Only three," I said. "Paul, a Russian astronomer on a Harvard fellowship; Tommy, an MIT senior, complete with Stanley steamer; and Harry, who has a yacht. On a cruise with him and his aunt two years ago I wrenched my back diving; the result is a weak spine, literally and figuratively."

"Blast those rich and successful chaps," Conrad growled. "Make me happy by blowing up Tommy's steamer and poisoning Harry. Don't you know it's dangerous to wear your heart on your sleeve?"

"Not at all," I said. "It's safer there." He sounded like my father. "Let's hear from you for a change. What about *your* amours?"

He refused the challenge while taking my arm going into the subway. I wondered if he felt at ease with women. Was it normal to shrink from the glances of strangers? Even allowing for a natural reserve, he seemed to hold the cards too close to his chest. I teased him about his shyness. He took it with good grace, simply saying he wasn't as bad as his British friend Martin Armstrong, the novelist. "*He's* hopeless. Incidentally, my children are very fond of him."

At least I didn't strike him as one of those "terrifying newshens." I hadn't been tough enough to last long on the Boston *Post*. At my lodgings we said good night with a self-conscious handshake. I didn't ask him in. It was late and there were things to tell Dear Diary.

First I blotted out Monday night's mush. ("To have found my Prince Charming at last, and he a *poet*, the supreme messenger of Zeus!! It's a heavenly dream, a fairy story . . . ")

On a fresh page, dated November 3, I wrote in purple ink:

All I need now is will power. WILL power. Once the interview is finished, I'll cut the whole thing off. I've done enough harm, can't risk more contacts if it means stealing a husband and the father of three. If he knew about Carl, he wouldn't give me a second thought anyhow. On the other hand, was it not fate, Karma, throwing us together? Think of the odds of meeting the one man in your life, and the opportunity to serve genius. Oh why did he have to be married?

When you're in love you love the whole world and wish everybody to be happy. I had grave misgivings, however, when Conrad insisted on my meeting his friends in Belmont. Wouldn't that compromise him? Not in the least, he said, arguing against his conscience, no doubt. Bill and Beatrice Taussig would love me, and I would see a fascinating house, mottoes carved over transoms and fireplaces. Bill had been his first roommate at Harvard.

Wrong guess. I was *de trop*, the atmosphere quite chilly in that hilltop home. Our host and hostess considered me a threat to Jessie, loving and admiring her as they did. Conrad made gallant efforts in my behalf, suggesting I try the piano, mentioning my latest interview with Henry Beston in the *Evening Transcript*. But nothing made me palatable. Conversation at the table limped and lagged. We left soon after dinner. Apparently their marriage was cracking up. And I probably underscored the fragility of marital ties.

The evening was salvaged by Conrad's friend Maurice Firuski, who had left the key to his doomed bookshop under the doormat—the building was to be razed. We sat in rocking chairs, holding hands and exchanging life stories by candlelight. Conrad spoke more freely about his boyhood but skimmed over his parents' tragedy, saying only that they had come to a sudden, violent end. Probably a car accident, I thought. Poor lamb, orphaned at eleven.

I delved briefly into my family history, no doubt upsetting Conrad by mentioning mental illness on my father's side. "Mercifully, much of my misspent life is a blank," I said, sighing.

"Why mercifully?" he asked. "You should dig up your memories, become aware of everything." His cigarette traced a parabola in the semi-darkness. "Pain, isolation, rancor, guilt, self-hatred—get it all out as I did in *Blue Voyage*. How else can you know who you are? The problem of identity and the multiple self is one I used in *Senlin*. Someone once asked me how God looked. I said, like my father when he smiles. He was a Quaker." In a warm account of his grandfather, William James Potter, a Unitarian minister in New Bedford for thirty years, Conrad expressed his own idealism. "He was a hero to his congregation. They followed him when he broke away from Emerson's orthodoxy to form the Free Religious Association, a doctrine embracing scientific discoveries like Darwin's theory."

The candles flickered and grew shorter. It was past midnight when Conrad blew out the last one. "Maurice may have an English edition of *Senlin*. If so, I'll pinch it for you. It's a Hogarth Press item, published by Leonard and Virginia Woolf." At the door he kissed me lightly on the cheek, as though more would shatter the spell. For him the evening was a flowering of two minds, though he left much unsaid. "You touch some deep chord of tenderness in me, a protective instinct, and God knows I've never been a protector."

Back at the Harvard Club, recalling my astonishment on hearing that he hadn't cried since he was five and "how with such a divine gesture of compassion you took me into your heart," he ended a thirty-two-year drought. The gesture eludes me now.

A nostalgic occasion, our last meal at the Hotel Touraine. Everything shone and glittered—the silver, crystal, jewels, bald pates, bare bosoms. Conrad admired my homemade forest green gown and apologized for his shabby tweeds. "I don't own a tuxedo," he said, staring down Boston dowagers until lorgnettes snapped back in place. He was still rueful about the football game we saw that Saturday, the score, Princeton 12, Harvard 0. He had kept his eyes riveted on the players, groaning and cursing, while I wondered if he was a good loser. We trailed a subdued procession out of the stadium.

While we enjoyed our broiled sirloin the string trio scraped away at "The Blue Danube." Conrad reminded me of my promise to play for him in the borrowed studio where I taught a few piano pupils. "But don't expect a virtuoso," I said. "I'm one of Goethe's *Wunderkinder*—the wonder goes while the child remains. I've always been torn between writing and music." Conrad thought I might have succeeded with someone like Walter Piston to spark me. "He's great fun, quite a wag, and a damned fine chess player. Just now he's in Paris, studying composition with Nadia Boulanger, but you must meet him when he gets back, if I'm here."

"That would be nice," I said, "but you're forgetting our pact. No contact after you leave, except for business." Dissembler that I was, no longer even pretending to be a journalist. The shift from professional to personal should have alarmed me. Who was I fooling?

I played for him in the S. S. Pierce Building on Copley Square. Not very well; I was too inhibited. Later, in the cab to Cambridge, his arm went around me. "Do you mind being called darling? I've never called anyone darling before, believe it or not." Then try, I said, and giggled as the taxi lurched, his kiss glancing off my nose. "That certainly missed fire." He looked chagrined. "To hell with the tragic view of life; your mild derision is much better."

We sped along Memorial Drive, past the sycamores lining the Charles. Tomorrow he would be gone. I missed him already. So much to ponder and weigh. The whole situation was unbearably anomalous. At my boardinghouse we embraced, I with the heightened intensity of renunciation, he with a reckless, "We must have each other, darling, I don't care how or when. If you don't come to England, I'll come back here. I've decided to ask Jessie for a divorce."

He silenced my protests with a kiss, then said shyly, "Expect roses tomorrow," and walked back to the taxi.

My "bon voyage" the next morning brought a tremulous thank you over the phone. "God bless you, too, and both of us," he said, "though it's obvious that God or someone has already blessed me." But Conrad's roses had thorns, and they pricked my fingers and my conscience. He was about to break up his marriage of fourteen years after five encounters with a woman who was anything but the calm, stable type.

4

M Y FIRST BATTLE with Father occurred while I was helping Mama with the Saturday baking. She was in her sixth pregnancy and nursing my little brother through scarlet fever. When our hired girl coaxed her to rest, she said, "I don't dare sit down, Helga, so afraid I can't get up again."

"Then don't sit down," said Father, marching into the kitchen. I got up and flew at him, pummeling him and screaming, "I hate you, I hate you, I wish you were dead!" The sting of his slap wore off in time, but not the feud. The daring of a six-year-old still has me marveling. After that episode I clung to Mother still more. "Don't ever die, Mama, promise." She had come close to it when I was born a breech case.

"The Angel of Death brushed its wings over her more than once," said Dr. Jermain. His warnings about more babies were disregarded despite her heart condition. "I'd rather have a dozen children on my bed pillow than one on my conscience." I was the third of seven, born January 28, 1899, during Milwaukee's worst blizzard. I waged war from the start, an *enfant terrible*, refusing the breast, throwing tantrums, and once rocking my highchair so violently that I toppled over.

A faded snapshot shows a barelegged gypsy with bangs and beads flanked by my elder brothers, Joseph and Richard, all three looking as if we faced a firing squad instead of a camera. We grew up in a climate of fear and friction, still paying for the hardships of our ancestors. European emigrés, peasant and patrician, they were all devout Catholics.

Both grandfathers were dour and forbidding. Robert Lorenz arrived here from Silesia with a dollar and his bride. Amelia, left motherless early, had been reared by an uncle, steward of a nobleman's estate, and educated along with the duke's children. I remember her dimly as a frail, bedridden arthritic, pining for her homeland. She had five children. Louis, my father, was the most enterprising. His sister and a brother were mentally unbalanced. We weren't allowed to mention them, though the small fry taunted us about "Crazy Auntie," who lived with Grandpa opposite our house on the north side of Milwaukee.

Our grandparents married late. They died before I reached my teens.

For all the emphasis on family life, there was little sense of continuity or candor between generations in that era. Birth, marriage, procreation, and death were scamped, vital knowledge withheld. Father's dolors and Mother's martyrdom became clear to me only much later, but conflicting information obscured the origin of our forebears.

My maternal grandmother, Gertrude Sonnen, was half French, her father a vintner in Châlons-sur-Marne. Like Amelia, Gertrude lost her mother at an early age and was brought to America by relatives. She married Peter Mich, an artisan from Luxembourg who failed as a farmer in Wisconsin after losing his savings in making good a friend's promissory note.

While the menfolk fled political persecution, their wives could never escape domestic tyranny. Most of the women in our family were appeasers. Ordinarily meek, Gertrude was a model of forbearance. But one day she lost patience with Grandpa's eternal grumbling and crowned him with a bowl of ragout. That single act of courage canonized her for me, and in later years I tried to break the mold of family placaters. My petite grandmother had ten children. Mary, my mother, was the oldest of four girls, a successful dress designer when Father came along.

Theirs was a stormy courtship. Though a trusting unworldly twenty-seven, she challenged the jealous, importunate suitor. When Louis threatened to jump in the river unless she accepted him, she said cooly, "Go ahead and jump, I wouldn't dream of entrusting my future to a fool." Her parents grieved at her "surrender" to a man who apparently demanded lifelong recompense for his joyless youth. Apprenticed at fourteen to his father's bakery, he had a grim boyhood and couldn't understand children.

I listened avidly to anti-Papa propaganda from Mother's sisters. "Your mama married beneath her, just like your grandmothers. She felt sorry for your papa. But she never forgot her true love, a prominent man in Iowa. He let a treasure slip through his fingers when he was persuaded against marrying an out-of-town girl."

I could charm everyone except Papa. That handsome, blue-eyed god with the fierce mustache, and a black leather strap, was not one to cuddle infants or coddle children. Ignored except when naughty, I fibbed, stole, tagged after boys, played hooky, and defied his edicts in general. I got the hairbrush, my brothers the strap. So began my vendetta, with far-reaching consequences.

From the first day at Saint Boniface, I took a dim view of education, after being sent home in disgrace for making a puddle. Sister Charista taught us first-graders to read and write both German and English by Christmas. After I discovered that German was *not* the American language, I refused to speak it at home.

"*Sprech Deutsch!*" "I won't!" "*Sprech Deutsch!*" "I won't, and you can't make me." Papa shook me like a rag doll, only reinforcing my resolve to be *echt* American. Everything German became anathema.

He never wanted us to have any fun, I complained to Mama, sulking and stuffing my pockets with gingersnaps. She kept the cookie jar filled and welcomed all our playmates. Grandpa and Papa, however, frowned on non-Germans—"Polacks, Pommers, Hunkies, and Irish riffraff." Our pranks and capers didn't amuse Father as they did Mother. I don't recall ever seeing him actually jovial, or hearing him laugh. He saw nothing funny about Joe wiring the front door to the pull-out flour bin in the pantry, an April Fool's Day trick. Or John, at a quilting bee, crawling behind Mother's guests and stitching the ladies' skirts together.

We clashed at almost every stage of my development. I concluded that Papa had no use for girls. Or tomboys. "Stop that whistling." Girls were to be seen and not heard, their opinions censored. I had nothing to say about my future. A wife and mother was the only possible career—*Kinder, Kirche, Küche*. A perfect homemaker herself, Mama couldn't make one out of me, dearly though I loved her. Being a *Hausfrau* appealed to me about as much as the macaroni business did to Joe, a chemist, or Richie, a draftsman-inventor. Papa's factory fascinated us. But the Macaroni Kids, as we were called, were literally fed up with pasta.

Father's prohibitions made an impressive list. The nickelodeon was *verboten*. So were poolrooms, pets of any sort, and trashy books (we hid *Peck's Bad Boy* under the bathtub and devoured Horatio Alger like peanuts). I longed for a pony but could never collect the requisite one hundred soap wrappers to acquire one. The next best thing was Old Tilly, the pensioned mare languishing in Grandpa's barn. Forbidden to ride her, I took a chance one day and was blissfully going along the alley when Grandpa saw me. Of course he tattled. I was punished and included him in my vendetta.

"An angel has him by the hand, a devil by the foot," Mother used to say of Father. In my judgment, people were either angels or devils, there were no in-betweens. I saw only the crêpe hanger, humorless and insensitive, doling out too little pocket money and too many indignities. There was the night he locked out Richie for violating the ten o'clock curfew; my invalid brother had bicycled twenty-five miles from relatives in Mukwanego. In contrast to such outrages, Father's virtues dwindled, in my eyes. He lived as he saw fit, a strict disciplinarian but a good provider, with endearing traits like giving us presents on his birthday.

To him I was a brat, nestling in Mama's arms, my refuge. He felt justified in straight-arming me. "You're your mother's girl," my aunts said thankfully. "There's nothing of your father in you." She fought our battles but not her own—a madonna and a lady, come what may.

If it's true that fathers form the masculine ideal and determine the daughter's attitude toward sex, my chances for a happy marriage were slim indeed. I learned little about the opposite sex, growing up with five repressed brothers, the only girl until age nine. Untrained in fair play with boys, I regarded males as rivals instead of competitors, had a chip on by shoulder, and hotly resented taking a back seat.

Happiness was brushing Mother's long hair. Glossy, jet-black, and worn pompadour fashion, it conjured up a remote period of grace and serenity. An unshakeable belief in an after-life of perfection sustained her. But I demanded instant reward and couldn't wait that long.

Being an only girl was tantamount to being only a girl. I identified with the pilgrim in Mother's song:

> I'm a pilgrim, and I'm a stranger,
> I can tarry, I can tarry but a while;
> Do not detain me, for I am going
> To where the streamlets are ever flowing;
> I'm a pilgrim, and I'm a stranger,
> I can tarry, I can tarry but a while.

I never tarried long at the white duplex across the street—a haunt to be avoided except in lilac time. Papa championed Grandpa as a generous man who had given the larger of the two church bells. And brave as a lion. When lightning struck the barn, he got badly burned rescuing Tilly. But I saw only a grumpy Grandpa, a partly deaf ogre glaring at me from a great height.

When lightning struck our neighbor's chimney one summer day, I made a beeline for the parish house nearby. Our pastor was not pleased at having his nap interrupted by a tot's clamor for confession. My belief in the Church's emissaries began to waver early, a cause for guilt in itself. One sin, never confessed, I committed at my first holy communion. Mother Superior warned us that blood would spurt from everywhere if our teeth came in contact with the Sacred Host. To test her claim, I bit into the wafer. Behold, nothing happened—no blood, no anything. She had fibbed.

The dainty feminine garments Mother made were wasted on me. Skirts and petticoats hampered my movements. I fancied myself in boys' clothes, felt more natural and free. "Oh let her alone," the nuns would sigh. "She's only a boy." They were known to measure our hemlines. Carnal thoughts were sinful, any pleasant physical sensation taboo. Modesty, prized above rubies, dictated undressing under our nightgowns. (I still practice modesty, trying to pee silently in public lavatories, but in my dreams I wear transparent negligees in the street.)

A trio of hoydens, Rose, Lula, and I played exclusively with boys. They couldn't shake us. I yearned to be part of a man's world. Joe asked when I was going into long pants. I watched his chemical experiments in the basement laboratory, fascinated, until shunted upstairs, Papa roaring, "Why aren't you doing your homework?" Upstairs I would bother frail, gentle Richie, bent over his drawing board. He admired my style at the keys, said I was almost as good as a player piano, that people stopped in the street to listen. Not Papa, however. He didn't even notice my acrobatic stunts on the turning pole in the yard, though an ardent member of the *Turnverein*. I was a brat to him.

The day after he punished me for buying gumdrops (my passion) with found money, a neighbor remarked, "What a cross-looking little girl you have there, Mary." Mama replied, "Oh but you're greatly mistaken. Clarissa may look like a thundercloud, but she has a heart of gold." After a spanking with the hairbrush, I could have any bed in the house to cry in. Mama made everything right again.

By age nine I was through with motherhood and looking after my younger brothers. When Aunt Elizabeth saw me in my teacup "surrounded by little ones," I said firmly that I wasn't having children. I would marry a man like Uncle Steve, who was childless. All the same, I was overjoyed when Dr. Jermain, my make-believe Papa, brought Gertrude in his black satchel. Throbbing with excitement, Rose and I waited on the front porch that August day. Girl or boy? I shadowed the red-bearded giant to the curb. "It's a boy, your auntie dressed her," he teased, cranking his Reo roadster, then shocked me by swearing at it.

It was a pleasure showing off Gertrude's delicate blue-eyed charm, taking her to the stores and public library in the coaster-wagon or sled. Papa's *Puppchen* was no howler like her big sister. She cried only when in acute pain, seemed to know that she had shortened Mother's life. I remember wavering between panic and jealousy while Father held her on his lap, waiting for the doctor to diagnose an earache. But for the nine-year gap in our ages, she might have had a stabilizing influence on me.

Denied higher education, Father revered it and took great pains to show his displeasure at my low marks. I could seldom concentrate on my homework when he was in the house. He would scold me for slouching, ask where was my shoulder brace; I would go upstairs sulkily for that instrument of torture, feeling put upon. *Arbeit und Pflicht* was his motto. Work and duty, which I shirked, though the nuns implanted a strong sense of responsibility and conscience in me. Each of us studied some musical instrument. Mother's fondest dream was of me becoming a concert pianist. Making up melodies, however, was more fun than practicing.

Her health began to fail, and two years after Gertrude's birth she died, aged forty-seven. The neighbors said God had taken the wrong parent. Why not Papa? We would never have missed him. I was convinced that he had broken her heart, hastened her death by his harshness. I moved into her room, trying to feel something besides vague relief at escaping convent school and the blue serge uniforms she had just finished. I never did accept her death. Prolonged spells of numbness followed sharp spasms of grief. My doting aunts assured me that I never lacked love or respect for her. "You especially realized how hard things were for her." Yet when I dreamed, many years later, of seeing an old woman abused in the street, I burst into tears and told a bystander that I once hurt my own mother very badly. How so? Breaking my promise to forgive Father? Killing her dream of a concert career? Refusing to learn in school?

My sense of self and worth nipped, I castigated myself for feeling nothing except the thrill of riding to the cemetery in style. After dragging that albatross everywhere for sixty-five years, I learned from Rose that it was my seven-year-old brother who said, "Goody, goody, now I can have a ride in a real carriage." Atone, atone, a stuck needle. "Guilt ruined your life," a friend said recently. I soaked it up like a sponge. Born seven hundred years earlier, I might have been a flagellant.

Shuttling between a punitive parent and permissive one, all of us experienced conflicts that erupted in nightmares and sleepwalking episodes. Mother's panacea was hot chocolate or chamomile tea sipped by the window while counting the stars. "Close your eyes and think of God's candles shining up there," she said softly. We fell asleep to her singing Brahms's Lullaby or hearing *Aesop's Fables* or *The Book of Saints*. Mother was on intimate terms with the saints. Wanting a bright day, she placed the statuette of Saint Joseph on the outer window ledge, since he didn't like to get wet. "Man makes the calendar but God makes the weather," she quoted whimsically.

Each of us was to be scarred by her premature death. Like espaliered plants starved for sustenance, we put out feeble shoots while straining toward the sun. Uncles might have imparted wisdom and knowledge, supplied a sense of continuity and history, but I for one had never seen Father's brothers, and Mother's six jolly ones were inaccessible.

We leaned on Aunt Margaret for comfort. Like Mother, she was tenderhearted and loved us. For the sake of her parents she had sacrificed marriage. How many tears were shed on her ample bosom, a bosom designed for more creative use! In her thriving business as a couturier, she made everything from christening robes to funeral raiment. Shoddy work she couldn't abide. *"Langes Fädchen, Faules Mädchen,"* she would say if I used too long a thread. Or, "As ye sew, so shall ye rip."

Aunt Margaret refused to run the house for Papa, much as she grieved for us. A year after being widowed, he buried his own father and was then obliged to "put away" his sister. We felt secretly relieved, my feelings tinged with sympathy for a sorely pressed man trying to grapple with seven children in a chaotic household. I had tried everything to win him over in the beginning. He seemed incapable of being pleased. At Christmas I spool-knitted watch fobs and ties for him, in summer picked posies, and the year round invented little waltzes. My efforts wasted, I began searching for a loving Papa, sitting on the front stoop and saying hello to every male passerby. No takers.

Outwardly gay and flippant, inwardly quaking, I retreated more and more into fantasy. I shrank from the grim realities of life—the blood-stained infant garments of my young brother run over by a dray wagon, the sight of a skinned dog in the alley covered with flies, our butcher chopping off a chicken's head and joking. Blot out the ugly and gruesome. Believe the nuns and priests who promise a heaven for the pure in heart; avoid hospitals, deathbeds, morgues. Leave corpses in their graves, family skeletons in the closet.

Since Father could never keep domestic help for long, I had to pinch-hit between hired girls. In my diary I addressed "Mother in Heaven," pouring out woes like asking Papa for household money. I sulked and mutinied, a grudge-bearer and emotional geyser, resenting authority while fearing it, be it Father, a teacher, our pastor, policeman, Mother Grundy, or God Almighty.

Having got my way, at thirteen I squandered time—my attention span that of a firecracker. Dr. Jermain was treating me for nutritional anemia and a thyroid disorder. Music lessons had ceased. My only distinction was accompanying the national anthem in assembly Monday mornings. My brothers were earnest, diligent students, I a disaster, flunking everything except English, stenography, and gym.

> Holes in my stockings,
> Holes in my head,
> I'll never be famous,
> Not even when dead.

Wrapped in daydreams, I threw myself into whatever sheltered me from reality. Fantasies about imaginary fathers filled diary pages.

Then Papa announced his intention of marrying his housekeeper, obviously in desperation. A mediocre if well-intentioned woman, she was barely tolerated among us—unfit to tie Mama's shoelaces. My frenzied pleas to forbid the banns failed to impress our pastor. An outlandish request. Faith in the Church dwindled still more.

The diary I kept under my mattress served as a safety valve. Of my stepmother, I said, "Everything about her is false—hair, teeth, heart." She found the evidence and passed it on to Father, his fury a painful memory. "So this is how you do your homework, blackballing a good woman, and writing lies to boot?" The lies referred to imaginary fathers I elaborated upon. (This journal was to cast long shadows over another one, whose privacy was likewise violated.)

The immediate result of Father's anger was that I was yanked out of high school in my senior year and put to work in a pennant factory, a job I loathed. Within a year or so, our stepmother deserted, the neighbors told that she couldn't live with Father or us. We gloated. *Schadenfreude*. My youngest brother still leaves the room at any mention, however remote, of that chapter in our history.

5

M Y ONLY LITERARY CONTACT in Milwaukee was an Irish poet, hellion, and sparkplug named Nancy Shores. Nancy goaded me into self-expression, using a carrot and a stick. Browsing in the public library, we took out a hodgepodge of volumes, from Maeterlinck's *Bluebird* to Elinor Glynn's *Two Weeks* (on the Index). We criticized each other's work, after my first short story appeared in the high school monthly, a terrific thrill.

Nancy loved to shock people and stick pins into the smug and hypocritical. Wild, precocious, with a gamin shrewdness, she thumbed her nose at the world. Father banned her from the house, and my brothers deplored her sacrilegious influence and flippancies ("Let's go into the darkroom and see what's developing"), which I thought the height of sophistication. She was the classmate most likely to succeed. But alcoholism claimed her in later years, and she was found dead in a New Jersey hotel surrounded by empty sherry bottles.

Her last letter to me read in part:

Dear Jiggs,

I still think of you as a serious and troubled high-school kid, thrown out of the nest too soon. I'd find you scrubbing floors or hanging out the wash or making beds or hustling to get the midday meal. You could do that, eat, wash the dishes and scoot back to N.D.H.S. inside of an hour. Remember the day you asked me to lunch and your Papa came home unexpectedly from the factory and gave you hell for inviting me? When you stuck up for me, he slapped your face. Your brothers always said he favored you. In that case, what did he use on them, the bastinado? Can I possibly persuade you to be good to yourself?

I was self-supporting over the next years, but hardly self-reliant. Except for sporadic displays of bravado, I couldn't cope with Father's hostility and so employed guerrilla tactics and engaged in "double-speak." Branded a *Schwindelkopf*, I decided my only asset was a pretty face, and that was God-given, as Mother had reminded me. "You can take credit only for your character." Which was in short supply.

Along with playing little mother again, I had crushes on older men like Dr. Jermain and our church organist. The beaux Father swept off the front porch didn't really interest me. I had little if any sex instruction and am sure my brothers didn't receive any from Father beyond the usual dire warnings about masturbation. When I began to menstruate, a terrifying experience, our aged Bavarian housekeeper merely said, "Well, now you're a woman."

The stork theory had sufficed, until Nancy belatedly revealed the facts. My stunned reaction was similar to that of the little boy who turned on his informant with an indignant "*Your* parents maybe, but not mine." The truth sounded black and menacing. I believed Nancy, since her stepfather was a physician. A traumatic episode in adolescence increased my dread and confusion. Marriage took on a sinister quality. Men were beasts, conjugal relations an assault, childbirth degrading and often fatal.

Nancy didn't believe in virginity. The rest of our group gave chastity the highest mark; we drew the line at "dingalings" and "smooches," while driving the boys crazy with imitations of vamps like Pola Negri and Theda Bara. "Nancy thinks it's all right to do whatever is fun," I told my diary, "but Mama would never have agreed. Oh Lord, I'm just a blob of jelly."

The war intensified my feud with Father and sanctioned my hatred of the German race. To counteract his militant pacifism, I volunteered as an ambulance driver in France, but the Red Cross turned me down. I knitted socks, collected peach stones for gas masks, corresponded with overseas troops, and sent them scrapbooks of current interest.

The war halted the Americanization of some two hundred thousand foreign-born citizens in Milwaukee. By October 1917 the German press was muzzled; by August 1918 the German language banned in grade schools. "*Verrückte Schweinerei*," Father raged. I saw nothing crazy in the Wisconsin Loyalty League ferreting out what they saw as apathy and treachery. Socialist Mayor Daniel Hoane broke up demonstrations and arrested offenders. By late autumn of 1918 most of the violence was crushed, but the hatred and bitterness remained. *Gemütlichkeit* suffered and withered. The traditions and customs so dear to Father were diminished.

My prejudices were somewhat modified just before the Armistice when Field Marshal Herman von Eichhorn, Mother's second cousin, was assassinated in Kiev by a bomb thrown into his carriage while he was partitioning the Ukraine and setting up a puppet government.

Meanwhile my second employer in foreign sales at the Bucyrus plant was a refreshing change from the first one, whose pawings had forced me to quit my job. Instead of firing me for incompetence, Mr. S played Dutch uncle. "Do you stutter from habit or for emphasis?" he asked, underlining a sentence I had typed twice. I seldom proofread my letters and couldn't brag about taking one hundred dictated words a minute or typing ten pages an hour.

Commuting the twenty miles in the "scooter" to South Milwaukee, I played penny ante with some of the other passengers, who dubbed me Red Ridinghood for my scarlet mackinaw and encouraged my antics and gaffes, such as chasing a ball of yarn in the aisle and tangling up the conductor. Each morning they flipped coins to bet on whose seat I would share. After rotating for weeks, I stirred up rivalry by choosing a middle-aged inventor with soulful eyes and a melancholy smile.

Phil was the first married man to pay me attention. He carried the world's injustices on his stooped shoulders. Though a pacifist, he swore to enlist and get fifty Germans if his best friend was among the two hundred American troops drowned on the torpedoed *Tuscania*. When the smoker grew too stuffy to breathe, we rode between the coaches, fairly congealed in subzero weather. Phil never took advantage of me, but enjoyed my frivolities and monkeyshines.

Father predicted I would run myself into an early grave. Aunt Margaret cited my complaints of headaches, vertigo, fainting spells. Couldn't I ever rest and relax? No. I had to experience everything, as did Nancy, now especially when life was all too short. More gold stars appeared in windows every month; more overseas letters were returned. I was determined to enjoy this world if it killed me. Up at five, I rushed breakfast, skipping it when I had overslept, caught the 8:10 on the fly, dozed through the lunch hour in the rec hall. Evenings were filled with dates, choir rehearsal at Gesu Church, organ lessons, or French at night school. I worked on scrapbooks, washed, ironed, mended, cleaned, and wrote in my diary, my erratic handwriting suggesting a disturbed person, possibly with suicidal tendencies.

As a wage-earner paying room and board, I expected freedom without responsibilities, mistaking license for liberty. Father's tiresome lectures were tuned out. He seldom relayed phone messages. Admittedly those were excessive. I had something like a beau-a-month club going. Richie suggested a card index. If Papa didn't care about me, there were plenty who did.

On his nights at the *Turnverein*, or a church affair, I had Nancy and other friends in for a *Bummelei*. We rolled back the carpet and danced to the Victrola or my accompaniment at the piano—"Dardanella," "Itchy Koo," "Tipperary." We played kissing games and musical chairs; the girls sipped lemonade, the boys beer. I always managed to send my guests packing and straighten out the furniture before Father returned.

Late in 1918 a new channel opened up. Nancy had moved to Chicago and urged me to apply for a stenographic job at Fort Sheridan, Illinois, where General Hospital Number 128 was being built for returnees. "There's no future for you in Milwaukee, Jiggs, either in writing or music. You'll stagnate." I longed to serve the heroes of the battlefield. The Marquette student whose marriage proposal I declined had yet to prove himself. He was about to join the Engineers Reserve Corps.

Nancy's suggestion was the finger of destiny, even if it left Father with no housekeeper (Gertrude was then at convent school in Saint Francis, Wisconsin). My army career began in a mere shack among piles of lumber, wiring, cement mixers, and Bucyrus steam shovels. A field auditor's secretary earned $125 a month plus lodgings. I shared a large room with a student nurse in Officers' Row in Lake Michigan bluff. General Leonard Wood, chief-of-staff, was a neighbor. Children of regular army officers romped and rode tricycles, their high-pitched prattle competing with the starlings in ancient oaks and elms in an oasis of beauty. White birches lined the ravine, a wide sandy beach made for moonlit strolls, amorous dalliance, and canters on horseback.

As the wards gradually filled up in the 400-bed hospital, I spent more of my free time with the patients. The crippled, the blind, the shellshocked stripped the war of its glamor. Anything I could do for them? "Yeah," grinned a redhead in a body cast, "gimme a new chassis." Would he settle for jazz? I sat down at the portable piano in Ward 57 and banged away at "Alexander's Ragtime Band," "Over There," "Hinky Dinky Parley-vous."

Whenever catching sight of me with Tinker, a stray mongrel I adopted, they would shout, "Here comes Jerry with her pooch. Sit right down, honeybunch, and make that keybox talk." If a piano was lacking, I strummed my ukulele. We had singalongs, the bedridden propped on elbows, crutches waving in rhythm, wheelchair patients beating time on leg and arm casts. "Don't be scared," they assured me the first day. "We're all through bayoneting."

Every other weekend I had pipe-organ lessons in Chicago and stayed with Aunt Elizabeth or Nancy Shores. My British teacher, Dr. J. Lewis

Browne, fired me with ambition. Talent must be taken seriously, he emphasized. A heady experience, practicing Bach, Karg-Elert, and Dupre on a four-manual organ of five thousand pipes and sitting beside the organist of Holy Name Cathedral on Sundays. By saving enough out of my wages I might afford at least a year at a music school and yet realize Mother's dream of concertizing.

I had begun forming a jazz band at Fort Sheridan. Transcribing letters about construction costs for forty-seven temporary buildings wasn't exactly fascinating. "You're no world-beater, but you're nice to have around, make me feel good," Major Q said. A softhearted cross old bear, he made *me* feel good, less of a deserter from the family. I found time for everything but sleep—playing hymns Sundays on the Knights of Columbus chapel's melodeon, ad libbing at the piano in the gym for the silent movies, or playing in the wards. They all smelled alike—paint, soap, carbolic acid, coffee, Dakin's solution.

Meanwhile my stenographic blunders mushroomed, for all my resolves, until Major Q said he'd had orders to fire me. "But I'd as lief fire myself as some people." Early in 1919 I saved him further embarrassment and myself disgrace by joining the Reconstruction Aides. There were occupational therapists and physiotherapists, arts-and-crafts teachers and writers among the first group. I was lucky to be assigned a weekly column in the *Army Recall*, and with a genial editor in Lieutenant Robert Wright. His assistant was Eugene Jolas, who would later achieve fame as editor of *Transition* in Paris. Eugene became my mentor. "Little Jerry is forever blowing bubbles," he wrote in my memory album, "but they are bubbles of mirth and laughter."

Most young women in that era were employed as stenographers, teachers, nurses, or seamstresses. Reporters were thought of as coarse, bohemian. But we "Bluebirds" in blue cotton dresses, white aprons and caps were looked up to by patients and staff alike. One of my fondest memories is of Helen Hillhouse, a fellow-reporter and my tennis partner. She poulticed bruised egos.

We were billeted on the reservation, some of us on the north shore. My roommate, Ruth, predicted I would be a nervous wreck by age thirty. I pushed wheelchair patients everywhere except to the contamination buildings, morgue, or psychiatric section. I took on assignments I couldn't fill, such as reporting amputations (I keeled over in the operating room). On the go from 5:30 A.M. until midnight, I ran errands, collected news, trekked ramps and twenty-two miles of corridors. I became inured to the squeak-and-thump of crutches, to hospital pallor, bloodstained bandages, basket cases, profanity, and trench argot.

"Hey, Mincemeat, got a cig on you?" "Hell, a pegleg's not so bad, you can step on nails 'n everything." "When my buddy's arm is hacked off, we'll be a two-handed piano team, see?"

Morale was high among the maimed and paraplegics—at least among those I observed. I wrote letters for the heroes of Soissons, Chateau-Thierry, Verdun, and Saint-Mihiel, for the armless and the illiterate. I sat with the dying and read to the blind—mostly nonsense literature like "Letters from a Rookie" from the *Dere Mable* series. I learned to spot the potential suicide, the boy brooding over the families of innocent Germans he had killed.

They showed me snapshots of their sweethearts, wives, kids; told me their domestic problems—a girl friend "PWOL" (pregnant without leave), or wives writing "Dear John" letters. I heard of medical miracles—a North Dakota youth regaining the use of his legs when forced to save his buddy's life, the Texas lad with a paralyzed throat, speechless until his girlfriend turned up.

Nancy Shores came on occasional weekends, bringing sweets, cigarettes, and badinage. Her husky voice, voluptuous movements, and raffish personality mesmerized the patients. "Autograph my leg cast, willya, babe? . . . Who says war is hell?" We made the rounds, including the psychiatric ward, which I had avoided. "What are you afraid of?" Nancy hooted. "Those shellshocked boys need us even more than the wounded. You can always play soothing numbers like 'Down by the Old Millstream.'"

"You're still an unlicked kitten, Jiggs," Nancy remarked about my two punctured romances. I owned half of Vergil's canoe, but not that Kansas patient's heart. And Jack, the fireman with the gorgeous tenor, never gave me a tumble—salutary setbacks for a swelled head! Nancy advised me to play the field. I did so, feeling a cheat accepting invitations to dinner, dance, or the opera at Ravenna Park, and rebuffing advances. We were just good comrades, enjoying music, sports, masked balls, beach picnics, and marshmallow roasts.

"A happy end to 1919," I wound up that year's diary. Visits to Milwaukee had tapered off because of organ lessons in Chicago, but I always stopped in Saint Francis to see little Gertrude. She was a model pupil and liked the nuns but became homesick and cried whenever she heard Brahms, Chopin, or Debussy, my favorites. Half of my army pay went toward her tuition—conscience money for having abandoned the family.

I saw a Milwaukee shattered by the war and devastated by Prohibition. Many saloons had already closed by July 1919, the deadline for obtaining new licenses due to expire January 1920, when national Prohibition went into effect. One tavern-keeper, August Kahlo, displayed a doomsday sign: "The first of July is the last of August."

If Father's letters were any indication, he was mellowing.

When you are away from home you are much in my thoughts. Not hearing
from you worries me. The house seems empty without you. I may have said
many things I didn't mean, but try to understand and remember the good
times. I miss you and your music. Wishing you happiness and success,

Your loving Father

P.S. I hope you find your way back to the Church.

Once a Catholic always a Catholic? I wondered. Praying to Saint Anthony for a dress lost in the laundry was simply a reflex, automatic. The
chaplain couldn't steer me back to the fold with books like *The Faith of
Our Fathers*. Why were religious doubts a sin against the Holy Ghost?
God gave us freedom of will, didn't He? And forbidden books, another
absurdity, smacked of totalitarianism.

Threats of punishment are an admission of failure. We make our own
hell and heaven on earth. For me, cantering on Dusty along the beach
under a dazzling blue sky was the nearest thing to heaven. Horses were
God's noblest creatures, as I told my diary, and this chestnut sorrel was
one of five magnificent Arabian steeds owned by General Wood. His
mounted orderly, Sergeant Beard, had taught me to ride. In Lake Forest
I took the bridle path winding through the McCormick estate, picked
trilliums or bittersweet for the patients, then galloped back alongside the
shimmering dunes. I never again recaptured that sense of exhilaration.

My pedigreed collie Scottie had replaced Tinker. He always kept pace
with Dusty, at a trot or a gallop. We were inseparable. He slept on my
bed, accompanied me on ward rounds and into the chapel. He also brought
me luck on the tennis court not long before I left Fort Sheridan to study
music in Boston. I had won a medal the previous year, but the July 1920
tournament was more competitive. A festive occasion, reported the *Army
& Navy Journal*: hundreds of spectators watching the matches, officers'
wives serving refreshments under an awning, General Wood to present
the trophies. After playing 110 games on the last day of the tournament, a
sweltering one, I headed for my quarters, too exhausted to wait for the
general's formal presentation of three silver cups. One of them Helen
Hillhouse and I had taken in women's doubles.

I cherish those trophies as much as the extravagant tributes in my
memory album. So much adulation should have generated self-esteem,
but we were a family of self-deprecators. Aunt Margaret once said, "Your
papa had a pot of gold in you seven children and threw it all away."

Father *was* impressed by the send-off given me by the Chicago *Tribune*,
a picture of his daughter on horseback with a story underneath that began:
"There are long faces at the Fort Sheridan hospital. 'Jerry' is leaving
today—'Jerry,' whose gladsome smile and cheerful, zippy disposition have

kept the whole place humming with happiness for the last two years, from the Commandant to the convalescent in the last cot, is going away to school." As a tiny cog in the machinery of rehabilitation, I learned two lessons: that life is indeed a gift and that happiness is a two-way proposition.

6

M Y HOPE of a musical career had brought me to Boston. It was a hope that had been revived when Dr. Browne recommended me for a scholarship to his friend George Chadwick, then director of the New England Conservatory of Music. In September 1920 I arrived with fifty dollars and my beloved collie. Since I couldn't smuggle him into the dormitory where I shared a room, I reluctantly lent him to a college student.

Fort Sheridan had given me perspective. My mirrors were beginning to turn into windows. But it had also spoiled me for serious study. Nothing I had done there escaped notice, whereas nothing I did in Boston attracted notice. Once the stimulus of a new environment wore off, I felt stranded. Still I made friends, one of them Anna, a girl from Hamburg who found that speaking German was still risky two years after the Armistice.

Anna and I would queue up Friday afternoons at Symphony Hall for the 25-cent rush seats or last-minute cancellations. If her struggles as a student were any criteria, I wouldn't last long. A "digger," wholly committed to music, she sacrificed all pleasure. Her textbooks carried the motto *Labor Omnia Vincit—Labor* instead of *Amor*. She lived in a three-dollar-a-week hall bedroom at the Student Union, practiced six to eight hours a day, and taught piano at one dollar an hour. Such commitment paid off in time. Years later she won the Mason and Hamlin piano prize, but a week before she was to perform the Tschaikovsky concerto under Koussevitsky she had a nervous breakdown.

Her experience shook me. It took forever to become a virtuoso, learning and memorizing nine concertos. A professional career demanded more stamina and emotional control than I possessed. Despite receiving two scholarships I couldn't meet the tuition, though I took various part-time jobs playing at rathskellers and elsewhere.

A long time later I heard from Nancy that when General Leonard Wood became governor of the Philippines he instructed his mounted orderly to turn over the five Arabian horses to some trustworthy person or else have them destroyed. Sergeant Beard tried to reach me in Boston, but at the wrong music school. I might have kept those horses in the stable behind the Conservatory, renting them out, and studied in earnest with more peace of mind. I almost wish Nancy's report had been apocryphal.

My piano teacher reminded me that I wasn't absorbing anything, whether a Bach fugue, Beethoven sonata, Chopin étude, or Brahms ballade. Raw talent was useless, my performances a million light years away from my aspirations. The plain truth was that I had never really learned how to learn. And worry disorganizes.

My morale sank to its lowest point, the more since my beautiful collie ran away, probably looking for me. Scottie was never found, though I ran notices in newspapers for a whole year. A dropout, with *Heimweh*, I used to go on long solitary walks in the Fenway contemplating suicide. Where was that plucky spirit Dr. Browne had admired? Anna pointed out that amateurs had something to offer, too. I had given pleasure to countless, and would continue to do so, God willing.

While playing for the patients in a suburban hospital, I met the medical director and his wife, a former nurse. Carl and Priscilla, a childless couple, took a fancy to me; their weekend invitations filled a crucial void. I had advertised for a bit of family life weekends in exchange for music and/or housework. When they asked me to make my home with them, I accepted with alacrity, never reckoning the consequences. They were the answer to my prayer, I thought: a lovely house and garden, all the creature comforts, piano lessons, a Latin tutor, orthopedic treatment for my spine . . .

But with everything to make me happy, I would wake up from nightmares crying out to my mother for help. The atmosphere had grown strained. I felt a subtle change in the doctor's attitude, something more than paternal. Incredible though it sounds, I didn't know what was happening—only that I felt cut off from my friends. In bed with the flu one day, I told Priscilla. She sympathized, asked about my beaux, and promised to arrange a party. Carl came into the room, his face inflamed. "If you don't care anything about her soul, *I* do," he said. His outburst startled us and I began to cry.

Still the portents eluded me. He had befriended my oldest brother, taking him hunting and fishing, and Joe felt part of the family. Carl was greatly admired, a devout churchgoer, of Puritan stock, a woodsman with a variety of interests, a delightful companion. I can't explain, much less condone, submitting to his lovemaking the day Priscilla was in town. I must have taken leave of my senses, a lapsed Catholic committing a mortal sin. Of course I should have packed my bags at once. I did try again and again to break away, but each time he threatened to kill himself. During one dreadful row, I remember, he ran out into the woods with his pistol. I stood at the window, petrified, not knowing whether to feel glad or sorry when he returned.

The situation became intolerable. I was afraid to stay, afraid to go. Finally I managed to clear out, taking French leave, the maid promising to forward my suitcase. For two weeks I lay in a semistupor at a girl's hostel, prostrated by hysterical seizures and convulsive weeping—tears that would never wash away my guilt or undo the harm.

I could not afford to continue at the Conservatory. Determined to discharge my financial debt, I took full-time jobs: writing copy for the *National Magazine* and covering the 1922 Disarmament Conference in Washington, working on a music journal, doing publicity for *Music Week*, and reading juveniles for a publisher. As a freelance I wrote magazine pieces and interviewed authors for the Boston *Evening Transcript*. The writer and former war correspondent James B. Connolly kindly offered to stake me, but I wanted no more loans.

Carl had signed up on a South American liner as ship's doctor after a protracted breakdown. Freeing myself from him proved harder than expected. By the spring of 1925 I began writing him, unable to ignore his anguished pleas, then spent several weekends with him. The sight of his ravaged face revived my pity and a sense of obligation. I only offended him by suggesting he adopt my little sister, for whom I tried to get a Radcliffe scholarship. He swore he would never give me up, though he had no solution for the impasse. Divorce was out of the question.

That was the unresolved situation when I met Conrad. After living in a vacuum, I had little to offer any man beyond an unformed character. A fugitive from school, church, and life, I had renounced my German heritage, neglected my talents, and lost God in the shuffle. To quote a contemporary psychiatrist, I had one foot in schizophrenia and the other on a banana peel.

7

CONDUCTING A ROMANCE across the Atlantic was exciting, expensive, and exhausting. Conrad's Marconigram sent from the ship carrying him back to England quoted Vachel Lindsay's poem, the words "darling, darling, darling, said the Chinese nightingale" just meeting the required length. Reading it gave me the swooning sensation of plunging down in a roller coaster.

What of my decision about no more contact after the interview was finished? I remained torn—torn for three years, in fact. Let the goddess of compassion melt my heart, he urged in one of his letters. Study Kwannon at the Museum. But compassion rightly belonged to Jessie and the children. Learning about us, she was unhappy but resigned, blaming him for

the whole mess, a nightmarish one of complexities amd misunderstand-
ings.

In a letter written late in December 1926 he told me that he couldn't
face the thought of abandoning his family.

> It is an agony to me. You must consider that—I don't, mind you, say that I
> *wouldn't*, but it's only fair to you and to me and to them to tell you (as of
> course you must have guessed) that my feelings on that score are profound.
> That's all I'll say here—of that much I think you ought to be clearly con-
> scious. This doesn't *begin* to sound all the complexities of my feelings. . . .
> above all remember that I love you as I have never loved anyone, and that to
> marry you is the one thing in the world that I desire with all my heart.

"You say you love your family but love me so much more," I wrote.
"That won't erase guilt or hatred later on. Frankly, you offended me by
suggesting I find a job in London with your friend Martha's help. *Are*
Americans allowed work permits? Anyway it would be sheer folly, and an
affair is out of the question, a clean break the only solution. You must put
me out of your life."

Conrad was bound to his wife. Still I kept on vacillating, seesawing
between heart and conscience. If he held on to the rough draft of the
interview I had done, I would be in the soup with the Boston *Transcript*.
Such an intelligent questionnaire I sent him, he wrote, when he couldn't
even add two and two. Would I at least look up his friends so as to see
him through their eyes? And let him know if Bob Linscott tried to influence me? His publisher friend had just returned from England. Conrad
assured me I wasn't taking anything away from Jessie. That had ended
long since. *Had* it? Nor would he be reconciled with her even if I withdrew, he said. As with me, it had also been love at first sight with Jessie,
the brilliant Radcliffe student from Montreal. Didn't she still love him?
Bob was cynically amused by my naive question. "After fourteen years of
marriage what's left of love?" he asked. Probably a great deal, on her part.

Maurice Firuski had told me that any woman Conrad loved would be
damned lucky. But Beatrice Taussig was less sanguine. "You'll ruin your
chances for a good marriage if you get involved with him. You can't build
happiness on the misery of others. He's given Jessie a bad time and he'll
break your heart, too. Creative artists can't endure peace or happiness. He
drinks heavily, is suicidal, and comes from an unstable family."

Well, so did I. I felt disloyal just listening to her, apprehensive, too. As
for his self-portrait, his description of himself as a neurotic verbalist and
egoist who had come to the end of his rope, hadn't I indulged in similar
breastbeating? It was a courtship ploy, I told myself, pure and simple.
There was a kind of poetry in his warning that he was "inconstant as the

moon, changeable as the chameleon." And don't, for heaven sake, he said, "ignore the Aztec in me—the cold, cruel, relentless, heartless, inhuman, brooding, self-centered and essentially fugitive animal (a kind of newt) that I terribly am. Not that I don't desperately hope that you will prove me to be something different . . . "

In his letters he played a desperate Cyrano, a clever devil's advocate, cajoled, argued, humbled himself for offering me little more than his love. I was too perfectly the woman he had always hoped to find. Why should a world that provided love deprive us of its enjoyment? He chafed at being at the mercy of time and space, haunted by MacDowell's *Water Lily* (which I had played for him), felt alien in his own family, frantic to return "home" to me, a remote creature three thousand miles away. In another letter he wrote that his love for me "is in conflict with something, I have a crazy desire to say something bitterly injurious to you—why? God knows. Forgive it—I do love you—let me merely dismiss myself as Injuriously Yours, Conrad."

Had Jessie been wooed with such ardor, eloquence, and persistence?

By mid-January 1927 my high-flown intentions crumbled. He wrote of returning expressly against my wishes, thereby absolving me of all responsibility. Jessie had consented to a divorce, if he still wished to marry me after a year's trial. Dwelling on her grief compounded my guilt. I surrendered to pressure, after trying to head him off at the last moment. Water wears away stone in time. But then, I could always bow out later.

Harry Murray had meanwhile been taking my psychological temperature. A biochemist, Jung-trained analyst, and associate professor of clinical psychology, he was well qualified to advise me. "Aiken is a law unto himself," he warned over dinner at the Fox and Hounds Club in Boston. "He'll take you to hell and heaven and back again. Are you strong enough?"

"Oh yes, I've got the constitution of a horse," I said airily.

His hearty laugh drew stares from fellow-diners. I had questioned his statement that men were the dreamers and women the practical sex. Wasn't I a daydreamer? He thought I might rekindle Conrad's creative powers, once my personality ripened and I developed awareness. He saw me as Brünnhilde and Conrad as Siegfried breaking through the ring of fire. Would the opera have the same old ending? Actually I paid little heed to his words. Harry brushed aside my fears of ostracism in Cambridge. "The hell with what people think or say," he cut in, with a wave of his hand. "Conrad's work is the only consideration. He's the only real poet in America."

The day of his arrival I stood on Commonwealth Pier in a turmoil. Gulls wheeled and dipped as the British liner inched into her berth. The raw wind cut through my muskrat jacket, the blue-jay wings on my hat vibrated like a buzz saw. Shoved and jostled, I scanned the passengers coming down the gangplank. Where *was* he? Had he taken my advice at the last moment and stayed put?

Fragments of that fateful day come to mind: the thrill of glimpsing a gray fedora and Burberry, waving my handkerchief and getting his jaunty hat-brim salute, a fleeting exchange of gestures before his face moved into focus, blue eyes smiling down at me through black-rimmed glasses, hands blue and chapped (he never wore gloves), carrying his old portable type-writer through customs.

The sight of his ancient, iron-ribbed steamer trunk strapped to the back of the taxi connoted permanence, settling down, home. Did Jessie pack it? I shook off the sobering thought. How could I hold him when she had failed? Would the children grow up to hate me?

The cab streaked under the Elevated past South Station, jouncing over potholes. We held hands, gazed at each other like besotted idiots. Wicked to be so happy. Dr. Prince would roast me for playing hooky, but it was worth risking my job.

The ice on the Charles was breaking up as we rattled over the Pepper Pot Bridge. Before long the Harvard shells would be slicing the water. Spring couldn't be far behind. But *he* was—with bills, Conrad sighed. Stone broke, in fact. His poetry was going begging as usual. *Senlin* had yielded a paltry $2.10 royalties. Only thirty copies of *Festus* had been sold in England, and he abominated *Nocturne, Earth Triumphant,* and *Turns and Movies.* He hoped to get a part-time job, meanwhile doing book reviews, short stories, perhaps an anthology. And I would type them. At worst, he could retreat to his Cape Cod cottage. A pity I hadn't used it, as he suggested.

The cab screeched to a stop on Plympton Street. Conrad had leased a two-room apartment in Hampden Hall, to be shared with his younger brother. While taking postgraduate courses at Harvard, Rob would be on field trips for his brokerage firm. The jovial, white-haired janitor helped carry Conrad's trunk into the elevator, remarking deferentially, "Your neighbor is another famous gentleman, sir, Professor Albert Bushnell Hart." How nice, I thought. I might learn American history at last.

An affair seemed inevitable. We came together with the propulsion of shipwrecked mortals famished after a long wait, quivering with unspoken promises, the secret language of lovers, clinging together and kissing with tenderness and passion. Happiness stolen, but with Jessie's knowl-edge if not sanction. His Christmas present of pre-Elizabethan songs expressed our emotions—"Christ! That my love were in my arms/ And I in my bed again!" That voice from the Dark Ages, he said, was his voice.

I would keep my room, ostensibly chaperoned by my brother and sister-in-law, who had moved into the building. Joe must have told the family in Milwaukee, for I was to receive a steady stream of Novena pledges, medallions, holy pictures, notices of Masses and rosaries said for my soul. (How many sleepless nights had I given Father? how many gray hairs?) Even if Conrad were divorced and we married, the marriage would not be recognized by the Church. That of course mattered little to an excommunicant. The real sorrow was hurting those I loved, and who loved me. "Don't tell anyone about Clarissa's scandalous behavior," my aunts cautioned as they prayed for their black sheep.

Already *persona non grata*, I took a rash step. "Living in sin" exacted a penalty. We were the talk of Cambridge, snubbed and whispered about at concerts and lectures. Rumblings came from the faculty. "That fellow Aiken is ruining his reputation, carrying on with another woman." Shortsighted of him, since he hoped to get a job at Harvard. But he loved to shock, as Walter Piston said subsequently, relished the tongue-wagging and rib-nudging. His comments about spouses cheating on the sly convulsed Rob, a married man who viewed human follies with humorous detachment.

Every morning—rain, snow, or shine—Conrad escorted me on the two-mile walk to Emerson Hall. One morning I came out tardily to find him grinning from a tree. The red umbrella I carried in a snowstorm turned up in a short story. " . . . the rosy light on her enchanting face . . . " We made fun of Harvard's wrought-iron gates. One exhorted freshmen to "Enter and Grow in Wisdom," while seniors could "Depart to serve better thy country and thy kind." The only "kind" I wished to serve was Conrad. When I had the flu he sent roses with a message, "At least these can see you if I can't."

When we were invited out I kept expecting some outraged matron from the Watch and Ward Society to pin a scarlet *A* on my bosom. I recoiled from the epithet *mistress*, as at Maurice's bookshop party where Robert Hillyer was overheard pointing me out. "That brunette in the green suit and fur toque talking to Bennett Cerf is Conrad's *mistress!*"

Falling in love with someone disguised as an interviewess was an O. Henry romance at its worst, said Conrad. At first he tried only to win over his friends, later wanting us both to be accepted. I was on probation with Bill and Beatrice Taussig. Their loyalties were with Jessie. I recall a summer evening when Beatrice berated him for driving over the petunia bed. "Why all the fuss over a few flowers?" he asked frostily. "Aren't human feelings more important?" She and Bill were still on the brink of divorce.

Heute rot, Morgen tot. Better to laugh than to weep. What delight having a renowned poet in pursuit of a nobody and appreciating her small talents. He confessed trembling all over when Harry mentioned my name, and remarked, "Outrageous, that one's conduct is separate from one's will." Precisely *my* reaction. We made spectacles of ourselves at concerts, exchanging notes comical or grandiloquent. We invented silly names for one another—Hamadryad, Esel, Daffy-down-dilly, Gollywomps. Conrad analyzed my dreams and the many flirtatious hoydens he found in my snapshot album, posing with ice skates around my neck, chinning myself on the turning pole, leaning on a snowman, clowning on a hayloft at girls' camp or on Harry's yacht, holding babies, kittens, chicks.

I made draperies and slipcovers for his apartment, which faced the Yard and was furnished on a shoestring. A scarred old beer-hall upright was honored by Walter Piston playing on it with fine abandon. There were several nice Japanese prints (Conrad being a connoisseur), a Marsden Hartley watercolor, a Gilbert drawing over the fireplace, an exquisite oriental lacquered cabinet which a seafaring ancestor brought from China, and of course books galore.

He drew up a list of reading material for me. The novels he recommended included *Moby-Dick*, *Ulysses*, *The Wings of the Dove*, *Remembrance of Things Past*, and *The Brothers Karamazov*. Earlier, while he was still in England, I had read *The Sun Also Rises* and had written Conrad that I found it depressing. Hemingway's novel *was* depressing, he agreed, but an honest author needn't avoid ugly or obscene themes like decay, death, and lust, provided he presented them with "a kind of powerful detachment," as he thought Hemingway had done. Anyway, that was the truth about the world, "and the honest author will not leave it out." It wasn't a great book, he said, but "a *DAMNED* good one," and his favorable review pleased Hemingway's editor, Max Perkins.

My beaux gradually drifted away. Life revolved around Conrad. I had eyes and ears only for him. I did worry about Paul. A wounded dove with a broken wing, the Russian astronomer dreaded returning to Tashkent in June, when his fellowship expired. His eccentric behavior first embarrassed, then alarmed me. I felt pangs of remorse for having neglected him. After stoning the windows of the Widener Library, he was carted off to Danvers.

I also worried about Dr. Prince's pupil, Forrest, an orphan raised by an aunt, a religious fanatic. He had lost God among the psychology textbooks. Shortly after claiming to be Christ and disrupting the class, he was committed in MacLean Hospital. One night he escaped, seeking refuge at my lodgings when I was out. My brother called the staff.

Conrad was more disturbed than I by my lame ducks. He speculated about my having helped to drive Paul and Forrest mad. By the same farfetched reasoning, would he add the doctor to the victims of a *femme fatale*?

8

Pandora's box flew open one February evening when I disclosed my affair with Carl. Conrad sat opposite me at the kitchen table, chain-smoking and fortified by gin. His eyes raked me. "Why didn't you tell me before, at the very beginning?"

"I hinted at it by *promising* to tell you about it," I said. The "very beginning" to me was his return with Jessie's sanction, which crystallized his intentions. Before that he was an anomalous suitor. "You advised me to suspend all ideas and judgments until you came back." Would he have remained in Rye if I had written him about the affair? Hardly—a pitiful Don Juan betraying himself by monstrous suspicions, as he phrased it. "If I'd known how important a virgin was to you . . . "

"It was vital for our future to begin with a clean slate," he broke in harshly. "I had a right to want to fall in love with a virgin . . . " (A right or a need?) "Instead of innocence I found something horrifying . . . " (Innocence is ignorance, why prize it?) "You deceived me, concealing the sort of life you led. That in turn made me jealous and distrustful."

"You had no right to my past whatever, especially since you kept *yours* secret," I said, already regretting having confided in him. "Withholding facts isn't always concealment or being untruthful." One doesn't hand a homocidal maniac a gun. Granted that mutual trust and honesty are essential in marriage, I couldn't believe Conrad's avowed purpose in pumping me was altogether tied up with "basic concepts of honor." I was feeding an insatiable voyeur.

"Didn't you use the doctor to settle old scores with your father?" Conrad persisted. "A man twenty years older than you?"

"No more than I'm using you as a means of revenge," I said. Conrad surpassed my father in self-righteousness. "The role of inquisitor hardly becomes you, since *you* also planned to seduce me."

"No red herrings. Your evasions and ambiguities won't wash. Stick to the facts," he said, "so I can absorb the whole wretched business."

"You *have* the facts." I couldn't condone or explain my moral lapse except as a possible revolt from a repressive religion. Amoral, perhaps because I had so little identity to offer. Why was it so important that I replace my father? Would I ever grow up to a sense of responsibility and achieve equal status with my peers? At our last encounter, Carl went into a frenzy, seeing Conrad's roses in my room. Driving his Marmon to Lock-Ober's restaurant that day, I told him of having fallen in love with another married man. He turned apoplectic, twisted the wheel, and sent the car crashing into a tree. We were badly shaken up though not injured. His parting words, "I predict great unhappiness for you," were equally frightening.

With Conrad, candor damaged us both. A jealous voyeur put me in penitential row, purification masquerading as his sole motive. Pure bluff, recasting the scenario of my affair as a morality play, tricking me into revealing things that he later used in his writing. We were already saddled with guilt. Mine was heavy enough to cripple a giant. Impatient, then insistent, it tapped like a blind man's stick.

As I write these words, I think of a good friend who later helped me gain perspective. "That you feel yourself to be twice a home-wrecker is just vanity," he said. "Sound, secure marriages aren't wrecked. Conrad's, like the doctor's, was already crumbling before you came along. Your defenses are precious to you. You'll either resist strenuously having them destroyed or you'll tie up the package with philosophical ribbons. You have enormous potential, but you'll never realize it or be a whole person until you dredge up the underlying reasons for punishing yourself and hiding your light under a bushel."

Conrad stepped up his grilling and drinking, chipping away at my self-esteem. He harped on my "promiscuity" at Fort Sheridan, pouncing on my relationship with men, ignoring the larger aspects of functioning in a world of fascinating dimensions. I had found beauty, courage, cynicism, hope, tears, and laughter in that veteran's hospital, a wide emotional range broadening my horizons. Discovering the joys of giving was a profound experience for a taker.

To Conrad this was all irrelevant. "Didn't Carl also suspect you of promiscuity, brought on by army-camp life?"

"Probably." A natural assumption. "The fact remains, I came away a virgin." We girls never lacked chaperones, I said. There was safety in numbers.

"No doubt your innocence was your armor. *Noli me tangere.*"

I ignored the sneer, got to my feet, and said, "It's a long walk home," as Memorial Hall clock struck eleven. "I'm tired, after two hours on the witness stand."

"Sit down," Conrad said. "All right then, stand. What disturbs me is your easy freedom and readiness to give yourself, no matter whom you belong to, as long as you're petted and get your saucer of cream."

"Guilty," I said. "I like to flirt. And you—are you simon pure?"

An early frost had blighted our romance. Abused nerves screamed for action, after sleepless nights. He was tearing me to pieces, destroying the most precious thing we had, degrading our love. He couldn't have given me a harder time had I held my tongue. I couldn't be natural with him any more than with other men.

"What right have you to play judge? Or God?" I raged one April evening. "Needling me and taking me apart? You're not qualified to analyze anybody. All you want out of me is confessions. I'm through. Find yourself another guinea pig!" I grabbed my coat and walked out. Beset by other problems like a missed period, I needed balm and poultice, not prod and probe. What was I doing anyhow, living with a married man? How did I get here—plunging into something I couldn't carry off? Was this a prelude to our future? By staying on, I would richly deserve the misery Carl predicted.

On the way to Emerson Hall the next morning I fantasized Conrad having drunk himself into a stupor, getting run over or falling into the Charles. Harry Murray, warning me of ricocheting from heaven to hell and back, had omitted mentioning limbo. I dangled in that void for months. Conrad and I made up again but only to agree to separate permanently. If he didn't return to Jessie, I would take a job beyond reach somewhere. By late April I was in disgrace all around. Dr. Prince had fired me and Harry's indignant "He has no imagination" was cold comfort.

I might have been an understudy for Christine Beauchamp, the famous multiple personality Dr. Prince described in his book *The Dissociation of a Personality*. A high-strung girl ignored by her father, idealizing and then losing her mother at fifteen, Christine ran away from home after three years of delayed mental shock. She suffered from headaches and nightmares, was given to morbid introspection, rushed around like a hysteric, utterly lost, unable to work or study for long.

My early years were similar to hers. An element of *grande hystere* ran along with a heart too soon made sad or glad. Alienated from my father, my attachment to Mother keeping me from growing up, a leaner dependent on others, I fantasized marriage as solving all my problems.

One Saturday I was preparing a casserole, Rob expected back from a business trip, when Conrad sounded off again about Carl. Instead of obliging him with more data, I reached into the fruit bowl and said, "Here, catch. An apple a day . . . " He knocked it out of my hand and slammed out.

How had Jessie coped with his jealousy and oscillating moods?

Rob found me in tears, asked what was up, and was sorry to hear we'd had a row, that I had put out the wrong foot. "Anything you care to tell me?" He fixed himself a drink after I refused one.

"What was Jessie like?" I asked.

"Jessie?" His blue eyes lit up. "Very pretty, short, petite, dark curly hair, and a mind of her own. She stood up to Conrad, wasn't easily silenced." He smiled fondly.

Good for her, I thought, glancing at the trim, slightly built figure. Rob might enlighten me about the Aiken family, I hinted. "Conrad said only that your parents had come to a violent end."

"Well, you're certainly entitled to know more," he said gravely, and began by tracing their lineage to the *Mayflower*, their forebears Quakers and Abolitionists. Soon after their father, Dr. Aiken, married his cousin, he moved the family from New England to Savannah. There was a strain of mental illness on his side.

"Each of us four had a Negro nurse," Rob continued. "Our parents became more vigilant after Kempton's nanny had him baptized on the sly," he added with a faint grin. "Mother was a statuesque beauty, a head taller than Father. She was already growing deaf by thirty-five, though she loved to play hostess and go to parties. Conrad once heard Father threaten her with another child unless she stopped gadding about. They were considered a charming couple, but he was insanely jealous."

Their bitter quarrels were climaxed that February morning when Conrad heard two shots, ran into his parents' room, and saw them both dead. He had made fictional use of the scene in his first novel.

> . . . Dr. Kiernan stated that when called in at 7.13 there was still a spark of life . . . she looked alive but extraordinarily still. Eyes shut. Mouth wide open, fixed in the act of screaming, but silent. TERROR! . . . Perhaps she knew I was there, looking at her, and then walking softly, quickly, away . . . 'Yes, William, I am dead. But I know you are there. Do you want to know if an accident has occurred? Yes. A dreadful accident has occurred. I am quite all right, now. Run and wake Nanny. Shut the door into the nursery. Wind the clocks on Sunday morning. And say goodbye to this house and world for ever . . . '
>
> *Blue Voyage*

I tried to digest Rob's information. Three of the orphaned Aiken children were adopted by Frederick Taylor, the first one Rob, as the youngest, then Kempton, then Elizabeth, who was later placed in a mental institution. Conrad had opted for New England. From a temporary refuge in New Bedford he was farmed out in Cambridge with his uncle, Will Tillinghast. He found little warmth, affection, or normalcy in that household (his cousin, Ruby, was mentally unbalanced).

Living under the shadow of his father's murderous act, haunted by an unmentionable scandal, a prey to whispers and jeers by schoolmates, he vowed early to avoid public appearances, keeping his literary self private. Ample reasons for his abnormal secrecy, but there was more to come.

"Oddly enough, he always felt poor and deprived," Rob told me, "although he chose not to join us. He resented our good fortune and yet the twenty thousand dollars each of us inherited saw him through Concord Academy and Harvard, paid for his Cape Cod cottage and trips abroad. After we separated I lost touch with him. He never wrote us at Boxly, though he came often to see his schoolmate Grayson McCouch, our neighbor in Chestnut Hill, Philadelphia. He didn't give a hoot about us. There was the generation gap, of course, and he never felt comfortable with our foster father.

"He visited us only once, in 1904," Rob told me. "I was eight at the time and he was going on to fifteen. I won't forget that visit in a hurry. He suggested playing catch, then threw a hard-core ball with all his might. It struck my forehead like a bullet, knocking me out." Rob shrugged when I asked incredulously, on purpose? "I can't get over the feeling that it was deliberate."

Conrad's fury mystified me at the time. He felt it disloyal and a betrayal for his brother to spell out their parents' tragedy, though he never vented his anger on Rob. Apparently I wasn't privileged to know what he had already documented for all to read in *Blue Voyage*, published that summer. He tended to choose people who identified with him; the closer the involvement, the more harrowing the relationship grew, and I was the one then closest to him. I had revived his suspicions of the mother he adored. but had yet to mention. He never knew whether she was innocent or guilty of infidelity. I was a stand-in for Anna Aiken on trial, with him as prosecuting attorney.

I grieved at being regarded as a rank outsider just when I feared I was pregnant.

9

WE SPENT THE SUMMER on Cape Cod in the home of Conrad's friends Jake and Joy Wilbur, who were abroad. Two couples shared it with us, the Kreymborgs and the Wehles. As staunch admirers of Jessie's, Harry and Kate Wehle deplored me, especially after an unwitting anti-Semitic slip I've forgotten had reduced Kate to tears, leaving me aghast. Alfred and Dorothy Kreymborg, not knowing Jessie, accepted me. Alfred revered Conrad as "the greatest Southern poet since Poe" and began an epic poem based on our clandestine relationship. Dorothy guarded his privacy with wifely zeal, reminding the other two lax males to take out the garbage on their day. Conrad wrecked another of Alfred's precious days by planting a dead mouse at the kitchen door. Dorothy had hysterics.

Back to square one, I longed to confide my pregnant state in a familiar, trustworthy person like Margaret, my brother Joe's wife. Those of Conrad's friends who predicted I would refuse him sex and hold out for marriage were now saying I would "nail" him by having the child. Stung by this baseless gossip and buoyed only by the irony, I tried everything imaginable to halt Nature—violent exercise, swimming, tennis, hiking, dancing, mustard baths—all futile including ergot, prescribed by Conrad's surgeon brother, Kempton. Conrad couldn't afford a love child, however gifted or beautiful. A conception was inadvisable with a history of insanity in both our families.

Meanwhile, I reveled in a Steinway grand and Conrad in our absent host's pornography collection. One night the local pharmacist nervously delivered Conrad's snapshots of me in the nude. It seems that mailing "indecent matter" was illegal. My privacy, an afternoon of sunlight and gaiety, had been invaded by hostile eyes. So many facets to Conrad—the romantic lover, intellectual, poet, gadfly, puritan, sensualist—all splintered by childhood traumas preventing him from being whole, but a boon to poetry.

With a pride of poets, bristling wives, and a mistress on sufferance, histrionics were inevitable. One weekend I gave away our relationship, if that was possible, to a New York editor. His bawdy after-dinner story started Conrad laughing and choking on his coffee. He blacked out in the living room and struck his head on the andirons, breaking his glasses. Instantly on my knees, I sponged blood and carried on like a tragedienne until first aid arrived. So much for my efforts to preserve his reputation.

Three months pregnant by July, I had to face facts. On a hot, humid day we set out for Manhattan. Soot-laden breezes drifted through the open train window from cranberry bogs and marshes. My lilac pongee clung to my skin. "We'll be limp as dishrags," I sighed, fanning myself with *Liberty* magazine. Conrad's ruddy face remained hidden behind the morning paper. "Pull yourself together, darling, it'll be all over by tomorrow." Yes, I said, "and I'll be respectable again," nettled by his blasé tone, though knowing he was just as distraught as I.

I lashed out at fate for shattering our ragged romance so lewdly. Conrad distilled it in "The Clover":

> Pray, time, what is our shame
> or what this blessedness without a name
> that the unknown of love should come to this
> animal birth embodied in a kiss?
> > *Collected Poems*

He mopped his brow, glanced out at Buzzard's Bay. "Christ, this bloody heat." His light suit gave off a shimmer, reflecting the sun, hair bright orange, the azure blue tie matching the eyes, one earpiece of his glasses fastened with a lingerie pin, his good spectacles broken in the accident. How many eternities ago had he said, "I'm as sure as I am of anything that we're made for each other. But what are you really like?" No longer swift, demure, impossible, now an Untouchable with swollen feet.

The train to New York was jammed, hot, and stuffy. We took separate seats. Out of Conrad's orbit, one could at least *think* craven thoughts despite a splitting headache. I removed my leghorn hat. Even the poppies on it looked wilted. Eyes closed, I saw myself in a sitz bath, trying once more to get rid of Conrad's child, while he stood over me, catechizing me about the doctor. "Now about that night in Manchester, how did he make love? Any perversions? Think. And don't use amnesia again as an alibi. You can remember if you try hard enough."

I had tried with mounting exasperation to surrender every shred of intimacy, recalling less and less, memories evaporating under pressure. Much of my life was a blur, some of it a blank. In music I memorized everything learned. But I had no recollection of incidents such as Carl renting a saddle horse for me, until told so by Margaret. Conrad admitted jealousy from our first meeting, hating the idea of any man just speaking to me. A marvelous lover, he invariably ruined our lovemaking by comparing his performance with Carl's, which he could only guess at. He was never convinced that his "rival" was no sexual athlete.

He wanted sex without any thought of my welfare and safety while perpetuating his father's hostility toward women, keeping my guilt alive for years. Put on the rack, I naturally blocked memories—amnesia, the narcissist's umbrella. "You badger me about my past, but I'm not allowed a glimpse of yours," I fumed. "You're ten years older and must have had more than a few affairs. I know you had a mistress shortly before we met."

"That's not the point" was his stock answer. "It's your *veracity* that's in question. You owe me a complete and explicit account of all your sexual experiences."

Owe? I became a prickly porcupine at any mention of the double standard. He couldn't ram it down my throat. If promiscuity was all right for men, why was it wrong for women? And since the ideal wife was a lady in the drawing room and a whore in the bed chamber, how qualify for the latter role when you've been raised in the Edwardian era?

"You'll never admit that men are after just one thing. But you make it damned easy, with your come-hitherish ways," he said. Three generations of Aikens took over. Beginning with the biological imperative that the predatory male scatters the seed, Conrad translated my defenses into Freudian jargon, whereupon his father exhorted me in the style of his cautionary letters to Anna Aiken, and his grandfather delivered a sermon on the importance of strict fidelity, spiritual and physical. Their oppressive clamor one day drove me out and heading for the river, which fortunately was at low tide. Dorothy, shadowing me, dissuaded me from getting my feet wet. A ludicrous spectacle for one who boasted of fortitude to Harry Murray. The "anima type," his term for an artless coquette, had little chance to develop with Conrad putting the lid on my *id*.

"Grand Central!" The conductor jolted me out of my thoughts. Conrad emerged from the smoker, Montaigne's *Essays* under his arm. For once his crooked grin failed to affect me.

Manhattan was in the grip of a heat wave. From our dingy hotel Conrad phoned the abortionist (recommended as "clean"), then sent an urgent wire to Harry Murray for a cash loan of $250. He was so agitated that evening, after ferreting out another detail about Carl, that I had to pull him back from the fourteenth-story window, though feeling anything but rugged.

The next morning we started for the abortionist's office on the West Side. Children were cooling off in the wake of sprinkling carts and around gushing fire hydrants. I trailed Conrad into the subway and milled with the crowds. A little girl smiled, showing me her posy of wildflowers. Suddenly she burst into tears, the flowers knocked out of her hand and trampled underfoot.

The waiting room was packed, girls and women chatting, giggling, smoking, all apparently unconcerned. The only male there, Conrad took refuge behind a magazine. I sat beside him, clutching my handbag, inert and frightened, my throat dry as chalk.

"Look at Flossie, healthy as a cow." The man in white tried to allay my fears, exhibiting a buxom, simpering wanton who was chewing gum. "And she's a regular customer, too." I mentally reviewed cases of acute peritonitis, then fought revulsion as the nurse led me through a long corridor to the operating room.

The ether cone descended.

I woke up to a mundane discussion about the high cost of gas and electricity. Then the nurse took my arm, leading me to the waiting room, where the abortionist said reassuringly, "No, you won't have to be hospitalized, sweetheart. Just take it easy for a few days."

Conrad paid the tab and led me out to the curb, muttering, "Disgusting old lecher." In the taxi he asked tenderly, "How do you feel, Critch?"

"Like an eviscerated fowl."

"Don't give up now. You've been simply heroic."

"Heroic?" I was a murderess, and he my accomplice. Letting me kill my child, actually feeling relieved, what's more. How far had I strayed from the obedient little Catholic for whom a whiff of incense was enough to send me to my pew saying my beads! "God's punishment," Father would have thundered. "You deserve to burn in hell."

On the five-hour journey to Boston I felt feverish, dizzy, and nauseated, though the anesthetic hadn't yet worn off. At South Station we had a long wait for Cape connections. Conrad ate a ham sandwich while I sipped a milkshake, then promptly lost it in the ladies' room.

That night I ran a temperature. "If anything happens to you, I'll kill myself," Conrad vowed, holding me in his arms. Within a few days the fever subsided in both of us, enough to celebrate the publication of *Blue Voyage*, his first novel.

10

WHEN OUR MÉNAGE broke up after Labor Day, I rented Conrad's cottage on Bass River for a few months, at a nominal sum, feeling an intruder using Jessie's kitchen utensils, china, and linen. Silverleaf poplars dwarfed the red-roofed house. He had taken his first job, tutoring at Harvard. Much as I missed him I needed a respite, a chance to recover my strength for the break that a terminated pregnancy had postponed.

He did come occasional weekends, raising eyebrows though staying with friends like Lucien Crist, the composer. His poetry readings delighted Jean and Leona, companions I found through ads, and who shared the housework. Poetic Leona, from New York, looked like a semicolon beside the hefty Jean, a Quaker teacher. We spent evenings around the fire, reading, roasting chestnuts, I darning Conrad's socks or playing the piano.

Conrad's domestic expertise impressed us. He repaired the kitchen pump, cleaned the kerosene burner, and tamed the combustible Franklin stove. But on the road his erratic driving made him a menace. The Ford yawed wildly one Sunday night in a downpour, my shrieks of alarm no help. We avoided collisions by inches and reached the cottage spoiling for a fight but too exhausted to bother.

When he was gone I shed tears enough to irrigate the Sahara. Visiting our trysting places, showing the girls Conrad's study in the Wilbur house, or thinking of leaving him all brought on more tears. "When I'm not there to see or touch or hear or smell or kiss you, you seem to fade away," he wrote. "Helen Linscott also felt something evanescent and elusive about you, something of the dryad or nymph." How does one become real *in absentia*? I never knew that separation could make you physically ill. As Emily Dickinson said, parting is all we know of heaven and all we need of hell.

Engrossed in my own problems, I had merely skimmed *Blue Voyage*, which he dedicated to me. His dream one night of our having a little girl touched off regrets and guilt. He starred in most of my dreams, hovering in the wings when others were onstage. I lost him, found him, defended him, shielded him. Standard nightmares of ceilings and walls collapsing alternated with more original scenarios. One night I awoke to a terrific crash, aghast to find glass shards on my bed. I had smashed the lithograph of the Madonna and Child over the parlor sofa where I slept. "Freud would have something to say about that assault," said Conrad.

Working on articles and short stories dissipated the blues, and so did physical labor. October brought glorious weather, the air intoxicating. I split fallen branches into kindling, mowed the lawn, puttied windows, and interested Penn, the Boston florist, in bayberries and alder. He wanted some at once, would pay fifteen cents a bunch, and promised large orders.

In my old riding breeches and Conrad's forty-league boots, I slogged through the Hyannis swamp, wading in slimy bogs, risking a sprained ankle, extricating one foot, and getting the other one stuck. A sly old hag said I could pick all I wished, but the choicest berries were beyond reach. Breaking through a network of briar in Yarmouth, I finally found lots of red ones, and drove home with enough for twenty bunches. I never worked harder for three dollars, though.

The village busybodies were on the *qui vivre*. "So you're alone this weekend," one Nosy Parker observed. "Isn't Mr. Aiken here?" No, alas. I would pretend to hear the magic jingle, hoping to see him at the doorstep with his Cheshire-cat smile, and tossing away a cigarette. The thought of spending Thanksgiving Day without him brought a dull ache. But then Jessie wasn't having any fun either.

It was clear from Conrad's letters that he still had Carl on his mind. "Dear Crosspatch," I wrote him. "What's your scolding about this time? Once more I beg you to forget the odious Carl business. . . . The skies have wept all day. Fritz D. came to tea. He brought his play for me to type and the latest gossip. When Henry Beston pumped him about us, he either feigned amnesia or changed the subject. Mrs. D. had already heard the rumor from a friend, who learned of it from that couple who made capital of your strangulation and my hysterics last summer—remember? I asked Fritz how his wife took the news. Calmly, said he, smirking. She even asked me to cocktails in Cambridge. I ate a turnip to compose myself. We've become infamous."

Conrad was bursting with sonnets and longing to break out in dithyrambs for me. I discussed his job with Lucien, who felt that teaching blunted a creative artist. Mrs. Bodley, my British houseguest, from Lincoln, Massachusetts, agreed. She thought his sonnets beautiful, heard his cry in poetry, thought his prose was just as poignant, and sympathized with his efforts to reach the unattainable. But our illicit relationship—no.

The days grew shorter. Nor'easter gales rattled the small-paned windows. The white clapboard cottage with the red tiled roof creaked and moaned. Whenever the Harvard bell struck the hour, Conrad wrote, he thought of me. Emerson Hall made him miserable. He was perishing with loneliness. And I with boredom.

"I want to throw Fritz's play in the fire," I wrote, "so tired of typing 'fire-gold, moon-green, year-worn, earthen beauty.' Gathering berries and battling the elements is at least something real and tangible. Sir, kindly spare me your dreams of infidelity. There's no Chester in my life, nor have I ever taken any man home from a ball at 3 A.M. Consider yourself crushed. And *applesauce* to Bob's boast that I laid myself in his arms with divine surrender, dancing. I'll go to the mat with him."

After five futile attempts to hire the scrubwoman, I told him, "I pitched in and cleaned the Wilbur house by myself. Eight hours' labor left me lame in every joint, my double curvature probably tripled, hands honeycombed with blisters. I could barely wiggle, but had a heavenly swim afterwards. . . . Hurrah, the Boston Transcript paid me forty-five dollars for my interview with Ben Ames Williams. I could have hugged the postman."

There were repercussions from Conrad's friends the Wilburs on their return from Europe. Joy Wilbur was incensed. Obviously she had lost the battle with Jake over letting us occupy the house. Her bedchamber had been "desecrated by an adulterous couple," she said—her home left a shambles. The drawing room floor *had* been badly scratched, the men using talcum or chalk in lieu of wax for dancing purposes. While I tried to explain, she hurled epithets at me—tramp, harlot, a disgrace to my sex. Jake wouldn't or couldn't stop her. Conrad finally cut short her tirade and we made a dignified exit, she threatening to sue him for destruction of private property.

Back at Harvard he wrote me that he would never forgive himself or Joy for exposing me to that ugly scene, and on our first anniversary. I had met a painful, humiliating situation with poise and breeding, and he never loved me more, he said. With a domineering wife, Jake lacked the art of putting a newcomer at ease, but there was no excuse for her, a shrew, an uncouth woman who didn't deserve to live in the same world with me. The sensitive are always abused by the crass, he said. He would be merciless until that "killjoy" apologized. (Her way of apologizing was to toot the auto horn when catching sight of me or the girls.)

In her shoes I'd probably have been just as furious if not as vindictive. Unaware of any nobility beyond indignation on Conrad's account, I marveled at my calm. But the hurt emerged in a dream, an example of obloquy which Mrs. Bodley predicted I couldn't handle. We were sailing for England and were late leaving the cottage when a grim-faced woman greeted

Conrad coldly, then glared at me, turning up her nose. Who was she? I
asked. He said, "Somebody's sister." In that case, why snub me when she
didn't even know me? I felt saddened, bewildered.

Had I not responded too plainly to Jake's "strength"? Conrad asked in
one of his letters. That fear gnawed at him. He implored me not to let
Jake "take away my bloom," as he once did Jessie's. Or was he wrong
about this? Absolutely. I hadn't thought about Jake since that dreadful
morning. If I seemed detached, it was simple fatigue again. My last letter
heartless? *Triste*, perhaps, recalling our quarrels last summer.

"Dear Wishful-Thinker," I wrote him. "I can't enthuse over your quix-
otic notion that Martin Armstrong replace you with Jessie. Such things
happen only in fiction. What's this about your warping me? Harry would
say you hatched me. You're not a monster, but you cannot go on nagging
me about the Doctor . . . "

There was no laying Carl's ghost. I warned Conrad that continual self-
disparagement and doubting my love would weaken it. I wearied of trying
to convince him that his lovemaking eclipsed that of his "strong, silent
rival." Don't despair, he replied. He would always respond to affection,
and love me the more for my charity. I was a miracle to treat his absurd
inanities with such a light touch, the first creature with enough maternal
patience to cherish a damned nuisance. All the same, he urged me to hurry
and clear up the Providence weekend with Carl. It was vital, along with
more data in general. He could now absorb it, I needn't be afraid, and
we'd be the better for it.

Then again, I might get a bullet in my head, like his unloving mother.

II

AN ESCAPE HATCH was indicated. I made inquiries. By the time our
trial period reached an impasse, I had applied for a secretarial job at
Amherst. Mesmerized by the poet, I despaired of the man. Between avow-
als of devotion Conrad continued the inquisitor, his opening gambits
either jocular or transparent. He even admitted having driven over the
same routes I once took with Carl! Would Joe like to lunch with him?
Why not ask him? I replied, knowing that he only meant to pump my
brother.

One gloomy morning, the rain playing pizzicato on the roof, I received
a letter from Conrad telling me he had sent Martin a long detailed analysis
of my sexuality, even thought of mailing me a carbon, but decided that
might be too distressing. I couldn't believe my eyes. What on earth possessed him, taking liberties with our intimate life and involving his bach-

elor friend? Why didn't he ask me first if I'd mind? What could Martin do about it anyhow?

He wondered if my struggle to break away from Carl wasn't the physical hold he had on me. He wanted me particularly to note his inferiority feelings toward Carl's "animal force and vigor." Though he, Conrad, suited me better in general, just imagining Carl's gigantic sexual affrays brought on periodic impotence. He longed passionately to surpass his rival, thereby demolishing him. If I could only make him feel that his technique was more cataclysmic.

This confession of sporadic impotence was to be the only one he permitted himself. It reopened the stale, tiresome business of Carlitis. I began to share Mrs. Bodley's views. She echoed Beatrice's warnings. There was no likelihood of happiness with Conrad. I was ruining my chances of a wholesome marriage and motherhood. Did I truly want to shape my life, instead of letting life shape me? Then job-hunting among eligible males was a sound instinct. Havelock Ellis declared that we would never have a perfect society until the selection of mates by women was left untrammeled. It was time that women chose the father of their children.

I tapped this lofty ideal in my dilemma. Amherst's personnel representative was soon due in Boston and would contact me. This time I didn't deny trying to shake off Conrad's spell. Meanwhile, our confrontation in Cambridge had to be postponed, Louis Untermeyer had turned up from London and Conrad asked me if I minded him dining with us. Of course not, I said. But it proved an awkward, strained reunion under the circumstances.

Louis's love life had also hit a snag. Torn between wife and mistress, he was inclined to return to his wife Jean, though his mistress, Virginia Moore, had had a child by him—a rough analogy of our problem. But Conrad swore he never seriously considered reconciling with Jessie, though he loved his children dearly. He could never forgive himself if he warped my life more than he had already. We debated the delicate issue by mail, my letter crossing his and skirting the central problem, a long-winded, sentimental, watered-down version of the original draft. How hard it was to be honest without hurting others! I had too long deferred to people, men in particular.

If the Amherst job were the writing on the wall, I wrote Conrad, I would be angering the gods to ignore it.

But I'm just as divided between you and marriage as you are between me and the children. I asked if you wished to make my going or staying an issue, and you said no. Yet that's what your reproaches signify. I do need a breather after so much turmoil, and a job elsewhere would be a test of our love. Deep

down in my heart I know I will always love you. Otherwise I'd have walked
out the first day you began grilling me about my affair.

   Louis Untermeyer's ambivalence and compunctions about his wife have
not affected me, merely emphasized our precarious situation and the opinion
that divorce would be disastrous for all of us. My friends say you want [to
have] your cake and eat it, too, unwilling to give up one prize for another.
Mrs. Bodley thought it a pity we continue, not on moral grounds but for
practical and psychological reasons. I couldn't live without society's respect
and good will, not tough enough to fight opposition . . .

What an anticlimax if Amherst should now turn me down! Conrad's
reply was a torrent of desolation and self-abnegation. Disarming. My
impulse toward a college of men signaled doom for him, he said. The
thought of Amherst snatching me away paralyzed him—a terrible surrender, suicidal, giving up the most beautiful thing in his life. What would
be left of him? But if I was really trying to escape, he could only be
resigned and reasonable, say God bless you. He had no rights whatever.
What could he offer? Nothing but an unstable love, divided allegiance,
notoriety, and financial stress. His deepest longing was that we have one
another the rest of our lives. But I must follow my instincts. "If you can't
heal me, no one can . . . I do love you, and if I lose you I shall lose my
soul."

   He endowed me with more willpower than I possessed. While I wavered I began reading *Blue Voyage* more carefully. Mrs. Bodley couldn't find
a copy in Boston and heard that it was banned. I noted my initials,
C.M.L., in the dedication. A self-portrait pure and simple, he said, that
ought to cure me of any remaining shred of respect for him. "But if so, I
shall perish." Jessie, he said, found the novel "very amusing," a reaction I
questioned. Some of the interior monologue to Cynthia was hilarious,
but there was nothing funny about the character of the protagonist, an
outcast condemned to wander forever, leaving decisions up in the air. That
he couldn't love anyone for long was there in his own words. He lived
only for his work. Human beings were secondary.

   But it was the passages referring to his childhood that were the most
painful.

   . . . I was disliked and distrusted. I was cruelly beaten. I was humiliated. My
   pride and will were broken before I had come to my seventh year. I was in a
   state of continual terror. I sneaked in and out of the house, mouselike and
   secretive, my only purpose to attract as little attention as possible. My fa-
   vourite story . . . was the story of the ugly duckling. . . . I would revenge
   myself . . . by turning into a swan. . . . What gifts had the good fairies given
   me, that I might some day astonish and confound my cruel father, my

forgetful mother? . . . Could it, perhaps, be wisdom? This was conceivable. . . .

. . . Ashes to ashes and dust to dust. Would you like to kiss your father? No. The others were lifted up and kissed the dead face, surprised. Why did I refuse? Shyness and horror. . . . Then we sat in the carriage . . . feeling that we oughtn't to talk or look out . . . Trot trot. Clop clop. . . . Being pushed forward, in the crowd at the cemetery, to the edge of the grave. . . . My father. My father which art in earth. It was just over there he took my picture once, on the bluff by the river. In the white duck sailor suit. Hollow be thy name. . . . He was thirty-seven.

Blue Voyage

The wounded artist turning in upon himself, the poet crucified. While I complained about my father's "meanness," Conrad spared me his horrendous childhood for reasons more profound than I yet know. I couldn't forsake him, he wrote me. Motherless waifs must stick together. I would try to make up for his suffering. "Save me, Critch." How could I resist that *cri de coeur*? His jealousy? Make allowances for a tormented soul deprived of a father in the critical, formative years. Possessive? But also generous to a fault, wanting to buy me luxuries—perfume, jewelry—not to mention encouraging my writing.

My interest in writing began in high school and developed through our years together and after—feature stories, a column, articles, essays, author profiles, book reviews—in short, journalism. My noble resolve to part from him boiled down to a wistful glance over the wall at self-determination and independence, if not common sense.

By early December I had capitulated. I would be going back to Cambridge. On the surface at least I was tranquil. Conrad had little luck apartment hunting for me. A two-room flat was too steep at $75, a single one for $42.50 on the Avenue too noisy. He offered to pay the difference in rents, having just received $250 from *Scribner's* magazine for "Spider, Spider." I refused. If only the berries Penn wanted immediately weren't so scarce, I could have earned more than by typing. But the season *was* short. And I wanted to write.

After Jean and Leona left, I braced myself against ghosts, whistling while getting dinner. The kettle chirped, logs crackled, the clock ticked cozily, and lo, I wasn't a bit daunted by the solitude. I ate a veal cutlet in the warmth of the lamp-lit cottage, my only fear that of losing my voice through lack of use. Talking to the cat was the solution.

Conrad finally found an inexpensive apartment in his building. We would share the grocery bill. What could be nicer? Two can live cheaper than one. "I shall miss this dear little house," I wrote him. "Bless you for letting me have it. Wish I could buy it. Don't look for me until Saturday

late. I may not be ready what with cleaning, washing, packing, and getting
off the remaining orders for the florist. But I'll hustle, and leave the place
a bit neater than I did Jake's. P.S. Where on earth will we park our tin
Lizzie?"

12

SETTLED IN HAMPDEN HALL, I began editing John Ruskin's letters to
Rosa Bonheur for two elderly sisters. Temporary harmony ensued.
After months of cafeteria fare, Conrad appreciated home cooking. He also
enjoyed his tutorial courses, though irked by red tape. Some members of
the faculty felt that the author of *Blue Voyage* was an undesirable molder
of young minds. But loyal friends rallied around him—Maurice Firuski,
Bill Taussig, Bob Linscott, Walter Piston, Gordon Bassett, Jake Wilbur,
and Harry Murray, who hailed him as a sage, magician, and psychological
detective. His verbal pyrotechnics awed me, though he read poetry with
little passion, even words like *murder*, seldom raising his voice.

The apartment became an intellectual salon for poets including Theodore Spencer, Robert Hillyer, John Holmes, and Kenneth Patchen. I
would ask Conrad for sonnets as casually as a housewife orders lamb
chops, and for a time he obliged with flattering dispatch, still insisting my
deafness to poetry didn't matter. My soul emerged in music, after all, and
I was all the poem he needed. He had me by heart, he said, a Divine
commedia, rich, complex, magnificent.

Why can't I recall more happy interludes? His brother Rob had the
impression that we got along well together. At times I suspected Conrad
of playing a cruel hoax. True, he dodged meeting a rich and beautiful
widow whom Harry suggested. All who met him were charmed. Jack, the
janitor, handed me our morning mail with a conspiratorial wink, retrieved
our parking space, and guarded our precious Ford. Visitors buzzed and
dropped in (the phone was still a luxury for Conrad). Walter came for
chess and played the beat-up piano, growing more antic and witty with
each drink. He was to make his debut in Symphony Hall that year, 1928,
Koussevitsky at the podium.

Liquor flowed, dubious bootleg alcohol diluted with canned grapefruit
juice. We feared our revelries and squabbles were audible to Professor
Hart and his sister, next door. But there were no complaints, even on that
February day when I found a drunken Conrad brandishing a pistol in his
bedroom. "I've been doing a little target practice," he said, leering at a
tiny hole in the wall. "That bullet may have killed old Hart." I was afraid

to ask why he kept a pistol. Blue-eyed men made the best shots, said the U.S. Army. He handed me a note from Jessie, who announced her engagement to Martin Armstrong. She took sole responsibility for the impending divorce, said she'd been living under a magnifying glass the past year, and so it had all been arranged by correspondence. "A pity it all had to end this way . . . " Conrad had got his wish. Baffled, I said, "But darling, this spares you making a painful decision."

"Oh Christ, your obtuseness . . . can't you see that my children are now irrevocably lost to me? It's a double betrayal."

Because of losing both Jessie and Martin? Martin in whom he had confided my sexual life? No doubt I was obtuse, not grasping the nuances, but there was more than ambivalence here. Had he merely been waiting for a misunderstanding with Jessie to be cleared up? Weren't we engaged? What about our year's trial period? And what did the year mean to *me*? I hadn't realized yet how sick he was—a romantic suitor already disenchanted, gambling his family, according to his aunt, for "a passing fancy," deflowered and thus unworthy of sacrificing his children for. And this coupled with the parallel of the cruel father, absent mother, and threat of insanity.

"I'm both yellow and secretive," he wrote in *Blue Voyage*. "That's the fate of the self-conscious. Also manic-depressive. Advance one day, retreat the next."

Thank God for my resilience. Decades later I learned that he had discussed our relationship with Margaret over cocktails, at the Lincolnshire. My sister-in-law told me that she singed his ears like a Scottish grandmother. The real sin was not in living together but in exploiting a vulnerable partner totally committed to a permanent relationship. What mattered was how it affected our self-esteem.

"I told him it was cruel to take advantage of someone ten years his junior. When he read me bits of Jessie's letters, I asked how he could hurt anyone he had once loved. It was even more unforgivable to discard the mother of his children like a pair of old shoes. 'If you're that heartless with Jessie you won't be any bargain for Jerry.' He defended his actions, saying that a great love warranted great sacrifices. I couldn't understand his callousness. It filled me with disgust and alarm. But he kept coming back for more."

She was too hard on him. He was looking everywhere for his mother, as he said in *Blue Voyage*. He did suffer, did brood over the children, writing them regularly. At least he confided in someone who loved me. When Margaret learned about his grilling and my abortion, she called me a lunatic. "How could you have stuck with him so long, knowing he was that jealous? You were the only one to stand up to your father, you refused to speak German, and you broke away from the Church. What happened?" she asked me. A bad conscience, I said. She found something melancholy in my voice and "spunky smile" that saddened her, remembered a day when I sent a rejected short story right out again.

The "fatal interview" with Conrad finally appeared in the *Evening Transcript* that spring. In it I quoted Louis Untermeyer, who called him one of the finest verbal musicians in the country: "Mr. Aiken has outgrown the world he lives in. He is the harbinger of a subjective era, and he speaks that language. For this reason, the present generation think him a trifle mad, perhaps even dangerous . . . this very failure to reach his audience magnifies his sense of hopelessness, since he is automatically challenged to match his sanity against that of the entire universe."

In March Conrad was fired for "moral turpitude," four graduates objecting to him as an improper teacher of the young. (The class poet of 1911 took revenge on Harvard in 1961 by declining an honorary degree from President Pusey.)

That summer my work on the Ruskin letters took me to Maine. The quiet and beauty of Cape Neddick was a salutary reprieve. My employers would have been flabbergasted to know of my lapse from virtue. They lived the sedate, cloistered lives of those who master the art of doing nothing. Their quavering treble voices exchanging trivia echoed through the Victorian house.

Ruskin's love for Rosa Bonheur generated musings about Conrad. I pictured him pacing the floor deep in thought, making love, searching the financial pages for quotations on Sierra Pacific stock, swallowing aspirins in gin, swatting flies on the ceiling with a magazine—except in repose the facial muscles were taut, lips full, sensuous, and trained into a thin line, the eyes turned inward as if seeing the invisible.

I sat down and wrote him:

Dearest love,

Each time we part, I fall in love all over again. Does this weary you? Writing you conjures up romantic images of our first five days before I knew anything about you. I work in a spacious, gracious room overlooking the garden. A Baltimore oriole serenades me from a spruce. Beauty abounds. Wild flowers intoxicate one, and the roar of breakers dashing against the rocks at night sound unbearably poignant. I hear Cathy's wild cry, 'Heathcliff, Heathcliff'! . . .

I'm reading Murasaki's *Tale of Genji* and wish you'd send me the second volume. I could consume all four in a week. I want passionately to perfect myself, conquer the faults that annoy you.

But his mind was still on Carl, and a weekend in Manchester that I had told him about—a letter that was followed immediately by a note.

"Dear goose," I replied to both:

> Br-r-r, what a cold letter your Sunday epistle was. I dissolved in tears, cursed you roundly, then tried to forget you. As lief try to blow away the clouds. The sun hasn't been out even for God. How can you bring up the Manchester trip again, after telling me you had spent that same weekend with Carolyn? Were I ten times as culpable, it wouldn't be worth wrecking our love. At this rate you'll have me hating Carl. If I'm to hang for my sins, you'll have to poke your head through the noose, too. . . . Your note served as a poultice after I had groped my way through your frigid letter. Oh you can be so angelic when you want to, and so diabolic otherwise. Let me know if you've heard anything yet from Jessie.

13

THAT AUTUMN I began working at the Dunster House Bookshop, then managed by Al and Winifred deLacey while Maurice was in Reno. Conrad had sailed for England, against everyone's advice, to "negotiate" with Jessie. He offered to fatten my three hundred dollars from his anthology advance. I mustn't stint on meals, must tell him if I needed help. He was making amends for having "wrung" my neck, he said, over what I can't recall.

In one letter I mentioned that Harry Murray and I had had an illuminating talk. "He's coming Tuesdays and Wednesdays whenever possible to tailor my soul and mind FOR YOU. Was amused to hear that you trusted him among a few. 'That's no compliment, is it? I'm proud of having been the cause of all this.' He thought I had broken through my shell, said you're the only poet worth a pot of beans, that your work will be considered a milestone in literature . . . "

Conrad's response was to ask me what Harry and I talked about. "You, you, you, and me, me, me," I wrote.

> He's teaching you to appreciate me. . . . What will happen to us? I'm glad you felt the relief of getting away. We were in a state of dry rot the last six months, doing each other harm. Whenever you moan about Carl's ship letters I pity you, mark you down from precious to semi-precious. I can't recall one word of his logs but can quote yours until doomsday. Fie on you for intimating that you're left with no new experiences to give me. Hang your head. There's so much to enjoy, and so little time without wasting it in wrangling about the past.

Conrad had meanwhile taken a beating in Rye. Jessie refused to talk to him. Her friend Margaret Game had him over a barrel, calling him an egomaniac, while little Joan asked, "Who's that?" Checkmated, he retreated to London, where he could see John and Jane on the school holidays, probably reliving his own orphaned boyhood.

He wrote me that he had found a nicely furnished apartment with tall French windows, in Brunswick Square, for thirteen dollars a week including breakfast. Dining in cost a mere two shillings and sixpence, and he could write there. He admitted being drunk most of the time, partly to keep warm and sane throughout days of gloom and fog. One evening he summoned his "future husband-in-law for five hours of sheer candour," before throwing up. Martin, apparently benumbed by the court martial, would be underwriting the children's education. His novel, *All in a Day*, was selling well, and he had bought a house in West Sussex for his new family. Conrad suspected him of having been hypnotized by Jessie's friend, "a detestable maggot with sandflea eyes, wet skunk's hair, and a razorblade mouth."

He destroyed Jessie's letter proving collusion and turned over his entire income for the children, *sine die*, when advised that nothing would be gained by delaying the divorce. Monstrous of her, he wrote, expecting him to furnish evidence of adultery when she was getting everything she wanted. In fact, he said, "she needs to be beaten! If she were a man, nothing would give me more pleasure."

"I have met the enemy and I am theirs," he wrote Bob Linscott. "I surrendered on every point. . . . Trusted my soul to bloodhounds, . . . all of them frankly determined to see me walk the plank as publicly as possible, and Jerry with me."

I commiserated with him on several levels. Frustration and confusion were compounded by discrepancies in time, unreliable mails, and erratic ship schedules. He had set his watch to synchronize with mine. Keeping up with a daily correspondent was a full-time assignment. Besides my job, I did homework, practiced on the piano, and wrote articles. Walter Piston thought I should work seriously on my music, Beatrice having shown him some scribblings. So did I, but free time was scarce and writing meant bread and butter. Despite Conrad's disapproval I resumed my diary, trying to find myself in the thickets of narcissism. His objections and incursions would seriously dent our relationship later on, and I would make concessions—a big mistake.

Heated rebuttals came from London on the score of appreciating me more. Hadn't Harry at first regarded me as a passing phase, underestimating my "incalculable riches"? Conrad asked. And remarking to John

Gould Fletcher that it wouldn't surprise him if I outgrew Conrad in five years' time?

My letters grew less objective as Conrad blew hot and cold. Defeated by Jessie, he needed a scapegoat and I was it. He didn't miss a single male I had ever met. To him all were my lovers. The Victors and Marks were not our sort, he said. Be nice to them but keep them at a distance. He didn't want to come back and find Victor a regular visitor. Otherwise he would "wash him out instantly." I'd been drifting into such easy relationships all my life, and he bet dollars to doughnuts that Victor was in love with me already, had been playing the piano all evening, taking me to dinner, the movies, *und so wieder*. "I shall be driven to murder . . ."

His letters read like those of an inquisitor with an inflamed imagination. I was rebuked for not mentioning my innermost thoughts the day I dined with Mark Potter—the tiniest detail, what I felt, what we did later on, how the relationship ripened, et cetera. It was my concealment and deception that brought on his jealousy, he said, not being square with him, sharing that craving the minute a new male became interested. Had I developed these minor flirtations in Carl's time? I'd better drag it all up, confess the excitement he could actually divine in me.

Well, he could whistle for any more recollections of my sex life. Dolt, not knowing what every author's wife should have known: that it was fair game to capitalize on the follies and folderols of one's mate. I could look forward to a series of attack-remorse-reconciliation syndromes, the artist requiring constant aggravations, like a bird gravel for digesting food. I had got *my* wish—a romantic longing for the privilege of serving the muse.

"No wonder you didn't ask me to type those two short stories," I had fumed after reading "A Man Alone at Lunch" (a despondent suitor lamenting the power of his fiancee's former lover) and "A Conversation" (the anguish of loving a promiscuous woman). "You're not interested in my moral welfare, only in whipping up excitement for scenes."

"Everything is grist," he replied. "An artist must be free to write whatever sparks him. What about *your* story on Carl?"

"That was my own experience. I wasn't using your past." Skullduggery, I called it. Now he was cooking up more of the same brew.

I wrote him that his suspicions were completely groundless. Eyewash.

I haven't seen Mark, Victor, Fritz, or Belknap recently. But I wouldn't let your childish threats or snobbish attitude interfere with my cultivating them. Victor—"that sort of person"—happens to be a decent lad and extremely talented. You put the Indian sign on him, then suggest I share my thoughts with you when I see him or Mark. What for? To furnish more copy for your typewriter? . . . I shouldn't really dignify your charges with any comment. You have a penchant for twisting the knife, insinuating that I may be merely using you as an escalator to the next floor. Sniping and then trying to forestall my retort. Saying everything you think or feel isn't always honesty, it can be self-indulgence. How quickly you would condemn such impulses in others. Did your vituperative letters to Jessie and Martin gratify you? Their silence must make you uncomfortable.

Suppose you pour out your poisons to Harry instead of Jake, a pushover, and work on your *Book of the Dead* instead of chewing on my past. I am not Mary Dugan. Keep a memo by your typewriter: "Dec. 8, all my suspicions revived after seeing *The Trial of Mary Dugan*; sent Critch a bruiser. Dec. 9, She's plainly a whore, may she fry in hell. Dec. 12, Her angelic letter sobered me up. Am sorry now I tore into her. I do love her, after all. Dec. 14, Cabled 'Disregard latest blast.' Feel better . . . "

In a frenzy to get off the hook, I stepped on tender toes. Conrad had begged me to "make a clean breast" of my sex life from 1918 to 1926; it was "now or never," letting Jake and Beatrice question me. When I humored him I got the brushoff from Jake. "I'm Conrad's friend, not your father confessor." His letters were a replay of 1927. I'd had enough of his stews and tempers and prying, my confidences turned into ammunition. The wellsprings of compassion were drying up, replaced by headaches, nightmares, fainting spells. The time had come to say, "Either accept me as I am or else forget me." I was the sum of all my experiences, and they included the opposite sex. His jealousy was a sorry joke among his friends. Three of them, and Rob, helped draft a reply.

I echo your "Now or Never," and propose that you judge every act and word of mine on its own merits. I will make a full confession on my knees, but of love, not imaginary sins. What fills *me* with despair is your refusal to believe me. Do you honestly think your neuroses were caused by my "betrayal"? If you want a straight answer to a silly question, you had them all before. Neither a virgin nor a prostitute can wash away guilt—dirty hands in search of a clean towel. A virgin would have been horrified living "in sin." Since you and Beatrice decided I was the "mistress type," whatever that means, all this hullabaloo about my non-virgin state seems superfluous. I've told you every essential fact from 1918–1926; the matter is closed. I'm going forward, with or without you. I love you as deeply as any mortal can, but I no longer fear you.

My declaration of independence drew blood. A horrible mistake, he wrote—that holier-than-thou attitude a false note, dramatic, haughty, and hot from Belmont (meaning Beatrice Taussig). Beatrice didn't understand the delicate balance between two souls. He had told her to keep hands off the whole "honour-jealousy problem." My reference to dirty hands haunted him. A son of Belial? He could easily be one if he wished, "darlinged" as he was all the way to Russell Square by "barking woo-woos." He was gladly surrendering his wife, children, friends, and home, so they might be safe from an egomaniac's depredations. Instead of expressing remorse at the psychic injury done him, he said, I cursed him for his jealousy. He would never get over it.

My genius for blundering. But it was sanity rather than vanity that led me to ask for help. I was goaded into it. Quoting his friends *was* maladroit, to say the least, humiliating to him. I should have told him in my own words that I could not continue feeding him erotic memories. He was perpetuating his father's paranoia.

Four excellent persons, he wrote, "wasting such wisdom and sympathy on a fat, pale, spineless worm." Must he always dredge up his sick conceit with whimpers? Would he ever learn to keep his mouth shut? He implored me to cable assurances that I wasn't abandoning him. Only I could make him sane and keep him alive. Music meant nothing to him except me. He wanted to dance with me, went crazy with desire thinking of my various dresses, hats, shoes, or remembering me brushing my hair before the glass. Was it too late to be the angel he knew I was? I had people, he said; he had none. It was my treatment of him that brought on periodic attacks of searching for my true identity. Threats or shrugs would not determine his ability to love me trustfully. He might end by leaving me.

Ashes were heaped on my head. I received a love letter in French, achieved without a dictionary, and Stendhal's *Chartreuse de Parme*. He had scoured London, on chilblained feet, hunting for *genêt fleuri* in vain. His pendant earrings arrived while Ted Spencer was present to exclaim at their beauty. "I now feel a genuine concubine," I wrote Conrad, and asked him to thank Elizabeth for helping him choose the hat and scarf at Liberty's. He had told me about Elizabeth the year before—that she had been his mistress, for how long he didn't say, a married woman living in Oxford. His 1928 letter told me that she had lunched with Martin Armstrong and had been fed the usual propaganda about us, but began changing her view somewhat after hearing Conrad's side of the story.

14

OUR EXCHANGE began taking on a more rational tone. We admitted having behaved badly. The important thing was that we loved each other and could work out our difficulties with time, patience, and common sense. If the divorce went through on schedule, said Conrad, we might be married the following fall, provided I still wished to marry him. He warned me about the horrors awaiting a literary chap's bride. Read the diary of Dostoevski's wife.

Or *Blue Voyage*:

> What if it were at last possible to talk of *everything* with a woman? To keep no secrets, no dark recesses of the mind, no dolours and danks, which could not be shared with her? But then she would have ceased to be attractive. It is simply because we have to *pose* before her . . . to pretend to be angels . . . the angel with the sword? . . . *Ah, the awful fixed curve of determinism!* MIS-ERY . . .

He was anxious that we live somewhere accessible to my monthly supply of ergot, initially prescribed by his surgeon brother, Kempton, before my abortion. I had been taking this forerunner of LSD ever since without his knowledge and unaware of the dangers. A fungus in rye, ergot had been used by medieval midwives to induce peristalsis, but like LSD it short-circuited the mind when taken to excess, and could be fatal. Apparently Conrad didn't regard our unfortunate heritage an impediment, for he asked if I could wait a few years before having a child.

In one letter he sent me a news clipping about a brilliant London chemist who lost all faith in women after seeing his fiancee talk to another man in the street, and kept his vow of celibacy unto death. "Worse than me?" Conrad scribbled in the margin.

Houston Peterson's proposed book, *The Melody of Chaos*, gave Conrad cold feet—better written after he was dead, if at all, he said. His elaborate dream-fantasy featured me depriving him of drink and his typewriter for an indefinite sabbatical. He said he might really get down to work if I joined him.

Five letters from him came in one mail. "Five letters this morning," I wrote, "and all of them *mad*. My poor dear, your abysmal doubts and desponds will give me heart failure yet. Try to be patient, and realistic. I'll answer your last batch tomorrow. I'm sorry I exasperated you again with my bungling cable, 'Stop drinking trust me.' I'm still trying to unriddle your reply, 'Will you cross or I.' If you won't take your doctor's warnings, how could I help you in London? And wouldn't my presence bollox up the divorce?"

Before I could decipher that cable, Conrad announced his imminent return. When he arrived early in the new year he looked ill, drugged with fatigue. "Courage," he said bitterly, his small income depleted, "we'll soon be in the poorhouse."

We sought refuge in each other, trying to compensate for loneliness and fear. I pursued my journalism and typed poems for his forthcoming anthology. That spring he developed a skin disorder and jaundice. Mistaking the latter for ptomaine poisoning, and blaming bad oysters and bootleg gin, he proved a difficult patient at the mercy of a squeamish nurse. When his ear had to be lanced, I fainted.

My ignorance and naiveté about authors imbibing inordinately, among other things, stirred up hornet's nests. Drunkenness was practically unknown in Milwaukee during my childhood, and my European antecedents were all abstemious beer or wine drinkers. Hands off, I was warned. Keeping Conrad functioning was a full-time job. His moods fluctuated constantly, up and down, up and down without a plateau. For several months I recorded them in my diary. If a definite pattern emerged, I could foresee the inevitable chill-and-thaw cycle. His graph showed such erratic jumps that I suspected he knew about my monitoring and dramatized his afflictions.

Feb. 7 [1929], miserable with the flu; 8th, very melancholy; 9th–11th, weak but civil, even affectionate; 12th, postflu depression, remote, bored, brooding over his family sacrificed; 13th, lethargic but cordial; 14th–16th, more scenes anent the Doctor; 17th, quarrel patched up; 18th–23rd, amiable; 24th, recovering from the bottle; 26–27th, cheerful; 28th withdrawn.

March 1st, brooding over loss of Harvard job; 2nd, caustic about my refusal to drop Victor; 3rd, suffering a hangover; 4th, recovered; 5th, loving; 6–8th, more anti-beau lectures; 8th, truce; 9th–11th, jealousy, battle; 14th, atmosphere clearing; 15th, peace; 16th–17th, psychic separation; 18th–23rd, peace, joy; 24th, tiff; 25th, atmosphere brighter; 26th–28th, ditto but avec a nocturnal spat; 29th, recovered; 30th buoyant, 31st, goose hangs high.

April 1st, harmony; 2nd, spiffed and abusive; 3rd, neutral; 4th ditto; 5th–6th, chipper. 7th, detached; 8th, slight tiff; 9th, topside again; 10th–11th, civil; 12th, jealous of Rob; 15th–17th, serene; 18th, combative after a party; 19th–24th, cheerful; 25th–30th, the indigo blues, skin peeling and flaking, followed around with brush and dustpan.

May 1st, jealous of Dr. T; 2nd–3rd, morose and queasy; 4th, arctic; 5th, very, very low; 6th, jaundice diagnosed; 7th–10th, quite remote; 12th, reviving; 13th, ditto; 14th–17th, skeptical of my illness; 18th, open warfare; 19th, calmer; 20th ditto; 22nd, distant; 23rd, intolerable (driving me to flee to Gertrude Townsend for a rest); 26th, find C. sodden drunk; 27th, jaundice relapse; 28th, weak; 29th, recovered and affectionate; 30th, physically recovered; 31st, row over my considering a job in a boys' camp.

June 1st, frigid; 2nd, fair and warmer; 3rd, a chill of 40°; 4th–5th, almost normal; 6th, almost meek; 7th, friendly until request for repentance refused;

8th, off again; 9th, peace until evening, frightful tiff over men and fibs; 10th, I capitulate, declining offer of boys' camp job; 11th, truce; 12th, very nice; 13th, chipper, angelic; 15th, jealous of fellow-tenant; 16th, cool, nasty; 18th, reduces me to tears; 19th, stoical; 20th–30th, longest amnesty yet; brighter prospects of mutual understanding, he a positive merry andrew.

Starting life over again at forty during the Depression was something no one relished. Conrad had decided at twenty to write poetry until he was thirty-five or forty, when his poetic powers and ambitions would wane. Then he would switch to prose. That is roughly what happened. But he lacked the novelist's ability to see life in the round, and didn't think he could acquire it. *Blue Voyage* was obviously a failure, he said, and he couldn't kindle any enthusiasm about tackling another novel. "Must I go back to the silly business of trying to write poetry, of which I've already written far too much?" he had asked in an early letter. "Anything done from habit is despicable."

Reviewing books yielded a mere pittance. His sense of humor and irony was his saving grace. A British request from *Town & Country Life* for a biographical sketch came just as his novel was remaindered. For a young southern belle on shipboard he had autographed a copy, "From your *faux pas*."

15

ONE ARDENT ADMIRER of Conrad's novel was destined to affect our lives profoundly. Malcolm Lowry's letter dated March 13, 1929, reached Conrad via Rye.

I suppose there are few things you would hate more than to be invested with any academic authority. Well, this I shall say. Next October I am going to Cambridge for three or four years to try and get an English Tripos and a degree. Until October I am more or less of a free-lance and a perpetual source of anxiety to a bewildered parent. The bewildered parent in question would be willing to pay you 5 or 6 guineas a week . . . if you would tolerate me for any period you like to name. . . . Let me hasten to say that I would efface myself and not get in the way of your inspiration when it comes toddling along, that my appetite is flexible and usually entirely satisfied by cheese, that although I can't play chess and know little of the intricacies of gladioli, I too have heard the sea sound in strange waters . . . and I can wield a fair tennis racket. . . . do you mind reading this letter sympathetically because you must have been pretty much the same as me in heart when you were a kid. And I do want to learn from you . . .

Selected Letters of Malcolm Lowry

When Malcolm arrived in Cambridge during a July thunderstorm I was in Old Lyme, Connecticut, doing publicity for the colony's twenty-eighth annual art exhibition. Conrad's letter to me described him as grimy, dilapidated, wearing dirty tennis shoes and carrying a broken suitcase. He was penniless, having spent all his cash in Antigua on a young mulatto girl. Much as Conrad needed a vacation from me, sharing it with a wild collegiate would hardly be restful. I had heard rumors of college capers involving Conrad and the editors of the *Hound & Horn*, Varian Fry (expelled for a year after putting up a For Sale sign on President Eliot's grounds) and Lincoln Kirstein (the wealthy poet-scholar addicted to the ballet). Innocent mischief, I gathered, whatever the binges. But now I had to worry about an irresponsible young dipsomaniac.

Conrad laughed at my fears, though after a night of carousing he was bent over like a candle pointing toward Lyme. He cautioned me about venerable artists such as Percival Rousseau, the dog painter, making passes. "Don't get spoiled or forget yourself by playing the piano too boisterously. You're at your best when gentle, though entrancing when rowdy, too." My letters were "brilliant, heavenly," he said, and he intended bagging some of them for a possible novel. *That* was permissible.

I ascribed his euphoria to Malcolm's worshipful presence. He had crossed the Atlantic to meet the author of *Blue Voyage*, intrigued by the book's dedication. My initials, C.M.L., were also his before he lopped off the Clarence. He saw something mystical in this, a sign pointing straight to his mentor. His suitcase bulged with notebooks and the manuscript of a first novel, *Ultramarine*, which chronicled his seafaring year as a coal-trimmer on a tramp steamer. My snapshot of him later that summer showed an athletic, wholesome-looking youth, a cherubic smiling face, brown wavy hair, and nautical blue eyes. Nothing suggested the alcoholic who documented the horrors of alcoholism in his novel *Under the Volcano* and eventually destroyed himself like Dylan Thomas, with whom he had much in common.

Conrad put in several weeks on Malcolm's novel, deleting passages that read like a parody of *Blue Voyage*. The two hit it off despite a twenty-year age difference. Malcolm turned twenty that summer; Conrad, forty. "We spoke the same language and were astonishingly *en rapport*," said Conrad. Too much so, I concluded, when his telegram arrived, telling of the accident. I took the first train back, after wiring for details and receiving a cryptic note about a drunken brawl that had left him with a concussion and a broken nose.

"Let this be a lesson to me" was the convalescent's wan greeting. Propped on pillows, his head swathed, he was nourished by the Grolier Bookshop below, which supplied sandwiches.

Rob described the scene to me. "I found Conrad on the floor, about

11:30 P.M., two pools of blood where the eyes normally are. He had tried to wrestle the porcelain w.c. lid away from Malcolm, but it broke and struck him in the face with such force that he went down like a felled ox. I called Dr. Taylor, who took him to the hospital and stitched up his forehead."

For all my maternal feelings toward Malcolm, ten years my junior, I could have killed him. "The beginning of a beautiful friendship," as magnanimous Conrad said, after his protegé returned to England. Rob and Kempton were alarmed by their brother's alcoholic intake; they suggested he have an examination and will his liver to medical science. After a physical checkup, Conrad exulted, "I'm sorry to say there's nothing wrong with my liver."

The misogynist surfaced whenever he drank, turning him into a demonic stranger. One spring evening soon after our marriage I was making polite conversation with Kenneth Patchen while waiting for Conrad to arrive. When he came, on unsteady feet, he pointed a finger at me and said with heavy sarcasm, "There sits the girl who calls herself my wife," leaving Kenneth acutely embarrassed and me nonplussed. Since I'd been told that a high-voltage personality must insulate himself, Beatrice Taussig's initial warning about his heavy drinking went uncontested.

She and Bill were both being analyzed by my employer, Dr. H, and Conrad reminded her during a powwow on psychoanalysis that I had access to the patients' case histories. She blanched, picked up her gloves and handbag, and left abruptly. I upbraided him. "That was a wicked thing to do—totally uncalled for." Within a few days my embarrassed employer asked if I didn't agree that it was unwise having a secretary who knew his patients socially. That depends on the secretary, I replied. "I had no intention of prying." He said, "I believe you," then gave me two weeks' severance pay spiced with profuse apologies. One more occupational failure to chalk up. (A gallant friend years later said he should have discharged the patients instead of me.)

Outraged, Conrad threatened to sue the Taussigs for slander and for jeopardizing my livelihood. That floored me. "Such a move seems out of order, since you baited Beatrice in the first place," I told him. I wondered if his motive was to prevent my reading the analyst's notes about his own relationship with Beatrice. His story "Spider, Spider" was a clue. A sophisticated Gertrude competes with a simple country girl, May, for Harry's love. "The counterfeit makes its way. And the genuine is spat upon . . . " Gertrude, bent on tearing May to pieces, scoffs at a gullible Harry, suggesting that May is only after his name, money, and prestige—a hypocrite who wouldn't be above blackmail. He succumbs to Gertrude and is caught in the web—a shrewd treatment of the love game.

My job lost, I redoubled the freelance writing, though a full-page news-paper feature paid only twelve to fifteen dollars. (If memory serves me, the *Bookman* and *Saturday Review of Literature* still owe me for essays and criticism.) Meanwhile I felt sanguine about marriage solving our prob-lems—joy through suffering. My optimism almost equaled that of Harry Murray. It was Harry who tipped the scales whenever I wavered about remaining with Conrad.

By January 1930 I was emboldened to speak up for myself, the more as Conrad had advised Louis Untermeyer to divorce Jean and marry Virginia Moore, the mother of his son. High time, too.

"I'll decide when I'm good and ready," Conrad said. He seemed af-fronted. "I won't be pushed or bullied into it. Just like a woman, only interested in marriage."

I did get my engagement ring. It resembled a pants' button, a pale green jade in Dalmatian silver claws. But I treasured it like the Kohinoor diamond. Three years of courtship through the wringer was enough. Jessie and Martin were married already, so Conrad could "regularize" our relationship. He had won the Pulitzer for his *Selected Poems*. And he had sold his Cape cottage for $6,700, at a slight profit. While I helped auction off the furniture, Joy Wilbur turned up with a bland smile, her eye on the marble slab for candy-making. Conrad later berated me for selling it to her. She had recently alienated his and Bob Linscott's friends Edmund Wilson and the Burton Rascoes by turning them out of the house as it were. "Jake is merely a claw extended by her in my direction," Conrad said through clenched teeth.

Lady Luck had favored him in 1929. I had no business sense and knew no more about his financial affairs than about his women, but he did say that he was badly burnt in the stockmarket crash, that his brothers had refused his request for a $15,000 loan. He was on the phone downstairs constantly, wearing a grim do-or-die expression. Forty years later, how-ever, Rob told me that Conrad had made a phenomenal killing just before the market blew up, between June 1928 and mid-August 1929—his first speculative venture. "He cleared more than $65,000, after selling 1,350 shares of Sierra Pacific Electric, and bought 250 shares of First Investment Counsel Corporation at $130. Those securities he left with me for safe-keeping before returning to England in 1930."

Rob told me Conrad was terribly upset to learn that Jessie had heard about his gambling in the market and might attach possible winnings for the children.

Conrad and I were married in February 1930, a civil ceremony at Ruth-erford, New Jersey, our witnesses William Carlos Williams and his wife, Florence. My shoes pinched, I felt silly in a fur toque and eye veil, my otter jacket, a hand-me-down, decorated with an orchid. Throughout the ceremony I reflected on the absurdity of the marriage vow; pledging to love and honor one another seemed as asinine as guaranteeing sunshine every day of the year. I certainly couldn't have felt *more* married. The ceremony was mere abracadabra, like adding a cupola to a gingerbread house. Half of me craved a church wedding, tearful relatives, orange blossoms, bridal gown, veil and bouquet, with tin cans clanking behind a limousine and a honeymoon in Niagara Falls.

The Williamses toasted us with beer at lunch, wishing us happiness in a world gone crazy. Conrad recounted an exchange at the marriage licensing window. When he explained himself as an adulterer, the jaded clerk said with a shrug, "Hell, aren't we all?"

Part Two

16

THE LAST BUGLE CALL alerted our friends. Draining their paper cups of bootleg gin, they wished us bon voyage and left behind a huge basket of S. S. Pierce delicacies. I swallowed Mother Sill's Seasick Pills in chlorinated water and prayed for a smooth crossing, my first and Conrad's twentieth. Out on deck we watched the bustle and confusion of imminent departure for England.

"Boo-oo-oo—" The deep-toned siren was like a physical blow. Engines throbbed, bells pinged, propellers churned, and a Western Union messenger jumped four feet from ship to shore to rousing cheers. While the *Scythia* edged away from Commonwealth Pier, Conrad's short story came to mind—"Farewell! Farewell! Farewell!", my favorite. August 1930, a memorable date for my diary. Farewell to three years of turbulence.

Conrad was maddeningly vague as to where in England we would live. "I'll tell you once we get there," he said, polishing his glasses, the blue eyes naked and vulnerable. I pictured a thatched cottage, Sea Bells, with a garden, fruit trees, and a music room for two pianos. Would I be cold-shouldered by our mother-in-law, as James Russell Lowell called Great Britain?

Next morning's gong was superfluous, with heavy seas rolling. I had lain awake much of the night, our third-class tourist berth rocking to the gurgle and slosh of basin water. Conrad ordered a cold bath from an admiring steward. His austere manner commanded deference. Several passengers recognized him from news photos. The Oxonian accent misled an Englishwoman. She thrilled me by asking if he was about to replace the late Robert Bridges as poet laureate.

We searched for companions while playing deck tennis and taking constitutionals. On the third day Conrad found a fellow-Harvardian, David McCord, poet and essayist, author of five books. He was bound for Scotland with his widowed mother. Conrad steered him into the bar, murmuring, "With Hoover threatening even stronger Prohibition enforcement, it's about time I shook off the States."

With a Pulitzer Prize and a book-length study of his work in process, Conrad felt more sanguine despite the Depression. We could count on at least one intermittent paying guest, Malcolm Lowry. The English exchange rate was in our favor, $4.82, and with luck I would sell more author profiles. I had done only a dozen since meeting Conrad.

We disembarked in Southampton, having accepted the McCords' invitation to join them for a week's tour of Scotland. The train ride to London intrigued me, the locomotive whistle almost two octaves higher than its American counterpart. My "Oh's" and "Ah's" at English scenery amused the McCords but pained Conrad. "No, Critch, Bovril is not a railway station, it's a broth." Victoria Station was enveloped in a yellowish gloom. An acrid odor permeated the cavern—my first glimpse of London, the fog blamed on soft bituminous coal belching from a million chimney pots.

After arranging the morrow's excursion with Dave, Conrad dashed off to a phone booth. Newshawks wore aproned placards reading "Will the B.B.C. Ignore Jesus?" I gaped at stalwart bobbies in shiny sou'westers waving white-gloved hands at traffic that moved on the wrong side. Conrad returned beaming, having spoken with his children. When would I meet them? "Before long" was the cryptic reply. Our cabby, a Bruce Bairnsfeather character out of *Punch*, brimmed over with British cheer, something sorely needed in that drizzle. A porter with an egg-shaped head and blue chin met us at our Bloomsbury hotel with an umbrella.

We groped our way through a dimly lit lobby reeking of codfish to an upper chamber detected by sheer clairvoyance. Bleak, cold, damp, it contained an iron bedstead, marble washstand, and fumed oak wardrobe with a stuck door and a cracked mirror. The gas heater, fed a shilling, produced a feeble gleam. The bath and w.c. were miles apart; coal smoke poured through a window that would not shut; and the door couldn't be locked. Pinioned against the tub when closing the door, I gave up the notion of a bath.

We awoke next morning to a pale disc in the heavens. Behold the sun that never sets, or rises, on the British Empire! While struggling with a leathery kipper, Conrad explained the British currency. But not the telephone system. I shouted myself hoarse trying to reach the McCords before noticing the fine print. "Press Button *A* after you hear your party."

When Dave and his mother and Conrad and I arrived in Edinburgh via the *Flying Scots-Man* a heavy mist—haar—shrouded the city. Conrad felt the need of taking his scotch internally, but taverns were shut tight by 10 P.M. "Tightwads," he grumped. "When a Scot opens his purse, a moth flies out."

I fell in love with everything—Edinburgh Castle, the brawny bagpipers in Royal Stuart tartan kilts playing "Scotland the Brave," the rosy-cheeked children, and gorgeous fabrics displayed along Princes Street shops. Dave at the wheel, we drove through the hilly lowlands where sheep grazed in fields of purple heather. I searched for my dream cottage among the stone farmhouses, but Conrad wasn't putting down roots wherever my fancy roamed. We dawdled in Luss (pop. 1,517), because Wordsworth spent a night there with his sister and Coleridge. Conrad improvised a limerick about the Lass of Luss, after Dave's mother scolded him for giving her too much for a bouquet of roses. "Americans like you spoil travel for tourists on a budget."

Conrad was mollified on finding a palindrome in a public garage: "Rats live on no evil star." It served to sum up his philosophy in a forthcoming poem based on the line "Evil is the palindrome of live."

We parted in London, Dave promising to visit us. Conrad showed me the landmarks—Westminster Abbey, the Tower, Parliament buildings, Mme. Tussaud's Wax Works, and Buckingham Palace. All of them awesome but not as embraceable as his artist friends in Saint John's Wood. Dame Laura and Harold Knight, a childless, middle-aged couple, were to become a blessing. Though Laura covered a variety of subjects, she was best known for her circus paintings. Warm, vibrant, spontaneous, she symbolized Mother Earth to me, her china-blue eyes sparkling with fun, her yellow hair looped around her ears.

We sat in the studio with cocktails and cigarettes. "When I was elected to the Royal Academy," she said, "the *Times* said it was an honor attained by few of my sex. Stuff and nonsense. I get so annoyed with male R.A.s who patronize me with their little gallantries. Artists should be judged by their work, not by their gender."

Conrad disagreed, his antifeminist views a bone of contention between us. Harold, a quiet, reflective, pipe-smoking man, defused the heated argument, then started another one at dinner, suggesting that inspiration became pure technique as an artist aged. Conrad took issue with that, his opinion seconded by Laura. But he thought Harold the better portrait painter and considered Laura too prolific and superficial.

I sat entranced in a new and glittering world, Harold launching into anecdotes, one about Augustus John "going dry" with the aid of champagne. If it was true that the British used speech to conceal thought, then the Knights were atypical. Before we left, Harold promised to do a portrait of Conrad as a wedding gift. "I'm also giving G. B. Shaw a copy of *Punch: The Immortal Liar* and saying 'Here, read this, by the greatest living poet.'"

Laura further embarrassed Conrad by embracing him. "I love him and always have," she said to me with tears in her eyes, taking me aside. "I know you'll be good for him."

17

THE NEXT EVENING we had an awkward encounter in Soho. "Oh Jupiter," Conrad exclaimed, walking into the Brice Restaurant. "There's Martin!" He hesitated before introducing me stiffly to a shy, bookish-looking man with a nutcracker profile. Armstrong rose and bowed. I shook hands with him, smiling warmly, then blushed remembering the analysis of my sexuality that Conrad sent him and the tongue-lashing Martin later got for marrying Jessie.

"They've settled in West Sussex," Conrad said caustically, after ordering *moules marinières* at a distant table.

"And where will *we* live?"

"I told you, we'll cross that bridge when we come to it." The blue eyes flickered. "Next on the agenda is Rye."

A sentimental journey? I was naturally eager to see Jeake's House (named after the original owners). But why couldn't he let me in on his plans? On the ninety-mile train journey the London suburbs gradually gave way to lush meadows and fields as cultivated as our national parks. Nature imitating art. Rolling through Sevenoaks I saw my first British deer posing in the woods at Knole, the fabulous 365-room castle on the Sackville-West estate.

"Now we've crossed Kent into Sussex," said Conrad, laying aside the London *Mercury*. As we sped south he became increasingly animated. "Now we're skirting Romney Marsh, a twenty-mile expanse of sheep-flecked marshland, part of it below sea level. Monks once lived there with their dependents." At our left, toy ships skimmed along the Channel. "Next stop, Hamstreet, then Appledore, then Rye." The sun came out as we rounded a bend, irradiating a pyramid, houses clustered on a sandstone rock. "Look at that, Critch, a Blake-ian vision!"

Conrad fizzed with excitement while we bundled into a dilapidated cab in England's most painted town. Rye swarmed with trippers, artists and easels cluttered the narrow pavements. I got dizzy and cross-eyed, trying to see everything at once. Grass sprouted between the cobbles on steep Mermaid Street. I expected to see Rip Van Winkle any moment. Red-tiled houses leaned crazily against each other, squeezed together in unBritish fashion. They looked compact enough to be scooped up and set down on Boston's Common without spilling a single house.

Our luggage stashed at the Mermaid Inn, we crossed over to a tall, narrow brick and stone house. Conrad grinned broadly at the To Let sign in the window. "Well, I'll be damned—what a lucky coincidence," he said, and tore off to fetch the key from the agent.

I gazed with avid curiosity at Jeake's House, now in trust for the children. It was flanked by a boys' school and a workmen's club, beyond which a spinning wheel doubtless proclaimed a knitting studio. A small plaque on the facade carried the date 1689 with three serpents, tails in mouth, emblems of eternity. Virginia ivy flamed up to the chimney. The foundation stones, said Conrad, were filched from Camber Castle, a sea fortress built by Henry VIII.

"Got it," he crowed, waving the key, the neighbors gawking.

I followed him into a bat's cave smelling of dust, mold, mice, and ghosts, the vestibule festooned with cobwebs, wallpaper in shreds. A dark passageway led to the kitchen, the only window over the sink looking out on the garden, a jungle of weeds. No heating unit in the L-shaped dining room adjacent, or in the rooms above except a wee potbellied stove in Conrad's spacious study. Leaded windowpanes, buckled floorboards, one bathroom for eleven rooms. How had Jessie managed?

"Not another old house like it."

"I believe you," I said. "Well, now that I've seen it, let's go hunting."

"No need, Critch. I've decided to lease Jeake's for six years."

"You what?" I gaped at him. "Good grief, you can't be serious. Why, we'd be cut dead for one thing . . . "

"To hell with gossips. I have a few loyal friends left—Robert Nichols and Paul Nash. You'll come to love it as much as I do."

"Perhaps," I said. "But will it love me?" It would always be Jessie's home. Eleven rooms for a childless couple living on a poet's income? I wailed all the way downstairs. Don't ask for whom the bell tolls—my lovely dream smashed, I had crossed the Atlantic filled with joyous expectations of making a fresh start in new surroundings, only to be hooked into history, our bones to mingle with those of the three Jeakes. Nothing would change. Conrad was determined to live in the past.

Malocchio, the evil eye, was upon me. I shivered, remembering our Nantucket honeymoon, when Conrad's wedding present, my lapis lazuli necklace, broke and I never did find all the beads. Hark, what was that weird ticking noise? Deathwatch beetles, Conrad informed me with a leer. "It's their mating call." How romantic. He removed the To Let sign, a challenging gleam in his eyes. I suspected he knew right along that the house was vacant. "How will Jessie feel about having us as tenants?"

He gave me a curdled look. "I'm preserving Jeake's for the children. It's *their* home. And *I* intend to run this marriage. Is that clear?"

"Crystal clear."

"The rent is only £125 a year," he added, locking the front door. "The ghosts make it a bargain."

And ghosts were catnip for authors, of course. I wrestled with my pride. Wasn't I also an author? I kept forgetting that I was indeed a professional writer, however minor by comparison. He had taken this important step without my knowledge—gone straight to Jeake's like a homing pigeon. To be sure, he had to live in an environment that stimulated him, since aliens were not allowed to take jobs or go on the dole. Moreover, if marriage was for keeps, I had to accept the breadwinner's terms. There would be far-reaching repercussions.

"Very well, we'll give it a try," I said. I straightened my shoulders. Whatever the bond between us, it was as yet too strong to break. What I should have done was go along with him, since a sense of home and place was so important to an orphaned boy, and then win his trust in me as an all-around partner. But then, as we used to say in Milwaukee, "We are too soon old and too late smart."

Conrad's return to Rye with me was a transparent move toward an unfinished marriage and winning back the children. More than twenty years later Alfred Kazin, reviewing *Ushant*, saw the author as "a man still imprisoned by the nightmares of his youth." His obsessive secrecy wasn't just the recoil of a murderer's son, but Oedipus thwarted!

18

GLANCING OVER MY SHOULDER at the early thirties, I see a host of memorables whose lives touched ours—the Knights, G. B. Shaw, Arthur Bliss, H.D., Thomas Hardy's widow, Phyllis Bottome, Marjorie Kinnan Rawlings, John Tunis, and among local celebrities E. F. Benson, Edward Burra, and Radclyffe Hall, who caused a rumpus by asking the Anglican Church to sanctify marriage with her lover, Lady Troubridge. A mixture of retired Indian colonels, working classes, and creative artists made up the population that remained roughly at 3,500 over the centuries, with a sprinkle of "gliglis," bridge-playing gossips (who were currently blackballing Conrad for his wickedness).

Before I could recover from Conrad's dictum, Malcolm Lowry turned up from Norway, where he had gone that summer aboard a Norwegian freighter. The Cambridge University student must have found an ungracious hostess floundering in chaos and upheaval. His father, a Liverpool cotton broker, staunch Wesleyan, and fox-hunting Tory, had engaged Conrad as teacher-therapist at $100 a month. Malcolm would be spending all his vacations with us.

I held my breath. Enough to live with one genius. Conrad still suffered headaches, souvenirs of the wrestling match over that w.c. lid. I associated Malcolm with catastrophe. He might set fire to his mattress, break a leg, or damage my husband still further. Just meeting him was a calamity, he admitted. Several months later, on a subsequent visit, he proved it by celebrating a sanguinary evening with Conrad at the pub in the Strand, at the foot of Mermaid Street. Rye's streets—Watchbell, Traders' Passage, Rope Walk—bespoke an ancient fishing and shipbuilding port. The fog had thickened. Dining alone, two hours later, I imagined the worst, but how would I know if something had happened? A phone in the house violated Conrad's sense of privacy, and the nearest call-box was in the post office several blocks away.

Around 9 P.M. a pair of muddied, blood-streaked apparitions staggered into Jeake's House. In their alcoholic euphoria they had staged a javelin-throwing contest across the narrow inlet where the Rother, Brede, and Tillingham rivers converged. Conrad, failing to release his weapon, fell in while launching it. Malcolm then tumbled in after him. Fortunately the tide was low. How they managed to scramble up that slimy wall remains their secret.

The scene recurred to me years later when I saw *The Scoundrel*, the ghost of Noel Coward draped in seaweed, rising from a watery grave to reclaim his soul.

Satisfied that no bones were broken, I drew a hot bath, laid out dry clothing, put on the kettle, and reheated the roast lamb. I doubt if Malcolm knew most of the time what he ate or wore. His idea of "banting" was to skip meals for brief periods, then gorge on everything except fish, choking on bones being one of his many phobias. I found myself catering to a gourmand and a gourmet, finicky Conrad expecting a Cordon Bleu cuisine. His breakfast egg had to be coddled three minutes exactly. His dislikes included "promiscuous salads," stews, casseroles and that unholy trinity of cabbage, cauliflower, and Brussels sprouts.

Problems mounted. Malcolm's presence complicated life at a time when I had to simplify it somehow.

My admiration for Jessie grew apace while grappling with a renovated seventeenth-century granary built by three generations of Jeakes named Samuel—mystics, scholars, inventors, and necromancers, one with levitation powers. Oh to rise above the damp, raw cold and that coke-burning hot-water heater appropriately called a bogie. How could Jessie keep Jeake's clean, dry, and heated? Everything from coal to colonels came through the front door. Mildew ruined boots and tennis racquets, and my preserves. Lugging coal, wood, and ashes up and down three flights for the three fireplaces at least kept one in trim.

We had a sweet time plugging mouseholes and treating beams for dry-rot, the trustees slow about making promised repairs. I found a char-woman to do battle with Conrad's folly. Mrs. Kipp had seen "wuss places." A dauntless granny with an 1890 face under a pancake hat, she wrapped some burlap around an ample waist and made the dust fly, eyes gleaming behind lenses in nine-penny brass frames.

"I'm 'appiest when I works, mum. Me old man says I even work in me sleep, groanin' somethin' awful. If I'm not scrubbin', polishin', bottlin', and fixin' up at 'ome, I'm doin' for others. But I must 'ave me proper tools. Now I need some hile, mum." Oil? Mrs. Kipp wasted nothing. Even her *h's*, dropped here, were added there. We held long, impassioned monologues, neither one understanding much.

Furnishing an eleven-room house on a pittance challenged my thrifty nature. I ransacked secondhand shops, kept tabs on auctions and rummage sales. Conrad retrieved his grandfather clock from the pawnbroker. He had stopped me from buying a crib. I asked for a cot instead of a camp bed. Would Freud allow for the language barrier? Two countries "divided by a common language," as Shaw put it. It behooved me to learn English. Thumbtacks were drawing pins, electric cord was flex, garters were suspenders, suspenders were braces, crackers were biscuits, biscuits crackers, and *I* soon to go crackers.

Marketing had its perils. Sedate old ladies zoomed through traffic on motorbikes, shepherds drove their flocks on High Street into the open butcher shop. A pig's piercing squeals pinpointed the beast being shoved in. I couldn't eat pork for a long time. The burly butcher, a Dickensian character, seesawed between "Real Riviera weather we're 'avin'" and "Dirty weather we're 'avin', ma'am." His prices came down for residents, and I had a charge account. "Mrs. Aiken to go down, 3/6," he'd bellow to the cashier, "the *second* Mrs. Aiken, mind." Two dowagers with dainty baskets and toy dogs stared at me. I forced a smile, seething inside.

Conrad called a snub a little murder. "Whoso that is without human nature amongst you . . ." But whenever I groused about being cut he said banteringly, "Good, we'll live in splendid isolation." He could talk—an Anglicized American, a loner and insulated introvert. As a newcomer he found it impossible to write "among those stifling, sterile, shut-in personalities." The cats struck him as more human than some of the people.

Our turn had come to live under the microscope, like Jessie. I had expected making waves but not being boycotted so virulently. I admired the British, their stoicism, manners, humor, intelligence, but stuffed shirts and patronizing gentry I couldn't swallow.

Ostracism had its comical side. I had only to step outdoors to see faces at windows. We trusted these Private Eyes so completely that we didn't bother to lock the door. One afternoon I returned from Hastings and found myself locked out. The catch must have slipped when Conrad left the house. The only recourse, without a key, was to go through the Spinning Lady's studio. She had already ticked me off about the rubbish-burning: "The smoke blackens my curtains and drives me indoors. I've spoken to your charlady, but presume she hasn't told you." (Mrs. Kipp advised me to "pay no mind to the likes of '*er*. What's an unmarried lady doin' with such a big boost anyway?" I couldn't answer that.) My neighbor muttered incantations as I climbed over the wall with my bundles, dropping some pork sausages, which she held as hostages.

Our opposite neighbor was the one to be cultivated—a bishop's son, whose white Angora cat inspected pedestrians from mullioned windows of the Old Hospital (it had sheltered Huguenot soldiers in the Napoleonic Wars). The half-timbered, gabled house, a gem I coveted, belonged to Mr. Ellis, a bachelor with a passion for Bach. Though Conrad had as yet to see the interior, our shy neighbor did once raise his voice in my behalf, helping a lady in distress.

Conrad's six o'clock pub-crawls with Malcolm set tongues wagging. Every evening I waited at the window, fidgeting. The dinner had dried up when they materialized, Malcolm weaving over the cobbles like a somnambulist, his striped blazer rumpled, hair tousled, a necktie holding up his white ducks. He tried hard not to be a nuisance. Though he called himself the runt of the family (he was the youngest of four sons) he was actually a great hiker and swimmer, had broken a record lifting barbells, and had won the schoolboy golf championship of England while at The Leys (where "Mr. Chips" was a master). He had allegedly been near blind for three years, with a chronic ulcerated cornea of both eyes, forbidden to read, write, or play games. Lest the bandages embarrass his family's friends, he was kept in school throughout that period. How had he spent all that time? "Well, every day I took the headmaster's dog out for an airing" was his explanation.

Despite my maternal feelings toward Malcolm, my diary gave him short shrift: " . . . A caged lion . . . never been housebroken . . . Definitely no mixer . . . How much longer will Conrad put up with this madman? . . . Between the two of them I'm fast going dotty . . . " Conrad devoted mornings to blue-penciling still more imitations of *Blue Voyage* from *Ultramarine*. The seafaring protagonist had had a rough time, shunned as a nancy and toff after arriving at the dock in a chauffeured limousine, given the scruffiest jobs, an Ishmael starved for comradeship, and ragged for his slovenly drinking.

The clink of the decanter on the sideboard made me wince. Conrad averaged four or five strong martinis before lunch and again before dinner. He needed no incentive such as Malcolm's chronic thirst. Periodic efforts to separate him from the bottle got me nowhere. "Don't try to change me," he said, though I was only trying to preserve him, and not in alcohol either. He reminded me that all good writers drank: "A poet without alcohol is no real poet. Swinburne's personality disintegrated, and his creative flow was damned up when Watts-Dunton banned liquor. To say I'm a heavy drinker is just one of your neuroses. I'm a normal drinker."

It took a heart attack in later decades for Conrad to decide that, far from enhancing a writer's awareness, excessive drinking destroyed perception and memory. Meanwhile, he admitted that he was never sober while writing the Preludes.

He liked to linger at table, sipping beer leisurely, whereas I wanted to do the dishes and retreat upstairs to read or sew. I had come to feel superfluous at his convivial literary powwows with a possessive protégé. That little seed of rebellion began taking root once more, as with my father. We were made for each other, the suitor assured me, while the husband said I needed a simpler man. I agreed wholeheartedly. And did he need a more complicated wife? If so, why had he walked out on Jessie?

19

I BREATHED EASIER after Malcolm returned to Cambridge. The children were expected before school opened, and Conrad could hardly wait. Meanwhile, Robert and Norah Nichols dropped in from nearby Winchelsea, looking me over with friendly curiosity. While Conrad apologized for the packing cases in lieu of chairs, I laid aside some slipcover material and rustled up tea. We sat around the fire in the large, half-paneled drawing room, munching "marmaladen" crumpets.

"How do you like England?" Norah asked. I dodged the question, saying it was too soon to tell, then citing Conrad's statement that he'd like it better if it were inhabited by Americans.

"You were thirty years too late moving to Sussex, dear boy," Robert badgered him. "A whole raft of literary greats lived within a ten-mile radius of Rye at one time—Joseph Conrad, Stephen Crane, Ford Madox Ford, Virginia Woolf, D. H. Lawrence, Henry James, Katherine Mansfield . . . " Robert sighed. "What a feast."

The poet-playwright was working on *Wings Over Europe*, the first play to mention the atomic bomb. He had held the Lafcadio Hearn Chair of English Literature at the Imperial University of Tokyo, the post Conrad declined partly because of his impending divorce. Norah plainly adored her husband. She sat in the background, smiling serenely—tall, svelte, the tweedy type, an heiress who indulged his whims.

After another half hour of talk about British food, Siamese cats, Winston Churchill, the Depression, and poetry, Robert waved his swagger stick at her. "Come along, Pieface . . . " And clattered downstairs with a jaunty "Tiddleybungho, we'll get together soon and have a honeymoon."

"What a character." I giggled. "No wonder Norah takes a back seat, living with such a live wire."

"Watch your step with Robert, he has only one thing on his mind," Conrad said darkly. "I would probably be the enthusiast he is, but for my courage or audacity to face truth and death hourly. The horror of all that fascinates him but also terrifies him. He's afraid of me, while respecting me at the same time."

Dear me. Another philanderer and rogue to beware of, apparently, was the distinguished painter Paul Nash, art critic for the *Nation* and the *New Statesman*. His paintings as an official artist on the battlefront were preserved in the British Museum and the Imperial War Museum. His wife, Margaret, collected his abstracts as a sound investment. Like the Nicholses, the Nashes were a childless couple with cats. They lived with Margaret's father, the retired Bishop Odeh, who had taught T. E. Lawrence Arabic. Their modern house perched on a cliff above the Salts and was furnished in exquisite taste, the walls hung with Paul's watercolors.

We had tea in the kitchen, scones warmed in a Dutch oven. Potted geraniums brightened window ledges, a gray tabby dozed on the hearth rug. I found Paul innocuous enough—a blue-eyed, black-haired aesthete wearing a fancy cravat and quizzical smile. Margaret, an Irish-Arabic mystic, seemed the stronger of the two. A cast in one eye gave her a piquant look. When I remarked that her jet-black hair reminded me of my mother's, Margaret glowed.

"Oh you should have seen *my* mother's hair—pure gold, and so long she could sit on it. It attracted attention all over Jerusalem. One afternoon she woke up from a nap on a park bench, startled to find her hairpins being taken out. 'What *are* you doing?' The Arab woman apologized, but simply had to see for herself if those beautiful tresses were real. She then asked for a lock and got one."

"I suspect you of having Italian blood, Clarissa," Paul said at one point, studying me intently. "With that pre-Raphaelite profile . . . "

Margaret, glancing at Conrad, sensed my discomfiture and changed the subject, giving me a rundown on social hierarchy in England. "On the upper rungs of the ladder are the squires, county judges, retired army personnel, professional men, schoolteachers, gentlemen farmers, and wealthy tradesmen. At the bottom are the shopkeepers and laborers. Artists are unclassifiable," she added with a twinkle.

She then offered me cooking lessons after I admitted my deficiencies. "Shall we say next Wednesday? Tuesday I'm taking Paul to a London osteopath for his asthma."

Conrad scoffed at that "quackery" and I rebuked him. Osteopathy had helped me enormously.

On the way home I thwarted him when he mentioned Paul's flirting,

emphasizing instead Margaret's kindness in putting her piano at my dis-
posal. "Why do you dislike her? You seemed to be allergic to her."

"She's a feminist," he said curtly. "The domineering type. Runs Paul."

"Maybe he wants to be run. You like Laura Knight and she's certainly a
feminist." I gave his arm a squeeze. "Come on, darling, don't be so stuffy."

He shrugged. Women were pegged as acquisitive, predatory, scheming,
and lacking perception. Lumping all females together as designing was
like condemning all men as bastards. He quoted the Oxford toastmaster
who said when women won the vote, "To the ladies, once our superiors,
now our equals."

Conrad had broken off his affair with Elizabeth of Oxford, he told me,
after she called him a heartless monster, but she was so much in love with
him that she called her husband Conrad. I found her letters, along with
his to Jessie and mine to him, in the box room off his study. He was
careless about leaving personal letters around. Had Jessie left all that
correspondence behind, assuming that he would return? *Was* it a lucky
coincidence, finding Jeake's House vacant?

With the exception of his pictures and books, roughly numbering a
thousand, Jessie "had taken every bloody thing out of the house," he said.
Not quite. There was his grandmother's china and her lovely patchwork
quilt, which we hung in the drawing room. (Poor man, he voiced the
same complaints when changing wives for the second time.) His desertion
of the three J's was explained in his story "I Love You Very Dearly" in a
volume dedicated "To the five J's"—Jessie, John, Jane, Joan, and Jerry.

When John and Jane finally arrived, a jubilant father brought them from
the bus stop. Joan was still too young to visit. John, sixteen, was a shy
towhead with a solemn twinkle behind spectacles, Jane a sturdy carrot-top
of twelve with bangs and a pigtail, her freckled face scrubbed shiny. They
took my measure when we shook hands self-consciously. I remember Jane
standing under the green witch's-ball, a wedding present, and piping to
Conrad, "Look, Cahoun, I'm all out of shape." An odd nickname, Cahoun. "Hang your coats in the cubbyhole, kids," he said, "and I'll give
you a guided tour after tea."

It must have been awkward if not painful to see a stranger in their
mother's place. Adjusting to a stepfather was less an ordeal, since they had
known Martin before. "You're probably famished after the long bus ride,"
I remarked, going into the kitchen. Conrad said they liked Huntley &
Palmer biscuits and ginger beer.

I saw a different Conrad altogether, a pied piper charming us with his
fantastic imagination and at times ribald humor. The walls resounded for
a solid week with our mirth. "Laugh, and you will be healed," he once
wrote Maurice. We were promised a second-hand piano, since John played

beautifully, besides being a wizard at chess, invited to matches with E. F. Benson. Father and son enjoyed the effect on Conrad's detractors when John was initiated into pub crawls. Tennis, Ping-Pong on the refectory table, bathing at Camber Sands, and excursions filled up most of the children's vacation.

John slept in one of the fourth-floor bedrooms, climbing a poop ladder, and Jane in her usual room next to Conrad's eyrie overlooking the garden. She helped me with the housework, chatting animatedly about school and other safe topics. We made a game of weeding the garden and hunting slugs with a jar of salt water. Old Mr. Gloss, the peripatetic gardener, suspected former tenants' children of importing marine snails to fraternize with the garden variety. "Them snails'n slugs'll see to your flowers, and no mistake."

Exploring the "Ups and Downs" of Sussex, I learned the meaning of signs like "Sheep-worrying, £5," among other things, and linked Leasam Hill with blackberry hedges, mistletoe bushes, sheep's wool snagged on fences, and Edward VII, who as Prince of Wales had been a frequent visitor to Lady Maud Warrender's mansion. (We were to hear more about Her Ladyship when I acquired her parlor maid.) Local excursions included climbing Ypres Tower for a superb view of the entire coastline from Kent to Sussex. On clear nights the lights of Cap Griz-Nez were visible across the Channel. I longed to go to Paris, but Conrad had been there and could take it or leave it. So he left it, and I never did see it.

Everything was cause for hilarity, such as seeing our milkman in a majordomo's uniform at the Electrical Palace. We sat in the flea-pit, where Conrad could smoke. The usherette sprayed the cinema with Shalimar, a futile gesture what with local yokels reeking of sheep dung. Prince George, in the newsreel, pronounced British apples the best. Jane held her father's hand throughout. On our feet, we sang "God Save the King," George V watching from the screen lest we escape prematurely. The children were embarrassed by Rye familiars greeting them cordially while ignoring Conrad and me, then inquiring after Jessie.

After they left I headed off the doldrums by reading aloud Conrad's letters to them from the States—charming stuff. I began to understand his deep attachment to them. They were enchanting, and had beautiful manners. When I remarked that I wished they belonged to me, he said if I had children they would probably bring me up. "Don't be horrid," I said. My child would now have been three, a blue-eyed, auburn-haired boy. That bottle of ergot in the medicine cabinet, later pronounced poison, was my safeguard against the joys and pains of motherhood. Just be grateful, I mused, if his children accept you and show you more charity than you did *your* stepmother.

20

M Y FIRST WINTER in England reminded me of an American visitor's
observation: Continentals have a sex life, the British have hot-water
bottles. That stiff upper lip is more likely to conceal chattering teeth than
reveal stoicism. The English system of central heating consisted of swilling
hot tea the livelong day.

"You make a fuss over things that don't amount to a nit on a gnat's nut,"
Conrad said when I complained. He took cold baths and thrived under
leaden skies. "Writers can't function in a land of eternal sunshine." He
claimed that my blood would thicken after two years so that I, a sun-
worshipper, could tolerate a 65-degree room temperature. But I noticed
that when we acquired the anthracite-burning stove he was lured into the
dining room from his chilly eyrie with the view through a large picture
window of schooners' masts floating past chimney pots. Oblivious to
noise and traffic, he wrote poems and book reviews while I slogged away
at the typewriter in the drawing room.

After a nap came a stroll, singly or together, or else a movie in Hastings,
the local cinema that we patronized at least twice a week. Tea was dis-
pensed with except for guests, Conrad indifferent to the tradition and I
begrudging the time spent away from my writing. Evenings he fed his
subconscious for the morrow's output, reading aloud the day's labors,
which I then typed, incorporating any changes. Or he might edit my
manuscript.

A bedtime ritual was massaging his neck and head, thereby easing
tension in both of us. Then came the rugged chore of wrenching myself
from the fireplace, getting undressed in a cold bathroom, and darting up
to an arctic bedchamber. A British bedroom is the coldest place on earth,
said Grenfell. Clad in a thick flannel nightgown and wool socks, I shook
my chemical pack into warmth. Making love was mandatory. It served a
dual purpose, the exertion restoring our circulation and dissolving hostil-
ities, compensating for myriads of frustrations.

Margaret Nash had become my "straightener," that exemplary character
in Samuel Butler's *Erehwon*. Despite unfavorable circumstances, I hoped
to make friends in England and be accepted by Conrad's children. They
were important to him and carried great weight. They would instinctively
judge him, monitoring his treatment of me and comparing it with his
treatment of Jessie. That surveillance might then curb his tendency to
manipulate me or put me in deep freeze or whatever. And all the while I
both feared and desired having a child, another part of him whom he
would love, and who might enrich life for us.

Unburdening myself to Margaret, whom I regarded as wise and trustworthy, was a vast relief, my only regret not having told her then about taking ergot. Her cosmopolitan outlook on life jarred me at times, but it was medicine for a romantic daydreamer. Rumors were circulating that after leaving Jessie and the children penniless Conrad had the effrontery to bring his mistress to the same house where he had lived with his family, that he was flaunting "that brazen young woman" in the face of decent, God-fearing folk.

"Don't let it depress or bother you, Clarissa," Margaret said. "Some day I'll tell you his version."

Coming home one November day from a cooking lesson at Margaret's, I began preparing Conrad's favorite dish, wild duck with orange slices, when his heavy tread sounded in the passageway. I hailed him, apologizing for not getting back in time to give him his anchovy on toast before he left for the pub. "Would you like it now?"

"No. What kept you so long?" he asked. His face flushed, he stood swaying between the sink and stove.

"Margaret showed me how to make Quiche Lorraine." I slid the bird in the oven, then measured some rice. "Afterwards I had a good workout at the piano."

"And what did Paul give you? The glad knee?"

"No, just the glad eye."

"I daresay you played right along with him, probably dissecting me in the bargain. If only I could believe you had a sense of honor," Conrad said. "God knows I want to, but I'm becoming more and more paralyzed with suspicion. Your whole history is one of promiscuity."

Oh God, I thought, here we go again. "From infancy to adultery?"

"Never mind the wisecracks." His eyes narrowed. "Do you wonder that I dream about your sex orgies?"

"That's your problem, not mine," I said. "Punishing me for your dreams will boomerang." I took the vegetables out of the cold box. "Why do you get so upset if I smile at a man? Are you so mean and prudish that you can't bear to see me enjoying myself? Do you condemn every woman who flirts with you?"

"No, but I wouldn't trust her if she was my wife."

"You make no distinction between flirting and fornicating?"

"None. One leads to the other," Conrad said.

I gave up. Useless to get rattled and exasperated. I decided next time we hassled to try the light, flippant touch. I could say, "I know you're simply itching to beat me to a pulp. Well, go right ahead, so all Rye can hear my screams. That'll make you even more popular around here."

My thoughts reverted to the summer before, when we were weekend guests, along with a roistering friend of Conrad's, of a highly nervous female writer on Cape Cod. Around midnight her screams for help sent him tearing below to rescue her from the clutches of "a drunken satyr." A spate of insults drifted upstairs. "You goddamn little tin Jesus, who the hell asked you to butt in?" Conrad's southern gallantry backfired. Recriminations filled another hour. Next morning, soul-searchings and abject apologies from a sobered and penitent libertine restored Conrad's *amour-propre*.

My deafness to poetry had begun to irk this *soi-disant* Nietzschean, to whom art was just another illusion. I earned a black mark the night we dined with the Nicholses. Armed with "torches" we trudged two miles, mostly uphill, through Strand Gate, past ivy-hung cliffs and holly hedges, to new Winchelsea (Old Winchelsea having drowned six centuries earlier). We arrived huffing and puffing at the Georgian brick house and were admitted by a starchy butler annoyed at a black Siamese cat that slipped out. Our exuberant host pumped my hand and clapped Conrad on the shoulder. "Hope you don't mind being the only guests, old chap, we're selfish and want you to ourselves."

Robert poured drinks for Conrad and himself, barley water for Norah and me, then aired his views on life, love, and literature, as though anxious to winkle Conrad out of his Calvinist shell. Like an apprehensive, doting mother, Norah watched him act out scenes from Shakespeare, afraid his exertions would bring on "a state of nerves."

"Robert can't survive without company," she said, smiling her tranquil smile. She showed me his study, a far cry from Conrad's austere one, the walls covered with autographed photographs. How could he concentrate with so many faces confronting him? Robert Graves, Vachel Lindsay, Aldous Huxley, Robert Bridges, "Papa" Ibsen in a silver frame, and Delius, the latter advising his young apprentice not to marry for love but a girl "who's in love with your art." Norah didn't understand Robert's verse, though her dowry made it possible.

We rejoined the men. Conrad was recounting his brief stay in Winchelsea years before, when Ellen Terry was a neighbor. I longed to try the Steinway grand, but the dinner gong sounded. The butler made me nervous, stationing himself behind my chair. We had ribald yarns with the vichyssoise, local drainage problems with the roast beef, the Depression with the salad, and Henry James with the cheese savory. Robert remembered the Master as a colossus calling on his father. "I was just a little chap, and he rumbled on and on about the precious innocence of children, laying a hand on my head. Believe it or not, he never did finish his sentence."

Robert was mourning D. H. Lawrence's recent death. "What did *he* get out of life? Mostly violent scenes. Hated his body and denied the angel in him. He wasn't the strong, rugged type who could laugh at women but rather the sort who beats them up. God knows, his wife should have been beaten at least once a week. A cow-pat, Frieda. Something out of the sea—and I don't mean Venus. She infuriated me. I wanted to take both heels to her backside. D. H. once said, his head in his hands, 'You know, Robert, I'm very fond of Frieda, but she is incredibly stupid.' Violent scenes were a psychological necessity for him, but his cloddish wife gave him reason for murder."

I studied Robert's faunish face, wondering what Frieda had ever done to him. While Conrad discussed cats with Norah, after dinner, Robert infected me with his drollery and persiflage. Feeling gay and devilish, I dredged up some risqué yarns, which he capped with more sophisticated ones. Giggling and having a grand time, I caught Conrad's withering glance while quoting the vicar. "He told me that Ruskin did all his work before breakfast, then read it to his family, first removing the toast rack so there would be no crunching."

The evening ended inauspiciously with Robert launching into verse. One poem he recited sounded vaguely familiar. He whinnied when I asked who wrote it. "Your husband." Silence fell with a thud. Conrad twirled his brandy goblet, seemingly oblivious of me. I simply didn't exist. Chagrined, I asked for a whiskey, which caused a slight tremor. He turned back to Norah with a bland, "You were saying . . . "

Homeward bound, he said icily, "If you *must* wallow in ignorance, at least have the decency not to advertise it." No use reminding him that I had typed so many of his poems I couldn't remember all of them. Wherever I put my foot was the wrong place. Jessie would never commit such a gaffe. I wished now that he hadn't told me she knew seven languages.

Later, after we had reached home, he said, "You have no inkling of what goes into verse, the intensity and pitch of consciousness necessary before I can function. Each time I write a poem I feel that so much blood has been given. You're all vegetables compared to me."

True. I knew little about the bitter battle waged to produce a superlative poem and keep poetry alive in a benighted culture. When he had finished, I crawled into the guest room and pulled the covers over my stupid head.

21

A CHANGE OF ATMOSPHERE was indicated. Boarding the train to London in a sloshing downpour, I mulled over Conrad's parting shot: "Don't be surprised if I'm not here when you get back." No forgiving pat or kiss. He never wanted me to go anywhere and yet made me feel in the

way. Well, at least the British Railway cared. They had recently held up
the 3:39 to Rye pending my arrival by cab at Hastings from Saint Leonards, where I mistakenly waited to board the train. The stationmaster at
Saint Leonards telephoned his counterpart at Hastings. Confidence flowed
at the memory.

For once I took the initiative with strangers and began chatting with
the only other passenger in the compartment, a forlorn-looking young
matron who got on at Appledore. By the time we reached Ashford, where
I changed trains, we had lamented a variety of social evils, like those
scoundrels cheating the system by finagling platform tickets. "I'll be in
touch with you," she said with a haunting smile, handing me her card.
Lady Tavistock? I blinked, making a mental note to ask Margaret about
her. A fig for smug Rye.

My Bloomsbury room was even more dismal than the drizzle. Chilblained feet suffered in new ghillie shoes. I escaped to the British Museum.
After doing research for a magazine article, I took a break, transfixed by a
sign in the washroom which I copied: "Stoppages having been caused in
the drainage of the lavatories through the closet having been used to
dispose of miscellaneous objects, it is notified that the provision of lava-
tory accommodation must be dependent on only proper use being made
of it." Cheers for Shakespeare's language! Conrad would relish that.

Remembering Laura's cordial invitation, I phoned the Knights and was
heartened by her tonic voice asking me to dinner and to stay the night.
My bag retrieved, I bought some delicacies for her at Fortnum & Mason's,
and a Burberry tie for Conrad. That would last longer than those pallid
figs wrapped in cotton. I hoped Mrs. Kipp was looking after him properly.

London engulfed me. I felt like Jonah inside the whale. Evidence of the
Depression was everywhere, beggars as plentiful as in the States. Welsh-
men shuffled in the gutter, carrying signs reading Unemployed Miners
and harmonizing "Auld Lang Syne." Fiddlers, round-shouldered from
poking their heads in tavern doors, were lucky to make two shillings
a day.

Heading toward Oxford Street, I got to Selfridge's in time to see a
liveried flunky darting to the curb. He opened the limousine door, releas-
ing Queen Mary, the Duchess of York, and little Princess Elizabeth. Flur-
ries and curtsies followed, a crowd gathering instantly. Simply glimpsing
the Queen of England was a thrill for a romantic American. I stored the
event away to share with Conrad, even during this psychic sabbatical,
though he was supposed to be anti-royalist, making no class distinctions
other than bores.

This was my day for toffs, I told Laura. First Lady Tavistock, then Her
Majesty. I arrived in Saint John's Wood footsore. "Chilblains are an old

plague with us," Laura said and insisted on bathing my swollen feet and massaging them. "We've tried everything—yeast, raw onions, paraffin. It's this damnable climate." What did I think of Rye? Were we being ostracized? Had I met the children? Jeake's House she called a damp, dreary hole.

Guests were expected for cocktails. The phone and doorbell rang incessantly. The studio filled with a bewildering assortment of artists, actors, ballet dancers, and circus performers. Celebrities in all the arts rubbed shoulders with Laura. "What a fascinating book your life would make," I said that evening after dinner, when she described sketching Ellen Terry at a Shakespearean rehearsal. "Get those stories down on paper, Laura. Write your memoirs. You must, absolutely."

"But who would want to read them? And where would I find time?" She promised to think about it. While Harold worked on a portrait, she recounted bits of family history. Her mother, an art student in Paris, had predicted Laura would make the Royal Academy some day. "I began to draw before I could walk," she said, chain-smoking and doodling on a sketchpad. "Grandmother became head of the household when my father died soon after I was born. We were poor as church mice, at one time living on gruel for several months. She used to say, 'Laugh in the morning, cry before night.' I was often punished for scrapping with rough-tough boys and coming home with torn and bloodied clothes. I had always wanted to be a boy."

"You, too?" With a sense of deepening kinship, I traced my lineage briefly, telling her about my maternal grandmother's two cousins, who married a count and a baron respectively, though the man she married— my grandfather—was a humble cabinetmaker turned farmer. Laura said, "I'm *all* peasant." We exchanged confidences until midnight. Being tucked in bed and kissed goodnight brought tears to my eyes.

The 2:25 to Rye was slow as molasses, taking three hours. On my left a nearsighted student read a book on sanitation and sewage. The ruddy-faced tycoon on my right ogled me and presently handed me a circular headed "Invincible Cycles, for Quality and Reliability." I thanked him while discouraging any notion he might have of treading the primrose path with me, either on foot or on wheels.

Back to my book, the diary of Dostoevski's second wife. Conrad had recommended it as a possible Aiken emetic. Anna never said *Boo* to her mate's fantastic demands or jealous accusations. She put up with gambling fevers, melancholia, epileptic fits, and persecution manias, concerned only about his peace of mind, and all this for fourteen long years. Before she died she deleted all signs of a tormenting and tormented personality from his letters, anything that might mar his image. Such nobility staggered me. She *was* the perfect wife the Knights had in mind when they said that Conrad's wife would have to be perfect.

My arms full of bundles, my head teeming with resolves, I hurried down Mermaid Street with a quick, light step, heart bursting with love and longing, and that giddy feeling floating on a wave of desire.

"Darling, where are you?" I called from the front hall. No answer. On the dining room table were an empty pewter mug, scraps of ham, and a rejected manuscript of mine. The kitchen sink was filled with unwashed dishes, there were grimy towels on a chair, and the bogie fire was out. I ran upstairs in a panic. "Conrad, are you there?"

I found him stretched out on the sofa in the November dusk, books on the floor, dying embers in the grate. "Are you all right?" I hurried over to him, asking if Mrs. Kipp hadn't come.

"Oh yes," he said, "and talked my ears off. I sent her packing."

"What a shame. I spent the night with Laura and Harold."

"Why didn't you tell me?"

I ruffled his hair. "No phone, no homing pigeon."

He grunted. "I've had a thin time of it while you were on a binge. But I discovered one thing—I don't really need you any more."

The bravado of a younger Conrad reproaching his "forgetful mother," about whom he kept silent? I hung the Burberry tie over the wireless set and went upstairs to change. For once dinner could wait. Being away from him had been a reprieve into sanity and peace.

22

THE SEASON OF FORGIVENESS was approaching, though the British didn't make a great fuss about Christmas. "So don't go all delirious, Critch," said Conrad. He was saving his *Ho-ho-ho* for the children. They were due after Boxing Day (which I learned had nothing to do with sports).

Young carolers began serenading us early in December. Choirboys from Saint Mary's sang for pennies, their faces like hobgoblins in the light of the hurricane lantern held aloft by the leader, the local dyke-cleaner and hedge-trimmer. Their epicene voices were oddly moving in the nocturnal hush of Mermaid Street. Mrs. Kipp said that some of them were beaten if they went home empty-handed. The Christmas spirit.

I remembered my family in Milwaukee with presents, and friends with Yuletide messages, meanwhile homesick on that green Christmas for the rugged Wisconsin winters, skating, tobogganing, snow shoveling. Father always made elaborate preparations for a German Christmas eve, when we got our presents. The season really began on December 6 with an invisible Saint Nicholas hurling bags of nuts, sweets, and apples through the kitchen door. Not the least of marvels was that of a Prussian autocrat transformed into a benevolent, lovable Santa, come to inspect us. Those of us finding more coal than goodies in our bags could expect fewer Christmas gifts.

On Christmas day Conrad and I started off loaded with presents for the Nashes. I wore my camel's hair coat, he his bargain of a Burberry. Accepting Margaret's dinner invitation was a concession for him. Turning into Church Square we saw E. F. Benson coming out of Lamb House, walking with two canes. He gave me a searching smile when we exchanged the season's greetings. Poor man, I thought. So many arthritics hereabouts, and no wonder. Living in Rye was like living under sea. "You suffer from sciatica," I mused aloud to Conrad, "and I from arthritis of the spine. That Virginia ivy is beautiful, darling, but so unhealthy. Won't you consider having it cut down?"

"Never. It's here to stay," he said stiffly. "The children love that creeper, and so do I. You're not to mention the subject when they come."

"That never occurred to me." I heaved a sigh, resigned to getting into my surgical harness again. Everything about Jeake's House was sacrosanct. Nothing must be changed. I envied the Nashes living in a bright, airy house with a view of the Salts, a playfield for rugby, cricket, circuses, and other spectaculars.

Margaret looked like some exotic flower in her rainbow-hued batik gown. Paul, decked out in a fancy Liberty cravat, glanced up at the mistletoe while taking my coat. He pursed his lips when I declined the gambit, and fetched the sherry decanter.

"May I help?" I followed Margaret into the kitchen. "What lovely smells. Bacon, spices, and something roasting . . . "

"Goose, stuffed with apple dumplings. I hoped to get some feathers for a pillow, but the old crone who plucked the bird claimed there weren't enough to put between two handkerchiefs." She tied on her apron. "We're expecting Johnny—Radclyffe Hall—and Una Troubridge after dinner. They live near the Landgate." Margaret shook her head. "What a chaotic household. Never a moment's peace or quiet. They have a butler, a maid, and a King Charles spaniel, besides a parakeet with a vocabulary of eighty-four words, so Johnny says."

"Goodness," I said, "that's more than I have. I'm dying to read *The Well of Loneliness*. A pity it's banned." Conrad called it *The Loneliness of the Unwell*.

Margaret's father lent a note of dignity, a laconic bishop, his white hair an aureole in the candlelight at the table. I groaned when she brought in the plum pudding. "From stuffed goose to stuffed guests." We were still sitting there when the doorbell rang. "Les girls," Paul said, winking and getting up.

A moment later a deep voice boomed, "Merry Christmas, dear Paul, we can't linger . . . "

I was disconcerted by Johnny's mannish suit, white ascot, and cropped gray hair, and stumped by her opening gambit: "Don't you agree that Rye lends itself to the Christmas spirit?"

She skipped from one topic to another, Conrad nodding like a tethered donkey. When Paul served the mulled wine and sloe gin, she was on physical fitness. "I'm an exponent of deep breathing and Plombiere's irrigation. Never touch salt. It gives you rheumatism. The last time I was ill I ordered a cylinder of oxygen. The neighbors thought I was dying, but I fooled them."

Conrad suffered. Chain-smoking, twisting an eyebrow, stifling yawns, he gave an audible sign of relief when Radclyffe rose and said imperiously, "Come, Una, dearest, we must fly." Lady Troubridge hadn't uttered a word throughout.

Conrad struggled to his feet and said deadpan, "We too must fly. Strenuous days ahead, with the children here."

"Oh don't go yet, Conrad, we haven't had any carols." Margaret's efforts were echoed by Paul. "By all means, come along, Clarissa, and do your duty." He marched me to the piano, leaning against the upright and murmuring compliments on the carols and English madrigals I played, followed by a Scarlatti piece, I whistling the refrain. "Lovely, just like a flute."

At the door Paul said boldly, "You should make Conrad take more notice of you." A poser, that.

"Christ, what a dull party," Conrad said as we left. "Nothing but gligliisms."

"I enjoyed it."

"Because it was dull."

I bit back a retort. Peace on earth, good will . . . Conrad didn't like to be told he was having a good time, said his aunt.

Our Christmas really began with the children's arrival. We all enjoyed a pantomime in Hastings, *Jack and the Beanstalk*, the women cast as men and the men as women. Jeake's House reverberated to frolicsome scuffles and shouts and the hollow pizzicato of Ping-Pong balls. A gray kitten donated by the Mermaid Inn added to the merriment. Male or female? No one knew for sure. I suggested holding out a pair of pants, and if it jumped into them . . . Conrad settled the matter by naming it Nero.

Conrad consolidated his relationship with John. There were long talks and long musings across the chessboard. Evenings, Jane curled up with a book before the aromatic peat fire, or joined us in paper games, charades, and limerick contests. Mine won the booby prize.

> There was an old dotard named Groodle,
> Who was a bit weak in the noodle;
> His wits he mislaid,
> So all the folks said,
> His kit he confused with his caboodle.

On the last day of 1930 I had a letter from my father, a rare event.

Dear Clarissa:
    I think you may forgive me for not writing. Now the Christmas spirit again awakens in our hearts and minds, the glorious ancient season when children gather expectantly around the green tree on holy Christmas Eve. But times have changed. My finances have shrunk. Houses stand vacant, rents dropped to a new low, thousands of workmen walk the streets jobless. How are you and Conrad? Do you prefer England to the U.S.? I would love to see the Continent, but that will never be. I wish you both a merry Christmas and happy New Year.

Affectionately,
Father

    The Germanic script blurred. Had I ever expressed appreciation for his admirable qualities—uprightness, integrity, self-discipline, devotion to his father and melancholy sister? Rebellion was all he ever got from me. I resented Mama's pleas: "Don't upset him, he's tired," or, "He's on the rampage," resented having to tiptoe around the house, seldom free to voice my feelings.
    Why had I never asked him about his childhood in old Milwaukee? Or about Grandpa in Silesia? I knew so little about those who had formed my character and personality, which meant I couldn't know myself at all. I recall one Christmas giving Father a Teddy Roosevelt souvenir plate rimmed with colored cigar bands, then breaking it later on, when spanked for some good reason. Subsequently I found the fragments in his desk drawer, each one neatly wrapped in tissue.
    His faults receded into the misty past, his virtues emerged to smite me. I began to get a glimmering of what he'd had to contend with, to realize that hating those once loved only destroyed the hater. My stubborn younger self was unforgiving. Asking his forgiveness now would at least be a start in the right direction. His letter might interest Conrad. I brought it downstairs.

He sat at the table, telling the children what a fine photographer Dr. Aiken was. Something analagous was happening to me and I longed to share it. But seeing Conrad absorbed in family reminiscences I lost courage, felt excluded from the magic circle, and went back upstairs.

23

THE YEAR 1931 was a grim reminder of the Chinese curse "May you live in interesting times." Reports came from the States of soup-kitchen queues, people reviving the barter system, the unemployed parading with placards, TRYING TO LIVE. We had a pleasanter impression of America from Paul Nash, one of three foreign judges of the Carnegie Exhibition. He returned raving about Manhattan's unbelievable skyscrapers and America's ravishing girls.

Lucky Conrad, to have earned £400 the previous year. Friends were told, "We remain serene." By Mrs. Kipp's standards we were prosperous. I was learning how the "underprivileged" lived. She had stopped the chimney sweep from selling soot to the nursery man. "No, Mr. Puttle, we can use it on the slugs." One day I found her winding up a discarded typewriter ribbon to use for bias binding. Sorting out the rubbish on her knees was her last daily chore. Joints and stays creaking, she salvaged gin bottles to be filled with dandelion wine, anchovy jars for her grandchildren's birthday sweets, corks to dip in paraffin and revive fires.

My economies were less stringent—use less electricity and fuel, do more dressmaking and knitting, re-block blue felt hat, save tissue from tomatoes, oranges, peaches; gather windfalls, pay Boy Scouts an apple instead of three pence for weeding. (A standard request in my childhood was "A penny's worth of whatever candy I can get the most of.")

When Conrad called me a tightwad, I blew up. "There's no pleasing you," I stormed. "You were extremely unpleasant when I got the Persian runner for £1.10 at auction. Do you or don't you want the house furnished decently?" He dodged the issue, leaving me up in the air.

There would have been no penny-pinching if he had told me about his $65,000 bonanza, and I could have catered far more lavishly to his creature comforts. Did he fear that Jessie might learn of it, or was it a case of dwindling confidence in his earning power? We argued about doing good creative work while unhappy. Einstein would have said it wasn't possible. But Robert Tristram Coffin once told me that a poet should have intervals of hardships. They were a spur to Chaucer, Shakespeare, and Dante, who struggled for a living.

One thing was certain, fellow-authors like John Gould Fletcher could always find a helping hand in Conrad. He encouraged them, tried to promote their works, and was unfailingly fair in reviewing their books. He spent tedious hours with his protégé Malcolm Lowry editing *Ultramarine*, excising more touches of *Blue Voyage*, and wryly suggesting that the title be changed to *Purple Passage*.

Malcolm juggled several projects simultaneously, his room a Sargasso Sea of manuscripts, papers, books, journals. However disorganized otherwise, he was a disciplined writer, and sober for long periods, as Conrad gladly reported to Lowry Senior. An excerpt from *Ultramarine* appeared in *Best British Short Stories of 1931*, a volume banned by some public libraries because of his contribution "Seductio ad Absurdum."

Malcolm's friends knew the manic-depressive as a comedian, a ham actor with the sly, sidelong look of a merry friar. It made me seasick just to watch his exaggerated nautical gait. Ordinarily jocose, sometimes bellicose, Malcolm did most of his heavy drinking at night. His lusty laughter drifted up to the third floor, waking me from uneasy slumber to toss about until lulled to sleep by the wheeze of his "squiffer" or the plaintive renditions of Negro spirituals accompanied by ukulele strummings. His genial, offhand "Hello, Jerry, how are you?" generally sufficed for the duration. In a rare burst of confidence he told me of his nanny whipping him with brambles until he bled. "I didn't complain because I thought it was the normal thing. She got the sack when the gardener told my parents he'd seen her holding me by the heels over my bath."

I can't remember ever seeing him conspicuously drunk while the children visited us. Gentle, shy, diffident, he seemed rather wistful about their prior claim to Conrad's affections. They in turn treated him with the cautious manner one would a natural phenomenon like Vesuvius. John and Jane had brought Joan, a violet-eyed, auburn-haired cherub, already writing promising verse at age seven. A precocious trio, Jane with her keen mind and imagination, John a chemistry student and whiz kid, and an enjoyable duet partner once we acquired a Steinway upright. I was taught nature lore—how a spider weaves her web, why birds don't get electrocuted on telephone wires, and why some bees buzz around as if intoxicated (they *are* drunk, on nectar).

The children came and went. A smokescreen rose around us, sadness and tension went underground only to reappear when farewells were said.

Time flew or dragged, depending in part on company. Walter Piston visited us that year and played symphonic duets with me, overlooking my clinkers. He urged me once more to get down my musical ideas on paper. "You have a nice way of talking at the piano. When will you put your talents to use?" In my next reincarnation. I was happiest improvising, and a useful accomplishment it proved to be when I played the pipe-organ in Boston for the silent movies. The day the organ conked out during a dramatic cliffhanger, I tried in vain to sustain suspense on a tinny piano. I should have studied a portable instrument like the cello. It's cozy and companionable. You could wrap yourself around it and feel the strings vibrating within your very soul. Playing in an orchestra was my idea of heaven.

Meanwhile we enjoyed classical music nightly, our opposite neighbor's records making up for his shyness—or anti-American sentiments? Our back-door neighbors behind the garden walls found us hard to take. Spiteful sounds drifted over to me as my muddy fingers tossed weeds on a compost pile. More sniping came from Jessie's old friends, the F sisters. After Conrad chided his son for having avoided them, John reluctantly revealed that they had pitied him and Jane for being obliged to visit "that dreadful young person."

The F's were responsible for most of the local gossip, said Margaret. "They spread those rumors of Conrad leaving Jessie penniless. When I asked if they could prove their assertions in court, they dried up. Conrad told Paul and me that he was about to give you up for the children's sake when Jessie announced her engagement to Martin. She refused to see Conrad in Rye or arrange terms outside the courtroom, instead hiring expensive solicitors and rooking him so that he couldn't afford to remarry or have more children, and making Rye unpleasant for him to return to. So he gambled his remaining capital in the stock market, tripled it, then lost it in the crash. That was what he told us, my dear."

Why should my spirits have sagged, when I had urged him right along to patch things up with Jessie? My sentiments reflected those of Elizabeth, his former love. He had no right, she said, in her letter to Conrad, to abandon his children for what might prove a fugitive passion. It would be different if his feeling for me would last his lifetime. That might justify setting up a second home and abandoning the first one. But he couldn't go through life scattering families and leaving them to get along as best they could.

Conrad had become increasingly indrawn and uncommunicative, as he described himself in a 1931 letter to Theodore Spencer. "I bark at poor Jerry, complain about the food, kick the cat, curse the stoves, . . . pay bills, dodge bills, dream about bills. . . . This is bad, Ted, this is bad—gor blymy it is." Maybe, he said, he needed a love affair. "But what fool of a female would take on a middleaged potbellied feeble shortwinded unsocial small-peckered sentimentalist whose orgasms are a mere fly-twinkle?"

24

OUR SECOND ANNIVERSARY in February 1932 was just another day to Conrad, as I confided in my diary. However, Old Sol marked the occasion by shining through purple clouds and turning a giant oak on Cadbury Hill to bronze. Our good friends brought delicate snowdrops, primroses, and delectable champagne. No rabbit pie was served that evening, but filet mignon and a dubious wait-and-see pineapple trifle. Spoons were furtively laid down, one by one—Norah, Robert, Margaret, Paul. Had I used bicarb instead of baking powder? Conrad suggested serving bicarb *after* my meals.

Memo to a *Schwindelkopf*: Keep your emotions wrapped in cotton wool. Defeated in the kitchen but glowing in a Patou gown of deep rose silk (a wicked extravagance plotted by Margaret), I enjoyed myself defiantly, a gay young thing, in Paul's eyes, "with lots of sex appeal." Before long, the shadow fell across the drawing room—chastity and prudery vs. sexual freedom. Paul believed in expressing appreciation. His compliments were construed as criticism by Conrad, whose tepid "Mm, you smell nice" became equivalent to a ten-gun salute. Robert, arrayed like a circus ringmaster, eased the tension by scattering broadsides over coffee and claret. "Sybil tells me she's given up whiskey, but I wager that vampire now drinks blood."

Norah smiled indulgently. Tranquil as a nun, she sat on the sofa beneath the kakemono of an ibis. The L-shaped room now had a lived-in look— Kerman rug, Windsor desk, monk's-cloth curtains, Japanese prints by Utamaro and Hokusai, Hiroshige's *Keso Mountain Snow-clad*, chintz slipcovers, homemade parchment lampshades, shelves along the wainscotting stacked with varicolored books, Henry James's works and Chekhov's near the fireplace, on the mantel an exquisite cornelian figurine, my thirty-third birthday present, which Jane would get at age twenty-one.

All of the men had had something published recently, and so had I— Conrad his Preludes and a short story, "Mr. Arcularis," Paul his illustrated *Room and Book*, and Robert his play *Wings Over Europe*, coauthored by Maurice Brown and now in rehearsal.

With the skill of long practice, Paul asked if he might sit on the arm of my chair and show me his book, which he had dedicated to Conrad. When I said no, he looked dashed. What was I afraid of—B.O. or S.A.? I felt churlish at that and relented, though anticipating a rumpus. Conrad was torturing an eyebrow. Margaret laughed later on, when I asked her to muzzle Paul. "I can't deprive him of free speech, Clarissa. Of course I've noticed how shattered Conrad is whenever anyone pays you attention. He

was just as jealous of Jessie. What she values in Martin is his reasonable-
ness."

Norah thought Margaret was "managing" Paul. True, if that meant
guarding his health, gratifying his whims, investing in his paintings, and
apologizing for his caprices—in short, cherishing him.

The conversation centered on John Gould Fletcher, then on the brink
of collapse. The American imagist poet had begged Conrad to transport
his books and clothing from Sydenham to London, where he was living
with a married woman. His wife, a divorcée with two grown children,
was now his "bane," refusing him his books unless he came for them and
when he did so pleading with him to return. Poor Daisy, losing all her
teeth and then her spouse. A jealous, bad-tempered witch, he claimed,
rude to his friends, locking him out at night. He feared a divorce scandal,
and his mistress's husband, a famous literateur, wouldn't tolerate publicity.

I felt sorry for Fletcher, even though he broke our chain-pull w.c. in the
garden. A lugubrious mortal feeding on gloom. Cheerfulness drove him
crazy. God pity all poets with *Weltschmerz* struggling to stay alive and sane.
I glimpsed the anguish of creativity while typing Conrad's story "Silent
Snow, Secret Snow," about a boy retreating into psychosis. He hoped
Harper's would buy it for $375. Instead, his agent let the *Virginia Quarterly
Review* have it for $75.

Conrad was in a "techy" mood, working on his second novel, *Great
Circle*. His fan mail was dropping off, his publishers didn't promote his
works, he felt liverish, his breakfast egg hadn't been coddled enough, the
suit he had tailor-made was too big, just £4 wasted, his tennis racquet
needed restringing, and those infernal housemaids clanking pails along
Mermaid Street woke him up at dawn. "Life," he said, "is just one goddamned thing after another."

What did I know about him? Only superficial things—height five foot
seven, weight eleven stone, hat size seven, shoes, eight. He clung to
threadbare garments, scorned woolen underwear, detested platitudes, baby
talk, or women's tears ("blackmail"), excelled at chess, was a baseball fan,
movie lover, music addict. Living with a gadfly was like having crumbs in
your bed. My inner landscape was almost as murky as his. I felt moldy
after the long winter, stranded in a damp climate with no central heat.

"Assert yourself more." Margaret kept after me. "Stand up for your
rights." Accordingly, I danced with Paul to "Limehouse Blues" at the
Nashes. Conrad had been laughing like a gleeful schoolboy on holiday
while we played the adjective game, our scenarios side-splitting. Once
home, the worse for drink, he ticked me off for engaging in a "cowardly
substitute for coitus."

I demurred. "Dancing might limber you up and free you."

"You've ceased to be of use to me," he said.

I swallowed hard. "If you really mean that, I'll go away tomorrow."

He should have married an heiress like Norah, though she, too, had ceased inspiring Robert, a restless malcontent. "As long as he has the energy to grouse, I know I can safely ignore him." Norah never knew when he would whisk off to Vienna or Bali on borrowed cash. Rebuked, he retaliated by spending his last sovereign on some geegaw for her. When she couldn't take his lifestyle, she visited her mother. He would then tell friends that she must be bored, because she had had him send her some soda mints and *The Decameron*.

That was the trouble. We were *hooked*. The following morning brought no reference to Conrad's pronouncement. How had I failed him—as a hostess, companion, housewife, sexual partner, or promoter of his works? Probably the latter. Deny it though he may, my blindness to poetry bothered him. His work was his whole life and I, a poorly educated partner, had no fruitful contacts. When the going was rough, the Little Woman wasn't there to restore his ego, no devices other than to commiserate—a Pollyanna whistling in the dark. It was largely a teacher-pupil relationship. My drawbacks only reminded him of his own. I still hadn't the faintest idea what made a poet tick. The care and feeding of a bard was beyond me. The magic of creation would have evaporated had he explained that he was generating poems and stories while he "loafed," strolled, chatted with cronies, or went to the cinema. A washout, I couldn't even drink along with him.

When Margaret quoted Jessie as saying that Martin was so reasonable, in contrast to Conrad, I found myself bristling. Criticizing one's mate was the wife's prerogative. And Conrad was a genius, after all, one of those on whom nothing is lost, as Henry James would have said.

Among the paragons I was to read about, Carl Sandburg's wife, Lillian Steichen, stood out—the model artist's mate. She sublimated her natural desires, though no strife is chronicled in the biography. What she did for her dear poet and comrade was almost saintly: always there, holding the fort when he came home, aware that letting him go was the way to hold him, making sure of his freedom to write without domestic interruptions. Indeed she sounded almost too good to be true. I suspend belief.

25

E ARLY IN APRIL I again followed Margaret's cue, asserting myself by spending ten days in Holland with Paul's gifted pupil Mary Howard. She offered to stake me, but I preferred going Dutch. Mary haunted Paul's

studio, interrupting his work and upsetting Margaret. She couldn't seem
to break away from her mad and wealthy mother to live her own life in
London. We had endless discussions, I impatient with her wishy-washy
attitude and deploring her lostness and "please-be-kind-to-me" smile.

Conrad had promised to get a physical checkup in London and see
friends like Fletcher and Eliot. We spent the night with the Knights in
Saint John's Wood. He remarked that Laura was developing that glazed
look, while Harold was growing old and crusty. I disputed that. The poor
man was simply exhausted after judging pictures for an exhibition at the
Royal Academy, examining up to twelve thousand daily.

I stole a look at Harold's unfinished portrait of Conrad, a blue-and-gold
study stacked next to one of Cedric Hardwicke. When Laura spoke of
painting me, I suggested a cartoon. But my features were too regular, she
found. "Patience," I mumbled, "time makes caricatures of us all." We
passed the evening concocting ideas while Laura sketched: Uncle Sam
scrambling the Golden Egg laid by a British goose; a military wedding,
the uniformed groom under an archway of swords, Death the bride; the
Almighty holding Satan by the tail and handing him a thunderbolt, captioned, "Put that in your pipe and smoke it!" Conrad's favorite remark.

We had parted with ill-concealed relief, a moist occasion, I with a
beastly cold and standing in a downpour at Victoria Station, where I
joined Mary in the boat-train. It was a smooth overnight crossing, freight-
ers gliding by the Batavia liner like jeweled caskets under a full moon and
leaving a silvery snail's trail on the Channel. The ship listed alarmingly. A
Dutch breakfast fortified us against capricious weather: eggs, sliced ham,
smoked beef, bloaters, groats, rusk, honig-brod, five assorted jellies, Edam
cheese, coffee . . .

At customs in Rotterdam a stout woman sadly surrendered a huge
frosted cake, sugar being *verboten*, and my most intimate garments fell out
of the gladstone bag when it was opened. Travel usually brought out the
worst in me. Our taxi sloshed through flooded streets, cabs and bicycles
skidding on the cobbles. Our hotel proved to be filthy, noisy, and in need
of disinfecting, the bedroom walls paper-thin. I panicked that night,
awakened by a male voice and the doorknob rattling. Mary calmed me.
No rape imminent.

It rained every day, sudden violent cloudbursts, the sun sporadically
piercing sinister black clouds like a torchlight before darkness closed in
again. The Dutch seemed to pay scant attention to the weather. There
were hardly any rubber boots to be seen, and few umbrellas. Coughing
and sneezing, I fretted about Conrad. He might catch the flu, be run over,
arrested as a dangerous pacifist, or meet another literary heroine like
Cynthia.

"Relax, for pity's sake," said Mary, shaking me. "Forget him for a change."

I couldn't. I scribbled notes about things to tell him—on trains, boats, stoom-trams, buses, autos. The shaven necks of men smoking strong cigars, the women shocked by our cigarettes, the colorful, immaculate barges, stolid skippers in pantaloons and *klompen*, their *Frauen* hanging out the laundry in the rain—to wash or dry. Holbeins, Breughels, Rembrandts come to life, the most interesting faces those of children, piquant and rain-spangled under hoods.

Why was I childless? Mary asked bluntly one day. What was the hitch? I hedged, loath to mention the main reason, our bitter legacy, and so invoked financial straits. Poor Mary, pining for a husband, home, and motherhood! I reminded her that the happiest parents had their griefs, as witness the Lindberghs' first-born, kidnapped the month before—a shocker for the whole world.

Mary felt herself growing into an ugly old woman, doomed to spinster-hood. She despaired of ever having a love affair. "I have to fight self-consciousness all the time, have no purpose in life, I'm just drifting. Paul is moving away from me, in search of more lucrative contacts. Margaret spoils him, buys him every bauble his heart desires. I know I'm not seductive, but—oh God, I *hate* the English with their pruderies and hypocrisies. I want to live in France . . . "

"If only you could break away from your mother and Rye," I said. You have so much talent." I tried to coax her out of the blues by reciting *my* gaffes, pratfalls, and romantic twaddle.

And yet in Holland our roles were reversed. She dealt with problems, making arrangements and decisions. Look in the mirror, Mrs. Aiken. Who was the "wishy-washy" one now?

The Channel was a witch's brew on the return voyage. Mary, exhila-rated, braved the tempest on deck. I lay in our stuffy cabin, eyes closed, determined to be seasick like a lady—no throwing up. The ship creaked, groaned, and pitched all night long. Toward dawn I snatched a catnap, then staggered down the gangplank on my friend's arm.

Mary read *Lady Chatterley's Lover* in the boat-train, I coughing and barking like a seal. "Conrad will be throwing me a smelt any day now," I said.

I found him in a state of nervous prostration. Instead of seeing his doctor and Eliot, he had rescued John Gould Fletcher from Sydenham, playing nurse for a solid week to an unshaven ghost in a spotted gray suit. "I fed him, gave him aspirins, mixed his bromides, swept up his cigarette ashes, flushed the w.c. after him, brought him drinks at the pub, posted his letters to his wife and his mistress, urged him to build up his physique for Daisy's successor . . . " All this with a literary renaissance in mind, the same advice Conrad had given Louis Untermeyer.

While I described my travel experiences, he asked if the ship's steward had fornicated with me. "No," I said with a feeble, mirthless laugh. "I was laid low by King Neptune. Is that *all* you can think of?" Neither one of us was exactly in prime condition. He later told me of having tried "a little asphyxiation" in the kitchen, driven by Fletcher's morbid litany of domestic upheavals, professional neglect, and fear of going mad.

My thoughts about Fletcher were unprintable. I decided that Malcolm Lowry was *not* the greatest menace to Conrad. But where was my compassion? Anxiety over a husband was no reason to hate a poor wretch, a Lazarus, even though he took every kindness for granted, wolfed his food, criticized the wine, and ignored his hostess. The crowning insult came after he had read my palm at Conrad's insistence. "Nothing there," he said scathingly, "nothing as remarkable as your husband's hand."

I now qualified as a member of the club, along with Ezra Pound, William Carlos Williams, Alfred Kreymborg, and Conrad Aiken, all of whom had suffered from Fletcher's irascible temper and eccentricities.

26

AMONG ENGLISH FARMERS, spring began when you could step on three daisies at once. For us, a variety of other portents ushered in the season of renewal: the young girl in the Strand with a lamb on a leash, the vegetable man from Brittany swaggering in a lei of golden onions, the fisherman at the door with baby flounders flapping on a board ("Can't buy sandabs any fresher, mum"), the bell-ringing muffin-man balancing his aromatic tray on his head, the bagpiper skirling his way to the next meal, gypsies selling water lilies and clothes pegs—all Gilbert and Sullivan characters.

Our garden put on a spring show with grape hyacinths and tulips, primroses to come. White pear and pink quince petals covered the flagstones of the upper terrace. What bliss in prospect, sunbathing in private, no peeping toms, only the soporific drone of schoolboys next door parsing Latin verbs.

Conrad had been working on *Great Circle* again after two months. That made me terribly happy. But he had to drop the novel in May when we netted two paying guests through *New Yorker* ads, besides expecting Malcolm Lowry. Ruth was a charming brunette from New Bedford, tall, slim, and *très chic* in a black sealskin coat, a movie camera slung from her neck. She was thrilled by Jeake's haunts and awed by Conrad. Edward Doro, who arrived later that month, had the lean, hungry look of the proverbial bard. A Sephardic Jew, he was the son of a California banker. Conrad said he wrote extraordinary verse, a compliment returned in generous measure.

Jeake's House braced itself as always when Malcolm showed up. In 1929 Conrad had said, "Now the fun begins." Since then he had grown less sanguine. One complication was Doro. Another possible rival for Malcolm was Ed Burra, Paul's promising protégé, a surrealist painter who had a show in London before he was twenty-one, although suffering from rheumatoid arthritis. "Never mind, Malc, the more the merrier," I chaffed, failing to perceive a lonely, ostracized youth terrified of being supplanted or forsaken by his father surrogate. One of three satellites, he strove and struggled for Conrad's attention.

Burra, a rich man's son, had been dining with us weekly. One evening he asked me for the uneaten pickled onions he had brought. Malcolm guffawed and ribbed him mercilessly. About all the two had in common was an aversion to soap and water. Ed apparently squandered his £400 allowance on other things than clothes, for his meager garments had to be forcibly removed for the cleaners while he stayed in bed.

As for Malcolm, at times he looked like a rumpled popover. "*We're* just a couple of bums, sir," he quoted his tactful valet at Cambridge. His underwear was truly unmentionable. Keeping him laundered and presentable took finesse. His socks created minor crises. One morning he left the house vowing to bury his argyles. "About time, too," Conrad grunted. "Only don't go near the gasometer, otherwise there might be another Neuenkirchen explosion." Malcolm's belly laugh echoed along Mermaid Street.

Paying guests meant more income but also more housework. We had a full house when the children came at Easter. Mrs. Kipp had been turning up later each time, overburdened at home, so I gathered. Explaining the need of a young daily, I felt a Judas. She took it like a trouper. "Long's you don't feel I'm unsatisfactory like, mum." We parted warm friends.

Searching for a daily, I passed up two duds—a tippler caught watering Conrad's gin and a cat-hater suspected of treading on our pet's tail. What happened to Nero I can't remember, but Squidge, the cat of one hundred names, was a genius in Conrad's opinion, even capable of playing chess. He retrieved Ping-Pong balls, went daffy outdoors, chasing shadows and pouncing on imaginary enemies. The instant Conrad sat in his fireside chair, the kitten leapt on his lap, purring like a sewing machine. The dialogue between them was endlessly fascinating.

I finally located a jewel. Demure, pink-cheeked Jenny worked half days for fifteen shillings a week, bicycling from Camber. Neat, clean, eager to please, she announced in a fluster the first morning, "Your cooker is kipped, mum." All curtsies and smiles, even when I cursed the ever-smoking bogie. Jenny doted on Conrad. One morning he called from his study desk, "That you, darling?", and turned to find her with the duster, blushing like a sunrise. She was learning to make Indian curry. He said, "If you teach her everything you don't know about cooking, I'll marry her!"

Meanwhile the three J's converted Jeake's ghosts into friendly spooks. They used a typewriter in the workmen's club next door and took over Conrad's study, staging an eighteenth-century ball, dancing to minuets and polkas. He maintained that ghosts were subconscious projections and could be exorcised, once you traced the source of guilt. My only ghost was Jessie. With Conrad's tutelage and fertile imagination, the children concocted a mystery, *The Jewel Seed*. It grew with each visit, and, though never finished, proved a harbinger of brilliant careers for both Jane and Joan. As always, we missed the three when they left.

In mid-May the Lindbergh baby was found dead in a thicket a few miles from the home from which he had been taken. The British felt increasingly repelled by American crime and violence. When Robert Nichols suggested that all American college youths be mobilized to clean up the gangsters in the underworld, Conrad said that would mean a wholesale slaughter of at least ten million.

I too had a sorrow, mourning the death of Mrs. Bodley, my English friend, who had urged me to break with Conrad in 1927. A valiant woman with a rare capacity for extracting the fragrance and essence of life, she saw beauty in ordinary things. Remorse overwhelmed me. I hadn't written her for ages—completely heartless, capable of loving only one person in the world.

I was outraged when Conrad found my diary in the desk drawer and read it. (That I had perused his love letters to other women didn't occur to me then.) His fury matched mine. Not only did he fear the journal would fall into public hands and become another scandalous exposé like *My Arnold Bennett*, but he had a right to appropriate anything from any source, he said. I reminded him that I was also an author, however minor, and had an equal right to say whatever I wished on paper. Had he been more receptive I might have *voiced* my observations and criticisms. I was apt to forget my own needs and rights. Self-expression was just as indispensable to a journalist as to a poet-novelist.

After the dust settled, I glanced at my latest entries. They seemed innocuous enough: "E. F. Benson suggested Tuesday for the B. Transcript interview. Only three days away. I tore around Hastings in a dither, collecting his *Mapp* and *Lucia* novels and the memoir, *As We Were*, about the nineties . . . Alas, little research was absorbed. Stymied by Mary Howard, who came to dinner and stayed interminably, debating the future of man with Conrad. His ruthless logic took the wind out of her sails. My yawns unavailing hints. Next evening she dropped in again, more precious time wasted in bridge and chitchat, until 11:30 when I told her I was retiring with a headache. Conrad then woke me up and took me to task for my bad manners. I insisted on postponing our tiff since Ruth was within earshot."

Our social calendar was fast becoming a battlefield. Conrad, who demanded certitudes, was himself unpredictable as the weather. With an invitation accepted, he couldn't settle down to work. Formal gatherings were a horror, mixed ones "spiritual slaughters." He hadn't the heart to turn away visitors. How protect him against interruptions? Tell callers to go home, my husband was in labor? He felt injured if I accepted invitations for myself. Include him and he went into a decline, sleeping less, smoking and drinking more. Any excuse served. He had no decent clothes, small talk bored him, his hostess only meant to exploit him. Shortly after ducking a lion-hunter's party in London by wiring that he was ill, he saw her on the street. "Served her right." He echoed Emerson's edict. Solitude was impractical but society fatal for poets. Still that didn't mean rusticating or premature burial.

Only fondness for Ed Burra induced Conrad to meet Ed's parents in Playden. The Nashes and Ruth provided support that Sunday and I was a willing and curious captive. This was, after all, our first nod from gentry—Ed's father was a county judge. Margaret said Ed had little to do with his family. When they entertained, he ate smoked haddock in the kitchen with the fifteen or so servants, guests told that dear Ed was buried in his art.

Conrad was tempted to use his cane on a pack of yelping pomeranians that greeted us in the driveway. We were shown into a manorial-looking house filled with Victorian furniture and objets d'art. Mr. Burra, excessively refined, gave me a limp handshake across a miniature replica of the Taj Mahal under glass. Petite, brisk, keen, outspoken, with a twinkle inherited by Ed, Mrs. Burra introduced us to three Amazons and a retired Indian colonel whose bosomy spouse resembled the Red Queen in *Alice*.

"I've known many Americans in my extensive travels," she drawled, "but somehow you don't strike me as one." Who was it said the ruling classes saved England from democracy? "Frightful, frightful," the colonel trumpeted, apropos the Lindbergh tragedy. "A dreadful country, no one safe. I'd rather see a daughter of mine disgraced than have her migrate to America."

Conrad winced throughout the table talk, which ranged from orchid-growing to Jew-baiting in Germany and the pernicious Hollywood influence. "Our young pick up all sorts of slang and vulgarities from American films," complained one of the Amazons. At that point Ed took pity on us and showed us his studio, a mere anteroom off the kitchen, the walls covered with lewd sketches, pictures of movie stars, and other pinups (*his* pictures were all at the Leicester Gallery), Queen Victoria's family, and notorious criminals like Jack the Ripper. Crime and the underworld were Ed's dish of tea. A prodigious artist, he worked to jazz records, pasting one surrealist painting over another. How those deformed fingers could hold a brush or pencil was a mystery. My admiration and sympathy were diluted with caution, however, as I learned later much to my distress that he was a mischief-maker.

"I've never cared much for Margot Asquith," Mrs. Burra said with bird-like gestures, "after seeing her paring her nails while in charge of the ices at a charity bazaar." Conrad gave me the high sign. Unfortunately farewells were aborted by a sudden downpour. He glanced wistfully at the Daimler idling in the driveway, then asked for a cab.

At home he poured himself a stiff slug of gin and swore never again. "The medieval rack is a pleasure by comparison." Even Ruth, our lightning rod, couldn't supply a rainbow by quoting Mrs. Burra's flattery: "How *can* Ed resist him . . . so magnetic and yet austere . . . "

27

CONRAD'S REVOLT left me with two choices: to decline invitations or go off without him, which of course disappointed the host and hostess. I remember saying defiantly, when he balked outright, "Very well, I'll go alone and make a fool of myself." Riding on his coattails was a far cry from the days when I believed people liked me for myself.

The fact that E. F. Benson had forgotten about being interviewed didn't improve my self-confidence. He did apologize profusely when his housekeeper announced my arrival at Lamb House, the former residence of Henry James. "Can you ever forgive me? And stay to lunch?" I could and would. He introduced me to Rameses II, a legless figure of rose granite in the foyer, smirking at my chagrin. "The legs were missing when my sister, Mrs. Sidgwick, bought it in Egypt."

Except for the twinkle, Benson resembled my father—blue eyes, white hair and mustache. A distinguished looking man of sixty-five, though crippled (he walked with two canes), he spoke in spurts, slurring words, but was volubly amusing, with a variety of facial expressions. In hopes of drawing a spark, or finding home base with me, he flitted from one subject to another—eminent musicians, lilacs, grapes, happiness—I had no challenging questions, and was in a dither about pulling off my first British author. Mouse meets lion: Son of Edward W. Benson, the late Archbishop of Canterbury, donor of the Benson Cup, a silver trophy for the best

I was ten and my brother John six when this picture was taken
at our home in Milwaukee.

Scottie and I, Fort Sheridan, Illinois, 1919.

My favorite photograph of Conrad, probably taken before 1920.

A portrait of me taken in Boston in 1925,
the year before I met Conrad.

Conrad and I in Cambridge, I believe 1927.

Left: Conrad and I in West Dennis, Cape Cod, 1927.
Right: Malcolm Lowry, Cambridge, Massachusetts, July 1929.

Conrad surveying his property in South Yarmouth, 1927.
Bass River is to the right.

Jeake's House as it looks today. The photograph was taken
by John Aiken's wife, Paddy.

Left: I took this picture of Jane Aiken reading and Joan studying chess moves in the drawing room of Jeake's House, February 1936.
Right: Squidge and I in the garden of Jeake's House, early 1930s.

Conrad (far right) at a garden party in Winchelsea, Sussex. The others (left to right) are Robert Nichols, Paul Nash, Margaret Nash, and Edward Doro.

Harold and Laura Knight at the Malvern Theatre with Sir Barry Jackson and Conrad, puffing on his pipe.

For nearly ten years after the breakup of my marriage I went around in a fog. "You're buried prematurely," friends lamented.

young chess player in Rye (John Aiken won it one year), and prolific author of novels and biographies.

Icebreakers began and ended lunch. Did I know Radclyffe Hall? Slightly, I said. She had assured me that I'd find "dear old Dodo," as she called Benson, an easy victim. Had I read her *Well of Loneliness*? Not yet. A remarkable woman, don't you think so? I nodded, at a loss for a reply. "I'm devoted to her," he said, while his butler stood behind my chair—to make sure I didn't slurp my coffee or Kümmel?

After consuming fishcakes, roast mutton, scalloped potatoes, spinach, and jam fritters, we adjourned to the garden room where James wrote some of his classics—*The Golden Bowl, The Ambassadors, The Wings of the Dove*. Through tall French windows I saw Rye's loveliest garden enclosed by a high brick wall—a charming room, with a fireplace and a grand piano, four walls book-lined. The master's retreat was destroyed by a bomb in World War II.

While I took shorthand notes, Benson sat at his desk stroking a white Persian cat and reminiscing about England's great captured between the covers of *As We Were*—Gladstone, Tennyson, Oscar Wilde, Lord Tavistock, Duke of Bedford, a fabulously wealthy man (my train companion's husband?). He said he wrote the book in four months' time entirely from memory, except for passages culled from his father's diary. In one such entry the Archbishop revealed being ordered by Queen Victoria to tell her son, that scandalous bon vivant the Prince of Wales, that he had better mend his ways.

Asked about work in progress, my host tapped a stack of copybooks containing the sequel, *As We Are*. I drew him out about Henry James. He said his father gave James the plot for *The Turn of the Screw*, a gruesome tale about evil spirits inhabiting two innocent children. "Henry was more British than the British. His butler was a real Jeeves. He found it necessary to educate at least one American guest, who began sipping the water in the silver salver proferred him the first morning. The butler, recoiling in horror, informed him, 'The temperature of your bath, sir!'"

I came away with a busy notebook and my *amour-propre* restored by his hospitable "You must come again soon, unprofessionally, and bring your husband." As I left a bevy of trippers reading the plaque near the door shrilled, "'Ooh, look at this, an American bloke, Henry James, once lived here!' Rye's future mayor shut the door rather hastily on their strident voices. I turned the corner on Mermaid Street, fired with renewed ambition to be a Successful Author, then teetered on high heels over the cobbles.

Conrad would be happy to meet his neighbor socially, just as I thought. "Perhaps he'll give me a job counting his wealth," he said. Money short-

ages dogged our days. Friends helped him out periodically, and also
his brother Kempton, until Conrad sent him a stinging letter in December 1933.

Late in May we tried our luck at the Derby. The omens were favorable:
a swallow flew into the study, and I found two four-leaf clovers. We set
out for Surrey in a downpour. Epsom Downs was awash in lorries, char-
abancs, bicycles—the British spirit soaked but indomitable. Throngs jammed
the barrier, rain beating a tattoo on umbrellas. The gong clanged. Contestants sprang off to a deafening clamor. Hooves pounded on turf, bettors
urged on their favorites. Conrad craned on tiptoe, quivering with suspense. I prayed, closed my eyes, saw myself at Fort Sheridan cantering
along Lake Michigan beach, then heard hoarse cries. "Here they come—
on the home stretch—by Jove, April Fifth is leading."

Conrad swore, "Blast and putrefaction," then trampled his parimutuel
ticket underfoot. Drenched and dejected, we sloshed through mud to the
bus stop. Never believe in omens. Why hadn't we listened to the Derby
over the wireless at home, or at the Knights's studio? Harold could have
used an extra sitting for Conrad's portrait.

Conrad felt jinxed. He remembered John quoting Jessie asking if we
seemed to be well off. "With $700 in the bank, and my work shot to hell?"
he said with a hollow laugh. "I wish life was over."

"No you don't, darling," I said. "Life's a gift, not a burden. Think of all
the exquisite poems you'll be creating for posterity." Another storm brewing. But he had reason to be bitter, after turning himself inside out for
mankind, as Houston Peterson said in *The Melody of Chaos*. The intense
concentration of creating the Preludes or the Osiris Jones poems drained
him. He would pace the floor, stimulated by the Gramophone grinding
out Mozart's *Jupiter* or a Beethoven symphony. With Doro and Malcolm
Lowry there, he was getting a much needed breather. But when they left,
he would be immersed again in his work. I told him he should have a
hobby to take his mind off literary matters—wood carving or gardening.
"Grab a trowel and dig in the earth," I said brashly. "You'll fall in love with
it. There's something about just kneeling . . ."

"Why not cut out paper dolls?" He uncorked the gin bottle. "You and
your simplistic notions. If you spent half the time on cooking that you do
on those crochetings that will never sell . . ."

"Those little crochetings have been my livelihood since I was nineteen,"
I said huffily. "Don't forget that we met through my writing." Or was that
one reason for his complaint? In behalf of all women childless or unful-
filled by homemaking, I resented his attitude. Was his superior achievement any reason why I should choke off self-expression? "You have genius,"

he had said at the start. Now, seven years later, "You'll never amount to anything, you're too normal." And would remain so, God willing, a writer of sorts and a musician manqué.

"Why not focus on your music, if you want an outlet?"

"Because I can't earn anything by it," I said, "especially in England, where aliens aren't allowed jobs, as you well know. Two writers under one roof may be one too many, but I can't and won't stop writing—ever. I already covered the Holland trip with my article on majolica. The wages I pay Jenny buy me precious time, and I've *earned* her."

"Then carry on with journalism and don't waste more postage on those two juvenile books," he said.

There it was again, my writing producing friction. A daydreamer trying to replace a warped childhood with a more palatable one, fantasizing and writing fairy tales or nonsense. Maddening to rack up near misses, the latest one almost accepted by the *New Yorker*. My literary agent in New York warned me about writing too much or trying to do too many creative things. "You'll soon be unable to find anything emotionally strong to put down. Whether you need a vacation from your typewriter or a personal housecleaning, I don't know, but *you* know, and I trust you'll do something about it. That buoyancy of yours is worth holding on to—hard."

Conrad rapped on the window, calling Squidge from the garden, then lured him into the corridor with a Ping-Pong ball. After setting the table, I took the cat's supper out of the cold box, cut up liver and lights, shoved the dish under the sink, washed my hands, scrubbed some potatoes, and started them on the gas range, then began toasting bread for Conrad's canapé. He followed Squidge into the room, planting himself as usual between sink and stove.

"You'll have to give me elbow space," I said, still smouldering at his disparaging remarks about my cooking. "You may not think me a good cook, but John does. When I do try to please you, I get no praise. Ruth and Doro found my *gigot en daub* delicious, but you merely asked why I hadn't served the green peas the pubkeeper's wife gave you."

"Exceptions prove the rule," he said blandly, munching anchovies on toast. "Your meals leave much to be desired."

"So do your manners." I groped for my handkerchief, thankful that Malcolm was out playing tennis with Doro, and Ruth experimenting with her movie camera. "*Your* day isn't broken up with domestic duties and interruptions. I've reached a point where I feel guilty about writing, snatching time from marketing, cooking, mending, dressmaking, and typing your manuscripts. I whisk the typewriter from one floor and room to another. If you were more helpful around the house . . ." Give him a dish towel and he would write a poem about it. "Paul hasn't lost his manhood, wiping dishes for Margaret. You gush over the cat and talk to him by the hour, but you never feed Squidge or . . ." The front door clicked. I turned from the sink. I had lost my audience.

28

"Your husband is a remarkable man," Ed Doro informed me tipsily one evening, as I grated cheese for a Welsh rarebit. "He knows too much to be a good poet, though I don't hold that against a genius. But his aura disturbs me. It's too powerful, I can't write in his ambiance." So others felt it, too. The dark, soulful eyes regarded me with sorrow. "I understand that you're governed entirely by your subconscious—kind-hearted, never hurting intentionally, just blindly."

My hand shook as I lit the alcohol burner under the chafing dish. Perfidious Conrad, telling a stranger intimate things while objecting to Margaret as my confidante. Actually, my subconscious was friendly and protective of him in my dreams, until I had that nightmare about the sword of Damocles falling on him. I woke up, screaming, "Look out!" When he grabbed my arm, I wrestled with him, thinking he wanted to kill me. That episode followed another row over my diary, as yet unresolved.

Meanwhile he expounded his credo to a large and admiring audience including the Nashes, Robert and Norah, with their houseguest Arthur Bliss, the composer, Ed Burra, and our three paying guests. Squidge on his lap, Conrad sat by the empty fireplace, cigarette in hand, a drink at his elbow, the black-rimmed spectacles accentuating his austerity.

Robert acted as devil's advocate. "You'll never get anywhere, my dear chap," he said, lolling on the sofa, feet on the window ledge, head resting on Ruth's shoulder, "squatting like Buddha, contemplating your navel."

"Oh yes I will," said Conrad. "If there's a purpose in life, it's developing awareness. The more aware one is, the less one talks; the less one talks, the more one thinks. One grows best by thinking."

"Sounds like transcendentalism. But consciousness must have quality, surely."

"Right. The more conscious you are, the better the quality. I regard myself as a disseminator of knowledge, of the world's news in poetic terms. Man has all he needs to evolve a religious credo, once he is liberated from dogma. He can, if he only will, become divine. When the half-gods go, the gods arrive," quoting his grandfather Potter's philosophy.

"Then you think Crippen the murderer is as good as Christ?" Robert asked.

"Why not? We're the sum of all our experiences, and they include everything we do, say, think, or dream."

"You deny any moral element?"

"Absolutely," Conrad said.

"Dead wrong. You can't live in a moral vacuum. We progress from purity of heart, not from the desire to be conscious. What stops you otherwise from slashing your wife's throat?"

"Damned if I know. Self-preservation?"

"No moral scruples?"

"None whatever," Conrad said.

"Don't fool yourself."

"I don't. We're all murderers at heart."

I chewed on that chilling statement coming from an avowed pacifist. It produced shock waves. Margaret quoted Balzac's "The heart must be within the domain of the mind." It was more important to be a good human being than a great one.

"No heart," Robert sighed. "That's probably why my play was a flop." *Wings Over Europe* had closed, despite favorable reviews by Shaw, Wells, and Barrie, doubtless all bought with his dinners, according to Paul.

Conrad then startled us a second time, even Malcolm who sat staring into his beer mug, by saying forcefully "Most critics are a lot of shits," echoing Eliot's remark to him about literary people. The ordeal of being an Englishman may have brought on Eliot's rumored breakdown, Conrad concluded. "The average public has no idea what a ghastly business writing is."

"I salute your courage," Robert said dryly, waving a cattail. "But to make a lifetime career of studying the horrors in one's soul seems daft to me. I say, take a good, hard look, accept the ugly and enjoy the beauty."

That made sense to me. I followed Squidge downstairs (he was allergic to dialectics) and rustled up more refreshments. Conrad's credo was as unpalatable to me as my meals were to him. Consciousness is "pure suffering," he wrote in his short story "Gehenna."

He was into religion while I passed around the cheese and crackers. "When Eliot joined the Anglican Church four years ago, he regressed two thousand years, becoming one of the herd, making himself null and void as an explorer of human awareness." Yet my atheistic husband took far more delight in having his portrait hung in the Unitarian Church vestry at Gardner, Massachusetts, than winning the Pulitzer.

"Music critics seem a little less obnoxious than literary critics," Arthur

Bliss rumbled. He was known for his *Colour Symphony*, and later composed film scores and many pieces for royal occasions such as Queen Elizabeth's coronation. The pudgy composer twisted and thrashed about, ruining my slipcover while expressing himself with his whole carcass. "They may be deaf, fat, and gouty, but at least they don't go into a huddle over No. 48, asking is it a fish or a fungus, and what shall we say about it. As for Catholicism, it's a form of witchcraft, of course, but I can entrust my physical life to the spiritual safekeeping of the Pope's emissaries and free my aesthetic self with monthly confessions. Not that I agree with His Holiness on secular matters like birth control. There the Vatican oversteps its bounds."

"Hear, hear!" said Robert. "I give Catholicism five hundred more years." He began to improvise a chanty about finding solace and absolution in the confessional, each stanza ending with, "There's always the Church waiting for you." Beating time with the cattail, he said blithely, "I've slept with lots of women, but Norah is love. She is peace." He raised his head from Ruth's shoulder. "It's like being out to sea in a little boat with the sun pouring down on you."

That little craft was in danger of capsizing. Norah's tremulous smile spoke volumes. She had my sympathy. While Robert played ducks and drakes with her money, said Margaret, he expected her to welcome various "fillies" he invited to Winchelsea. Ruth became restive, wedged between Robert and Paul, the latter alternately caressing her thigh and nibbling her elbow. Later that evening she giggled, admitting, "I'm glad I can prove to Malcolm that the bites on my arm came from Squidge's fleas and not from Paul's teeth."

Conrad's strained pun, "An aPAULing idea," mystified Malcolm. My matchmaking efforts had fallen flat. Ruth was shocked at my idea that she ask him to the cinema.

Malcolm was much too conflicted to take notice of either her or Jenny, their languishing glances lost on him. "'E's a real gen'man," said my daily, proving her devotion by saving all his discarded scribblings. He had written me a note postmarked Camber, on one of his solitary tramps along Romney Marsh, a humorous apology in rhyme for some forgotten misdemeanor, probably committed while tight. I suspected Jenny when it vanished. Sure enough, Conrad found it in her apron pocket. She had either taken it from my desk or else fished it out of the wastebasket.

Trial-and-error manuscripts filled my wastebasket. Conrad, I decided, had reasons for challenging my writings. We were bound to collide, our failure ricocheting. He hadn't the time or energy to play nurse to my literary bumblings. With a myopic outlook on life and mentally lazy, I wasted time on trivia, my ambition outdistancing intelligence. I lacked the capacity for sustained effort and perseverance (*Sitzfleisch*) in either the literary or the musical fields. I was a drain on Conrad's capital and brought him no dowry, whereas Jessie had an inheritance besides giving him children. Why not please him by spending more time in the kitchen, justifying Margaret's efforts as a cooking teacher? Experiment with dishes, collect recipes for a cookbook, and call it *Delicious Debaucheries*?

In bed we wrangled. It began with Conrad telling me that Paul had tried to lure Ruth into his studio, "And in Margaret's presence, what's more. Have *you* ever been there?" No, I said teasingly, "would you mind if I went?" I had no intention of going, wasn't interested, but flared up when he issued the usual warnings about infidelity. How could I ever develop more awareness when I wasn't allowed to express myself? Who was stopping me? he asked.

"You, yes, you!" I said. "I mustn't look at another man, mustn't associate with the 'wrong people,' mustn't waste time writing children's books, mustn't say Boo when you're drunk and abusive, mustn't keep a diary— *verboten*, everything *verboten*. You're my father all over again!"

"In a good mood he is an absolute angel," I wrote in my diary. "Loving and thoughtful. But it never lasts long." Conrad pounced on that sentence. "Don't think your obliquities fascinate me. They fill me with increased loathing. Put *that* down in your journal."

"I will. And your snooping fills *me* with loathing," I said hotly. "A diary is private and sacred." How often had I shut myself in our bedroom to pour out grievances, catharsis for a bruised ego. "I've been writing the truth, not obliquities, everything I feel. I was my real, candid self."

"I found little candor or soul-searching. It's rather a device to smear me. And how you enjoy the role of a wronged wife."

"I wouldn't need any devices if you treated me decently," I said. His bitter complaint to Jake Wilbur of being maligned brought a reminder that I had to have someone to talk to, after all. Evidently my impressions of him were the exception to his wish of stripping *himself* bare.

But *was* I being honest, or had I mixed motives? A close scrutiny would have revealed the wronged wife Conrad spotted, collecting grudges and complaints and alibis for criticism often warranted, and using guerilla tactics. They say an unexamined life isn't worth living. I might have grown in maturity and perception had I *tried* at least to follow this credo. Panic blocked me at the prospect of excavating reasons for guilt and amnesia— buried death wishes toward Father?—all the specters of a chaotic past. And so I covered my head with a shroud, as friends said subsequently, buried so deep in fantasy that even hypnosis couldn't recover memories.

Finally I agreed to tear out the offending diary pages (and never ceased to regret it). What a yammer, had I bullied Conrad into destroying parts of his manuscript! But I would continue jotting down my thoughts in shorthand, safe from prying eyes.

29

WE CELEBRATED Independence Day 1932 with verbal fireworks, touched off by Bishop Odeh, bedridden after falling off a bus. Though he rallied a bit, Margaret feared he would go on dying "for another two years." Conrad denounced her callousness. "The least she owes him is filial love. He pays half the household expenses, yet she and Paul treat him like an interloper."

"Margaret is tuckered out," I said staunchly. "She does her best with a high-strung, asthmatic husband and a senile obstinate old man."

"That's *her* version. She's a dissembler," Conrad said. "Stretch her any way you like, she'll snap right back. Her father deserves more than perfunctory attention."

"How can she feel any regard for him? His cruelty shortened her mother's life." Just as my father did Mother's life. I tried to forgive him but couldn't forget his treatment of her. Nor could Conrad ever forget that his life was irrevocably damaged by his father. Condemnation and hatred came through strongly in both *Blue Voyage* and *Great Circle*.

Margaret had trouble finding a satisfactory nurse. I volunteered to spell her occasionally, reading Orczy thrillers to the Arabian bishop.

Our lives were to be complicated by a flood of summer visitors, particularly one couple also named Nash, whom Conrad had met in the pub. White-haired, stocky Vernon, a rabid Communist, resembled Ben-Gurion. His young and glamorous wife, Deirdre, dominated the conversation. While their border terrier chased Squidge through the house, she raved about the sixteenth-century house they had recently purchased on Romney Marsh. "We got the Old Vicarage for a mere bagatelle, only £100, just what we wanted. Nash plans to make it livable."

"Yes, by Jove, no time to lose." Vernon shook his fist. "Back to the earth before the crash comes. Convert swords into plowshares."

"You *must* see it, Clarissa," Deirdre trilled, her tawny-green eyes on Conrad, her Irish voice and honey-colored hair enchanting him, though I found her quite resistible.

The bargain proved to be a picturesque ruin: a sagging thatched roof, two rooms sans floor, a leprous ceiling, windowless kitchen, huge fireplace stuffed with rubbish, and all overgrown by moss, lichen, and ivy. Deirdre, in high heels, scraped gunk off a wall with a penknife. "Oh please don't do that, Clarissa," she shrieked when a chunk of rotted beam crumbled in my hand like a biscuit.

"What this place needs is a roaring bonfire," Conrad said later, as we trudged waist high through weeds, sheep nibbling among the nettles. "Or else the Last Sacraments." He surveyed the godforsaken area, no other dwellings in sight. "They'll have to milk their nearest neighbor's bossy in the dead of night."

Within a week Deirdre appeared with Robert Nichols, her eyes swimming in tears. "The carpenter promised to fix up the place for £40, but now he says it's hopeless. What shall I do? Stay in Rye or go back to London? I'm sure Nash doesn't want me in town. But then again—God, what *should* I do?"

Scram, I thought. Let Robert take her on. I've got only one life to live, and it belongs to Conrad. He grinned when I said, "Watch out, that Circe has designs on you. Don't forget you're a misogynist."

We could no longer complain of social stagnation. The perpetual assault by visitors was devastating. Conrad couldn't balance work with relaxation. It was either a feast or famine with us. A full house of unrest. At one time all the beds and sofas were occupied. Jeake's throbbed with hijinks and drama. The two Nash couples squared off. Malcolm's alcoholic sprees worsened as Doro and Burra claimed more of Conrad's time. Trifles grated on my nerves: lights left on, windows left open in the rain, Mary Howard's boozy escort smashing a windowpane. I tried to keep a tidy house, compulsive about straightening cushions and furniture—physical order compensating for inner chaos. My sense of hospitality wore thin at the seams. I sped parting guests who lingered while drawling "I suppose we'd better be going . . ."

Conrad berated me. "Haven't you learned *any* manners?"

"No," I said. "Manners are wasted on parasites and freeloaders. You demolish me for trying to prevent people from sabotaging your work."

"Then stop meddling in my life."

"Then stop taking out your frustrations on me."

Jenny was so rattled one evening that she served fresh cherries in one bowl and the stones in another. Conrad's pun, "Cherries with stones are more to be pitted than blamed," raised a feeble laugh.

I didn't exactly jump for joy when Deirdre informed us that the Old Vicarage could be renovated after all, readied for occupancy by next spring. Neither was Margaret keen about that. She had taken a firm stand with Paul, whose work was threatened by a newcomer, a paid companion to a heroin addict.

"You can't afford to know *arrivistes* like Julia," said Margaret. "She's a psychopathic liar, and dangerous—the sort who expects men to go mad with desire and tear off her clothes. You're not to let her in if she comes here. I will not have that scheming female in my house. She tried to blackmail Robert for some trifling billet-doux, and then began ingratiating herself with Conrad." He described her as "radiantly insincere," telling the gentry that she felt sorry for Clarissa, "an old friend living in sin with an American poet." (No longer, now married—and I was no old friend of hers.) After that Conrad blocked her entrance, saying in his best *haut en bas* manner, "I think you'd better stop calling on us."

Prior to our boycott, we had been asked to be witnesses at her wedding (a civil ceremony) to a penniless poet turned chicken farmer. He appeared in the same baggy old flannels and sweater. At the reception, a motley gathering, I overheard the bride telling people that their union would be platonic. So I said blithely, to fill in a hiatus, "How many marriages do you suppose are consummated in the registry office?" My faux pas provoked stifled laughter, Robert cackling, Conrad shuddering. On the way home, he blasted me. "You're a great social asset. I can always count on you to embarrass me. Hell's bells, don't you even know the difference between *consummate* and *consecrate*? We've got one thousand books upstairs. Why don't you make use of a dictionary? Your incompetence and slipshod habits will drive us apart yet. You do everything in a rush and impulsively—typing, playing the piano, cooking, writing . . ."

True, true, true. His two-page, single-spaced list of book titles was gathering dust. I was as lazy and literal-minded as the day I asked the fourth-grade teacher who said the Church was indestructible, "But can't it burn down, Sister?" I seemed to be hatching an obscure phobia that attached itself to all situations. Fear of opening my mouth was the one I needed most. Was the ergot responsible for my lunacies? Conrad, enveloped in cigarette smoke, lectured me for my gaffes and rightly so, the intellectual sensitive about his reputation.

The latest entry in my diary read: "The walls begin to crumble. Scribner's Magazine rejected *G.C.* for serialization. If only I were of some use. Kemp cabled, 'Sorry, bust' to C's request for another loan. We're mired in petty quarrels and can't let off steam until we're in bed. I hadn't expected to cope with such a large house, or cater to so many boarders, juggling menus. It's home and Father all over again. Explosions are inevitable."

Ed Doro and Ruth had left Rye late in July after Doro's father went bankrupt. Malcolm outstayed his welcome for reasons all too apparent, though his quarrels with Conrad were conducted out of earshot. Brought up to be seen and not heard (like my brothers), he was a good listener when not up in the clouds and vague as a ghostly sound in the night. Whenever he went into a trance playing bridge or parlor games like mock murder trials, I would say, "Wake up, Malc," snapping my fingers, tempted to agree with Margaret. She regarded him an unproven prodigy, a dissolute maverick, and one day sounded off at length on the subject.

"Malcolm's too busy being picturesque and moody much of the time. His daemon is devouring him, so he must be forgiven, one of those sad, lost young men who can't live with themselves and with whom no one can live. That doesn't impress me. I can't sympathize with those who throw away their talents or corrode their systems with alcohol and drugs, shortening their lives. I prefer the organized artist—Beethoven, stone-deaf, composing monumental symphonies and sonatas, Michelangelo getting the Sistine Chapel ceiling painted in spite of physical handicaps and setbacks, Goethe at forty, beginning *Faust* and working on it until his death at eighty-two. Those artists respected their talent and the need to work. There has to be order within the chaos, not just a mood."

I rose to Malcolm's defense the more I learned about him. He was haunted by a fear of homosexuality, a curse as vile in his father's eyes as syphilis. He also had a deep sense of guilt about masturbating. His roommate in college threatened suicide when Malcolm refused to have sex with him, saying, "That's a good idea, why don't you go ahead?" Spurned, the boy went ahead and killed himself.

Malcolm never looked so alone as when part of a group—the isolation of an alcoholic on sufferance with society. His blanket was his ukulele. He strummed Negro spirituals on that long-necked instrument, favorite of Bix Beiderbecke, Joe Venuti, and assorted Dixieland exponents. I sometimes accompanied him at the piano.

"Three guesses how he'll celebrate his twenty-third birthday," Conrad said wryly when Malcolm left just before the end of July. "I fear my dream of seeing him stand on his head and drying out was just wishful thinking." Lowry received a weekly six guineas pocket money. He never saw his blood relatives again after age twenty-five. For his novel *Ultramarine* he wanted to use Conrad's dream, mentioned in *Great Circle*, of eating the father's skeleton, but was told that would be carrying things too far.

30

BEFORE MALCOLM LEFT RYE we were cajoled into attending the Ellen Terry Memorial performance. I was delighted, having read Shaw's romantic correspondence with the actress. Her daughter, Edith Craig, had previously shown Margaret and me the cottage in nearby Smallhythe. There, time stood still, everything preserved as of old: stage costumes, memorabilia, the children's school desks. Margaret lamented Edith's brother, Gordon, who expected their mother to support his numerous mistresses.

The Bloomsbury set turned up in droves, overflowing a garden fragrant with lavender and syringa. You couldn't breathe in the crush. Ladies in tailored suits looked over younger ones, while a blasé music critic ogled them through a monocle when not embracing them. Lady Sackville-West, large, formidable, and with a faint mustache, wore a black sombrero and gestured with a long cigarette holder. Her husband, Harold Nicolson, buttonholed Paul to ask whether Major Yeats-Brown, author of *The Lives of a Bengal Lancer*, was a fraud. "It seems so to me."

Scenes from *Twelfth Night* were performed on a candlelit stage in the thatched barn where Shakespeare had reportedly played during the Beaumont-Fletcher barnstorming era. John Gielgud starred as Orsino, Peggy Ashcroft as Viola, Margaretta Scott as Olivia. During the intermission the daughter of Alma Tadema, the painter, paid tribute to Ellen Terry, setting off an epidemic of yawns and belches. Conrad winced at phrases like, "This hallowed spot . . . drawn here by love . . . may her memory long live . . ."

A southwest gale was brewing as the curtain rang down. Our taxi was invaded by several strangers and a spotted dog, all bound for Jeake's House. I collected beer and cheese for a swelling crowd spilling over on the floor—among them Dicky Dixon, pianist at the Kit-Kat Club in London, and her housemate, Vilma, rivals of Radclyffe Hall and Lady Troubridge.

Esmé Percy (who played the Hungarian ambassador in *Pygmalion*) regaled us with theatre gossip, mainly about Mrs. Patrick Campbell. "Oh what a jealous cat was Mrs. Pat," said the long-haired Shavian actor in the Russian tunic. "She once begged a box from Noel Coward for the opening night of *Private Lives*, then dozed during the performance, snoring loudly when not crooning to her lap dog. Noel sent up a note entreating her to lie on the floor if she must sleep, so people would be spared the unedifying spectacle. The next night she sat in the front row, clapping his every entrance and exit."

Esmé went on and on, while Margaret drooped. I began dozing, too, as he boasted of having been alone for five minutes with the divine Sarah in her dressing room. Conrad kept afloat with gin. Once he came to bed, his moans and snores woke me up at intervals. Had so many sex deviates disturbed him?

. . . you might have thought me not sufficiently masculine? . . . A sentimental introverted weakling, with that tendency to sudden cruelty which all the injured manifest. But my trick of unexpected reticence, my impassivity of

appearance, my proneness to fatigue and indifference, the rapidity with which
I tire of people . . . these characteristics give an air of masculinity which
might have deceived you? Are you listening, Cynthia?

Blue Voyage

I had the jitters at the Graham-Watson dinner party. Major Yeats-Brown
sat beside me, suave and witty. As I was finishing my wine and brandy I
noticed that the guests all seemed to consider me amusing. I found the
reason in the mirror, having forgotten to remove my hat—too much
liquor and a touch of the flu, I pleaded later. Conrad took pains to point
out that our hostess knew Reine Ormond. The Cynthia in *Blue Voyage*
would doubtless hear all about the present Mrs. Aiken mislaying her wits.
Oh for a smuggler's cave to hide in. Conrad talked in his sleep that night:
"'I'll have you buttered,' cried the Queen."

Dear Diary:
    Coventry [the silent treatment] ends today, the silence lifted by a kiss on
the nose, C saying something kind. FEAR. Such a harmless-sounding word,
yet I wait for disasters. More nightmares, the days filled with domestic and
social pressures. Driven to the meadow for peace and quiet.

The children came in August. We tried the sortes Shakesperianae. In
three ventures at the Oxford Shakspere, Conrad twice put his finger on
the line "May you be happy in your wish, my lord." The atmosphere was
neutralized, thanks to John's blue-eyed twinkle and affectionate banter,
Jane's breezy common sense, and Joan, a quiet listener, entertaining us by
illustrating clichés. When Conrad heard that Jane was to be a cloud in a
Cupid and Psyche ballet at Hayes School, he threatened to attend. All
three J's writhed. John stammered, "But Jessie and Martin are going."
Conrad said with a diabolical grin, "All the better, a family reunion." I
told him to stop teasing.
    John measured me constantly and showed inclinations toward his fath-
er's antifeminism. His face was beautiful in repose, a blend of intellectual
and spiritual. His rollicking nature dispelled fits of dejection and rebellion.
A dream he revealed gave me an interesting sidelight on him: he was
teaching his young half-brother the alphabet but stopped short at *R*, since
the next letter was indecent. Mozart and Haydn broke the ice between us.
Sightreading Haydn's 99th was great fun, at the composer's expense.
    Joan produced a remarkable nature poem for Conrad's forty-third birth-
day. My Tunbridge-ware folio was appreciated, and we had a cake with
candles and an astrological glimpse of Leo—"kingly, heroic, generous,
ruled by the sun, tawny red hair, fine, sparkling eyes, a noble carriage."

But Conrad refused to don a bathing suit at Camber Sands one sunny afternoon! Was it congenital shyness or disappointment at John's deciding on London University instead of Harvard? I swung Jane around in the water as usual, though she was becoming rather heavy. When I sat on the shingle beside Conrad and asked if he wouldn't at least get his feet wet, he said no morosely. Nor was he amused to hear about the Camber postmaster who forbade his wife to swim there, then asked for a transfer, after a naked girl walked into the post office.

Homeward bound, Jane and I gathered sea poppies, wild foxglove, and pink mallow while deploring the trippers overrunning Rye. Shrill-voiced sightseers with kippered faces and abbreviated attire, they peered into windows and popped through open doors of private houses to ask, "How much for tea?"

Suddenly I became a target of criticism. "You're growing round-shouldered," Conrad said, "you slump and slouch in your chair, you mumble and swallow your words, and though you play like an angel you talk like poor Poll . . ."

Couldn't he have waited until we were alone? Embarrassing the children. A subdued quintet reached Jeake's House. I slipped upstairs, took a hot bath, then climbed to our bedroom, closing the door. Tears came unbidden.

"Jerry?" Jane knocked, then opened the door. "Oh, excuse me," she said, and withdrew. Mortifying to be caught crying. I'm sure Conrad was sorry, aware of the children's sense of fair play. Had he been comparing me with Jessie?

The surfeit of visitors continued after the children left. I longed to escape to the Knights, who spent their summers in Malvern. No one seemed to feel, with the poet Cheng Haio (A.D. 250), that August visitors should not be admitted. Everybody wanted to meet the American poet. The Nicholses brought weekend guests, the Nashes their friends, Mary Howard her lame ducks, Ed Burra his bohemian cronies. Conrad's classmate John Tunis spent a night relaying yarns about tennis stars—Helen Wills, Molla Mallory, Sidney, Wood—"with few real sportsmen among them."

Close on John's heels came Phyllis Bottome, the British novelist, an intimidating personage, white hair a striking contrast to the coal-black eyes. They flashed as she delivered a nonstop diatribe against her sex. Conrad said later that she threw away first-rate ideas like chaff; he only wondered why her novels weren't better. On the subject of flirtatious wives: "They lack domestic training and individuality, have no talents or techniques except coquetting. And what is more nauseating than an arch or kittenish woman of forty? Husbands are fools to indulge such wives."

Conrad's glance stabbed me. I visualized Deirdre and her staggering knowledge of erotic literature. He lapped it up. Busy or not, he didn't object to her dropping in at odd times and calling him "Aiken" with unlicensed familiarity.

I had been spelling Margaret, keeping vigil at Bishop Odeh's bedside, until 3 A.M. the day before he died. He was terrified, struggling for breath, the mottled hand clutching my wrist, the face under that nimbus of white hair ashen and shrunken, the eyes sunk in their sockets. Margaret, hollow-eyed, had a dreadful time with him. He had grumbled at paying the vicar fifteen shillings for the last rites. Ten was all he used to get. It took the doctor's shot of morphine to bring final oblivion.

An unnerving experience. I described my first deathbed scene to Conrad while altering my black dress in the little sewing room off his study. "You're a death hater, an old-age hater," he said vehemently. I asked if he was a death lover. "Don't be sarcastic," he said, "I've faced the prospect of death many times." He quoted Katherine Mansfield: "If you wish to live, you must first attend your own funeral." He believed we should meditate daily on death to give life meaning.

"How gruesome," I said. "Like Sarah Bernhardt sleeping in her coffin. The grave yawns for us all too soon." I glanced at Waldo Peirce's caricature of Conrad's poem "Priapus and the Pool," a nude, red-haired Narcissus gazing at his reflection. "I mean to enjoy life and taste everything. Plenty of time to think about death."

"You prate about wanting to experience everything but the ultimate drama of life. Death is as fascinating a mystery as birth." He had watched his second son being born, a stillbirth. But *our* child had even less chance than that red poppy sprouting from the crack in the window ledge. "You haven't learned much from my writings," he added sadly, going downstairs.

True. I couldn't grasp the way he dealt with human relations. But at least I understand some poems like "Hallowe'en":

> . . . it is our ancestors and children who conspire against us
> life unlived and unloved that conspires against us
> our neglected hearts and hearths that conspire against us
> for we have neglected not only our death
> in forgetting our obligations to the dead
> we have neglected our living and our children's living
> in neglecting our love
> for the dead who would still live within us.
>
> *Collected Poems*

"Lucky Margaret, to be free," Mary Howard whispered, during the vicar's eulogy of Bishop Odeh. Yes, but I dreaded the changes to come. Without her father's pension she couldn't afford a house in Rye and a London flat. Where find another Margaret? She and Norah and the Knights were the only friends who really cared for me, and I for them.

As if summoned by the funeral, a ghost materialized—Beatrice Taussig, separated but not divorced from Bill, and showing traces of anguish. After a long session in Conrad's study, she came downstairs, seizing my hand, and begged forgiveness. I assured her it didn't matter any more, losing me my job with her analyst three years before. At that she broke down, said, "I never dreamt of hurting you, have always been fond of you. The friends who knew about it won't speak to me any more, didn't believe me." I told her *I* did. "But Conrad doesn't. He called me a bloody liar and the world's greatest self-deceiver." *Conrad*, who instigated the whole mess?

The next time Deirdre came I gave her tea and seedcake but little else. Her tittle-tattle made my head ache. "Oh Clarissa, I feel all moldy and smoldery today. Our whole vacation is spoiled. We came down expecting to have you to ourselves, then find that my damned sister-in-law is staying on. Having to see her face at every meal—ugh! The damned vultures, they only come because it's cheap. I could kick myself for bringing her, but she was ill and tired. I'll never be unselfish again. The whole cursed family will be on our hands. Young Peter is a dear, but his father's such an awful old ass. Just imagine, he's never seen a nude woman except his wife. He'll interfere with everything, criticize our improvements on the cottage, and all our fun ruined. Oh God, it makes me furious. He has a passion for organizing . . ."

If only Howard would organize *her*. The opposite of his brother Vernon, he was a successful inventor, manager of European laboratories for the IT&T, the first to get a phone call from New York in 1924, when the transatlantic cable was laid. He came home to find a message, "America called at 10 A.M.," scribbled by the maid. She had no idea that history was being made.

As Deirdre feared, I much preferred her sister-in-law to her. She stayed until 6 P.M., hoping I would ask her to dinner, then went to the Ship Inn with Conrad. I had yet to realize that his favorite pub meant as much to him as to the average Englishman. Any wife contesting his right to frequent one whenever he wished, or betraying jealousy of fellow-drinkers, would be thrown down the nearest well.

Conrad returned, his eyes ablaze. "Why didn't you ask Deirdre to dinner? You deserve a sound thrashing. I'm damned if I'll let you interfere with my friends. This is *my* house. Deirdre simply can't understand your hostility. I said you developed violent antipathies for no reason."

"Yes," I said, "just like your violent dislike of Margaret. If I copied Deirdre's flirtatious behavior you'd commit mayhem. I've put up with your jealousy for years. Now that it's turnabout, you can't take it."

I filled his pewter mug and sat down, trembling all over. I was peeling an artichoke when he raised the mug and flung beer in my face. Speechless with shock, I ran into the hall, grabbed my jacket and purse, and began the two-mile walk to Winchelsea. The long summer twilight cooled me off somewhat. After killing more time at the cinema, I stole into Jeake's House like a thief. What had his jealousy taught me? Not a thing. It was the hatred behind the act that scared me.

That night I woke up at the window, breathing heavily, hearing myself say, "Don't jump!" In the nightmare, Conrad pushed me out of bed and was about to give Doro a signal to shove me down a chute.

Don't take genius too seriously, I read somewhere soon after meeting Conrad. Poets live entirely in their imagination and make their own laws. A thrilling way to live, I thought at the time. Conrad would write immortal poems which I would inspire. In return, he would take care of me. I had only to find that mythical being. The actuality was a strong mutual attraction but a mismating. When the energizing was self-defeating to both partners and the fantasy had run its course, what then?

31

OUR MARRIAGE began taking on a frenetic tone. We were two mules pulling in opposite directions. The tense silence lasted for days, unbroken except for essentials like driving to Winchelsea one noonday with Paul and Margaret. They talked of putting up their house for sale, a desolate thought for me, doing without Margaret's mothering. But I had to cut the umbilical cord sometime.

We sat around a glass-topped table on the veranda, sipping drinks. Norah and I barley water. The black Siamese cat chased a wagtail around the sundial. The sun was tonic. A tangy breeze from the Channel blended with the fragrance of newmown grass. E. J. Moeran, the Irish composer, was the current houseguest. A major work of his was scheduled for the winter, performed by Stokowski in Philadelphia. I had played a four-handed arrangement of his Suite with him. The ruddy-faced giant had endless yarns about celebrities. Sibelius, he said, could finish a quart of Scotch in one sitting. At sixty-seven he drank Augustus John under the table. On a holiday in Helsingfors he was the only sober guest, though drinking steadily from 10:30 P.M. to 10:30 A.M. A contest between him and Malcolm would have intrigued Conrad.

"England is driving out all foreign talent," Moeran remarked. "A brilliant Italian pianist I knew began her career as a protégée of Cortot. Now she's working as a nursemaid in London." We agreed that music was the poorest paid of the arts. And literature ran a close second. A batch of rejections was eroding our confidence. The *New Yorker* had returned Conrad's last two articles and *Blue Voyage* had yet to find a British publisher. He cabled the American bank for his last $200, then withdrew the remaining £36 from the local bank.

While Norah was telling me how boring it was to meet new celebrities, Robert said to Margaret and Paul that he believed in meeting all sorts. "I can always learn from people." Even from the Robin Hood beachcomber living in a tent in Winchelsea? Conrad asked, having met the slimy character with the dirty beard. "I have a bone to pick with somebody," he added, eyeing Paul and Robert accusingly, "whoever wrote that lampoon of me in the London *Mercury*."

They shrugged off any knowledge of the dastardly act. "I enjoyed your essay in the *Freeman*, old chap," said Robert, his faunish face all innocence. "But gossip writers like Gerald Gould are running the works nowadays. John Orage tells me the publishing business is dead."

"So I gather," Conrad replied morosely. He updated Moeran on Fletcher's plight in Bedlam. "I had found him comfortable lodgings here last spring, but he went back to Sydenham. Soon after, I heard he had jumped out of a window, injuring his spine. A month or so later I had a long, poignant letter. If his wife didn't have him committed, he hoped to escape her and his mistress and the tax people by going to the States. His next letter, twenty-five pages, was obviously that of an agonized but sane man. I thought it might be used to get him out of the madhouse, so I tracked down his doctor, who knew his solicitor, who appealed to the Commissioner for Lunacy, and there the matter rests."

Everyone expressed concern. Various schemes were aired for extricating the Imagist poet. For Conrad's sake I prayed that one of them would succeed.

During the al fresco lunch I learned why the figs ripening on the south wall wore tiny net sacks. Norah said it was to keep the bugs from pecking them. When I wondered aloud why the fig leaf was chosen to cover the male's private parts, Robert clucked in mock dismay. "Why, Clarissa, what a licentious mind you have."

"Not at all," Paul chimed in stoutly. "She has the highest moral tone. I can vouch for it."

Conrad gave me an inscrutable look. The talk pivoted on the awesome powers of the subconscious. Paul had a dream he asked Conrad to interpret. "I was walking up a steep hill to G. B. Shaw's house and saw several hideous old women, all naked, one with her derrière marked off in squares like a preliminary sketch. Only Shaw's pretty secretary was clothed. Now what do you make of that, Dr. Freud?"

"Too complicated and abridged as you tell it," Conrad said stiffly. "But I'll hazard a guess. The climb to Shaw's house might symbolize intellectual inferiority, the nude and unattractive old women suggest suppressed sensuality, while the fully clothed secretary could be the unattainable object of desire. Well, you asked for it," he said as Paul winced. "I happen to agree with Freud that dreams are the most important clues to the unconscious."

Paul's greatest ambition, according to Mary Howard, was to meet the right people. And why shouldn't he? James Thurber was to call him a keen collector of human curiosa, a man of humor and imagination.

"I also had a dream," Margaret said with a twisted smile, as we bundled into the taxi. "Father rose from his grave to reproach me for spending his money on asthma remedies for Paul."

"Tiddledebungho," Robert sang out, one arm around Norah, the other around Moeran. "Tomorrow I'm off to get an antituberculin bug." He and Norah would spend the winter in Vienna, Robert to rewrite an old libretto for Delius.

Coasting downhill, we pursued our separate thoughts, until Paul said boldly, pressing my hand, "Vilma asked me if you were ever painted as a madonna. Did I tell you that you have a Manet or Renoir-period face? Very dynamic, beautiful eyes, mouth, hair, and a spirit any sculptor would love. It's the kind many women try to imitate, but yours is the genuine article, and it has improved over the years."

"Along with a free-floating anxiety," I mumbled, blushing. "Must be my bangs. But don't mistake me for Shaw's secretary."

"*Touché!*" He wheezed, grinning.

The following afternoon I was playing duets with Dicky Dixon when Paul rang up, asking if I would drop by on my way home. When I did so, puzzled and apprehensive, a chagrined Paul greeted me, explaining that his invitation to tea had boomeranged. "When you didn't show up, I went around to Jeake's and found Conrad there, reading my note. Dashed awkward. He told me you were at Dicky's. I thought he had gone to Hastings."

More trouble. Oh Lord, save me. I trotted home with a sinking heart. Conrad, livid, wreathed in cigarette smoke, stood under the green witch's ball. The atmosphere crackled. "What's going on between you two? No use lying. *There's* the evidence," and he waved Paul's note before my nose. "Up to your old tricks again."

"Tricks are more in Deirdre's line," I said. "She could teach me several that go over big with you."

"Never mind your *tu quoque* ripostes. It's all of a piece, Paul deliberately flattering you, dancing with you every chance he gets, and you flirting with him. He'll be broadcasting it all over Rye . . ."

"Don't be preposterous. You talk as if he tried to rape me."

"I wouldn't minimize the possibility," Conrad said. "You seem to take pleasure in defying me."

"Defying? Did you forbid me to dance? Or command me to stuff my ears when he compliments me?" I didn't know whether to laugh or cry. The more Conrad sniped at me, the more I clutched at praise, hoarding it like a beggar trying on borrowed finery before the mirror. "All this fuss over a harmless flirtation. You may be running our marriage, but you're not running me."

Conrad started for the pub without his usual appetizer. I began dinner. He seemed to be *goading* me into being unfaithful.

Dinner was eaten in a pregnant silence but for the grandfather clock. The stillness was like a time bomb. The dishes done, I hunted slugs in the garden, then took my monthly dose of ergot and retired early, too distraught to read. Conrad had carried the gin bottle up to his study. Insulation.

Music drifted through the open window from the Old Hospital opposite—the third Brandenburg Concerto. Bless Mr. Ellis and his passion for Bach. Listening to the celestial strains, mesmerized by the rhythm, I imagined that relentless finger on the metronome whipping back and forth. It might have regulated the tempo of my life, helped develop order, logic, peace of mind. I felt the pangs of a fugitive, turning my back on "a talent that is death to hide."

Sometime later Conrad's unsteady tread woke me up. Switching on the light, he emptied his pockets, stacking coins in neat piles on the bureau, then said with speech slurred, "It's plain as a pikestaff that you and Paul are conniving against me."

"Oh God, don't start that again," I said. My heart pounded. "Just leave me alone. Please."

"Well, aren't you?" He stood over me with a gin breath, buttoning his pajama jacket, a manic gleam behind the spectacles. "I want to know where you two make love—in his studio?"

"You see lust in every man's eyes."

"Come on, confess, you goddamned whore!" He raised his voice. "Or I'll wring your neck."

The bed shook with my trembling. I huddled under the blankets. He pulled them off. His hands closed around my throat. "Tell me the truth." His grip tightened. I gasped, choked, saw pinwheels, then with a desperate effort managed to wrench myself loose, and cried hoarsely, "Help, help, HELP . . ."

My screams alerted our neighbor opposite. "Anything wrong over there?" he called. Conrad strode to the window, shut it with a bang, then fell beside me, cursing.

32

THE TURBULENT SUMMER of 1932 was taking its toll. Jeake's House exerted a baleful effect on us. Everything seemed distorted, out of kilter, like a bad photograph. Conrad could handle physical danger but not the prolonged stress of an indifferent public, strained finances, or reliving his childhood while working on *Great Circle*. Everything was an ordeal—Fletcher's literary reverses and marital entanglements, Malcolm's problems and Oedipal obsessions, my hallucinations and nightmares, with Paul's untimely overtures.

Ample warnings from Beatrice Taussig and from Harry Murray should have prepared me. And from Conrad himself. He admitted being a weak creature in need of help—"I'll be back to bibs and diapers before long"— but feared dominance and managing, afraid he would break down and kill himself out of shame. The April before, he had "tried a little asphyxiation." More recently he urged me to wash my hands of him. "I don't want to frighten you, Critch, but I really think I'm going insane. My mind does the queerest things. The words get all mixed up when I try to think or speak. My father's death should have freed me, but it didn't. I've been dreaming again and again of killing myself. I shouldn't really be alive. I've survived only by a series of flukes, protected in having enough money. But lately the struggle has been too much. I feel myself going under, and rather than end my life as a lunatic I'll commit suicide." He reminded me of someone in crisis or anguish, the lips compressed in a taut line, the eyes looking inward—a piercing gaze riveted on some intolerable spectacle. A man self-crucified.

Tongue-tied with panic, I could only think of platitudes—the children suffering just as he had on his father's account. His confidences made me feel all the more useless, after being shut out of his thoughts.

I took comfort, naively, in the fact that he had left his revolver with Walter Piston. His irrational behavior had of course long been of concern to relatives and friends. It must have troubled Jessie greatly—the drinking, excessive jealousy, abnormal shyness, the violent mood shifts.

Although he refused psychiatric help, he did accept professional counsel from three friends—Harry Murray, Jake Wilbur, and his old schoolmate Grayson McCouch, a gentle, soft-spoken Quaker who loved Conrad, helped him financially, and predicted the Preludes would make him immortal.

"The Old Bird" had true beauty of character, cared deeply about the human condition. He was the sincerest and most honest man Conrad ever knew. That angelic face darkened with Aztec fierceness when confronted with injustice or cruelty. One morning he put a field mouse out of its misery, after rebuking Conrad for watching Squidge play with it.

I remember overhearing the tail end of an argument one day about parental responsibilities, Grayson afraid Conrad would corrupt John by his life style and atheism. I took him aside and asked him not to interfere with the father-son relationship. "John influences Conrad more than the other way around," I told him.

Grayson didn't believe in psychoanalysis, but I'm sure he often discussed the issue of inherited mental illness with Conrad. *I* couldn't. My role was necessarily a passive one. My hands were tied. Merely voicing anxiety was unsafe. "Don't start dictating to me," he snapped when I said that three packs of Players a day would never cure his catarrh. "I'll do as I damned please." The idea of having him committed never crossed my mind. It would have amounted to *lèse majesté*. With his credo of total awareness, insanity was a calculated risk, the price of delving into the subconscious and creating a portrait of the human mind. I couldn't meddle with his life's mission as a priest of consciousness, however much he seemed determined to reenact his father's destructive act.

> Would I be afraid of him still? I am taller than you are. . . . Look! You see that scar? You gave that to me, holding my hand in the gas-jet . . . You see the unhappy restlessness with which I wander from continent to continent, this horrified and lack-lustre restlessness which prevents me from loving one person or place for more than a season, driving me on, aimless and soulless? This is what you did to me by depriving me of my mother . . . That's of course what *he* wanted—that poem he left on the table—the darkness—'*closer, closer all about, Blotting all the light of living out!*' Intra-uterine reversion. Perhaps the fact that *he*—will prevent *me*. Explode it. It was a sort of exhibitionism . . . Vanity.
>
> *Blue Voyage*

Explode it. I lived in perpetual fear of and for Conrad. He policed my activities, revived suspicions of infidelity, made me feel a criminal being shadowed. I would announce the day's schedule, shopping in Hastings, doing research for a magazine article, calling on Margaret, on Mary Howard, or going to the cinema. Then, bracing myself, as when I asked Father for housekeeping money, I delivered my speech and fled.

Another quarrel, one evening, solved nothing. Neither would the movies, but I had to get out of that stifling, oppressive house, and so left Conrad working at his study desk. The Electrical Palace smelled of cheap perfume and stale tobacco. I sat in the last row taking in little. The feature, as I recall, was one that starred Sylvia Sidney. About halfway through the picture I slipped out and ran all the way home, galvanized by a premonition.

The third-floor study was in darkness. From the front hall I could smell gas. The kitchen was alight, but something blocked the door. In a cold sweat I pushed with all my might and forced it open. Conrad lay slumped on the floor unconscious. A chair was overturned, a sheet of white paper on the table. I turned off the jets, opened the only window and the two outer doors, then poured gin into him, spilling most of it, after dragging him into the dining room. His gaseous breath nauseated me. I seemed to have split into two persons, one clumsy and hysterical, the other an impersonal nurse, coaxing him to breathe deeply. Suppose it was too late? Would the children and his brothers blame me, feel that I had driven him to it, that I hadn't heeded his warnings, overlooked or run away from each signal, left him and gone to the cinema?

His face had turned ghastly green. How call the doctor without a phone in the house? I didn't dare leave him anyhow. Where were his spectacles? The eyelids fluttered feebly. Then, with a convulsive gasp his eyes opened. He began coughing, retching. I knew nothing about resuscitation, but intuitively waited until his lungs had cleared somewhat, a long, anxious business, before tackling the exhausting job of getting him upstairs. It was the longest climb yet. I had taken a spill the day before, falling down several steps during a midnight hurry call to the bathroom, and laming my back fearfully. He hung on, panting, groaning, making strange sounds, I encouraging him. "Just a few more steps and we're there . . ."

He fell into bed, I on top of him. "Don't ever leave me, no matter what I say or do," he said in a faint, hollow voice, spacing the words. I promised, nerves screaming for relief from a turgid melodrama.

The kitchen smelled strongly of gas the next morning. I forestalled Jenny's curiosity by saying casually, "There must be a leak somewhere. We'll probably have a thumping gas bill." I can't recall whether it was an unfinished poem or a note that I retrieved from the table, or what happened to it. The terrible loneliness of taking that final step into nothingness, the endless seesawing, weighing pros and cons, the consequences— with his vivid imagination, he would have been plunged into the innermost pit of hell.

I took his breakfast tray upstairs. Would he express gratitude or curse me for sentencing him to life, as it were? Neither. He only marveled at my "miraculous return" from the flicks. Had he feared or hoped I would come back prematurely? He couldn't have foreseen my leaving halfway through the film. The attempt must have been genuine. Suicides who gas themselves lose consciousness fast, according to physicians. Describing it all in my diary helped to defuse the shock. But I broke down that afternoon at Margaret's.

"I almost wish he had pulled it off," I said. "Does that horrify you?"

"No, my dear, I understand perfectly. There's a limit." Margaret sighed. "You look like a ghost. I'll brew some fresh tea and put a stick into it. You probably feel as I do that we have a right to end our life. You haven't told anyone else? Thank God, it will be a secret *entre nous*."

Conrad would have been certified insane and hospitalized if I had called a doctor. I was mistaken in thinking that a suicide attempt was a crime in England punishable by imprisonment. Oh why hadn't I used shorthand in my diary? I made a mental note to tear out those pages before he found them.

Part Three

33

Signs of the depression were still apparent by December. In London hunger marchers rioted, the House of Commons was cordoned off, thwarted demonstrators hurled insults at Ramsay MacDonald and his Conservative Coalition cabinet, traffic was held up at Trafalgar Square as mounted police dispersed pedestrians, the hats of men arrested hung on picket fences, and passengers at Charing Cross were frisked, the gates locked after them.

I had been working in Saint John's Wood on Laura Knight's memoir. She had finally agreed to give it a whirl, though still skeptical about its popular appeal. Conrad's agent, Heath, had leapt at the idea. Wading through hatboxes of press clippings, I found that she had had adventures enough for a dozen women, and more distinctions than any other British woman past or present. The round, smiling face on cigarette cards was familiar to royalty and commoners alike. Her oils, watercolors, and etchings hung in galleries throughout the English-speaking world, and beyond. A tribal chief in Central Africa cherished her picture "By the Sea," showing two pretty girls whom he wanted for his wives.

Known best as the circus painter, Laura had been accused of imitating herself. A stranger looking over her shoulder jeered, "I see you're trying to paint like Dame Laura Knight. She does circuses, too." Laura was too prolific, said Harold. She had a finger in every pie—the theatre, ballet, boxing, racing. "I want to cover the whole world," she said, "splash paint on canvas everywhere. Life holds such wonderful possibilities, and it's all too short."

Her love of life and stoicism overcame most obstacles. Traveling with circus groups, Laura made about twenty thousand sketches. She disclaimed having been born in a circus or suckled by an elephant, but she had some narrow escapes. An elephant once backed into her easel.

I was inspired with every fresh discovery of her enterprises. Would *I* have slaved, fought, sacrificed, and struggled to develop my gifts, enduring hardships, even hunger and cold? She had the courage to be herself at all times. Shortly after she turned down a £1000 commission by Guinness because they demanded a preliminary sketch, the postman brought a check for £143 from the Olympia Exhibition in Los Angeles for her painting "The Boxers." A windfall, she jubilated. "The first sale this year." A sanguine Micawber, she banked on something always turning up.

Raised in Nottingham by her widowed mother, a fine artist, Laura learned early that life was no rose garden. At fourteen she put up her hair, let down her skirts, and took over her mother's art class, pupils all older than she, some aged forty. Since female students weren't allowed to study the nude, Laura couldn't compete for the one scholarship open to her. But Harold, a fellow student, did win one. They were married during the lean years.

The Knights shared the pleasures of painting and pinch of poverty, roughing it for thirteen years in Staithes, a remote fishing village where the living was cheap. Predictions of disaster with two artists under one roof proved groundless by dint of separate studios, mutual independence, and differences in approach to art. Harold was the portraitist; Laura painted all forms, though then the vogue as a portrait artist. (In the 1940s she would be commissioned to sketch and paint the trial of the Nazi war criminals at Nuremberg.)

We worked mornings until one-thirty. Kensitas and acid drops kept me going. Laura's studio was stacked with canvasses, in one corner a shaggy-browed pixie with a quizzical mouth and prominent red-veined nose— G. B. Shaw, my idol. Laura sighed. "The trouble I've had with that portrait! He's so changeable and difficult, one minute a tired old man of seventy-six, the next an absolute devil." He sang operatic airs and told fanciful tales. For instance, and she quoted him: "My nurse used to hold the back of my petticoats so they wouldn't act as sails and carry me away." This apropos of his big ears. "And have you noticed the projection at the base of my skull? Catherine of Russia had the same. I'm told it means excessive sexual development."

I envied Laura. Oh to be a mouse named Boswell, eavesdropping under a chair with a notebook.

There were constant interruptions—the printers, press, models, ballet dancers and acrobats, musicians, actors. Laura was frustrated but never cross, chain-smoking, blue eyes twinkling, yellow hair coiled around her ears. Once in spate, she couldn't dam the flow, and confessed to having the time of her life pouring out material to a willing ear, anecdotes about Harry Lauder, Queen Mary, John Drinkwater, Pavlova.

Laura's vitality, at fifty-four, put me to shame. Some evenings she kept dictating until 1:30 A.M., head buried in her hands and growing inaudible. She seldom retired before 2 A.M., sleeping on the porch throughout the

year bundled up like a Nordic peasant in sweaters and shawls. And reap-
peared bright and chipper next morning with my breakfast tray (a sinful
luxury), ready to continue the Niagara of memories.

Conrad must have told the Knights about his suicide attempt, for they
expressed deep concern. "Why do you two live in that damp hole?" Laura
asked. "Move to London, as Paul and Margaret intend doing. It's absurd,
rattling around like a couple of snails in a shell much too big for you."
Idle advice. Conrad would never leave Jeake's House.

I had been gradually unwinding. Fewer walls crashed around me. I
slept well until 6 A.M., when the wrecking crew came to tear down Maxine
Elliott's house nearby. I was grateful for the chance to help Laura with her
autobiography, a timely prospect dear to my heart. Bringing it off meant
everything, bolstering confidence with Conrad and hopefully keeping our
relationship on a more even keel.

My admiration for women had been increasing. I no longer took their
patience, kindness, endurance, and common sense for granted. Laura could
laugh at herself, remembering more gaffes than triumphs—wearing her
dress inside out at a party or taxiing to Saint James's Palace with three-
pence in her purse, which got her home on a No. 2 bus, the Duchess of
York would have been amused to know. Her vagueness was delicious.

By feminists like Dame Ethel Smyth, the concert pianist, Laura's elec-
tion to the Royal Academy in 1927 was regarded as just another belated
recognition of female achievement. Laura herself shrugged off the implied
chauvinism. What it signified to her was not the artist's sex but the work
itself. Women should win their place by merit alone. Months of hard work
lay behind her pictures.

At the Royal Academy presentation of scholarships, Laura was the only
woman member among rows and rows of white-haired venerables, some
with van dykes. What a collection of stuffed shirts, I thought, sitting
beside Dod Proctor, reportedly the next female R.A. A pompous venerable explained at great length why a student's monochrome I had the
temerity to admire was atrocious. When Laura introduced me as the wife
of a distinguished American poet, he hemmed and hawed, then drawled,
"Ah well, I daresay poetry has its uses." The Knights were disgusted at
the supercilious attitude in general, remembering their own struggles as
students.

Laura's radiance worked magic everywhere. She made people feel young
and carefree. If life was a gift, she was one, too.

She had astonished me by wanting to paint me, "to show you how
beautiful you are." When I said she would make me still more vain, I
replied, "And so you should be. It's good for your morale. Look at Shaw.

He makes no bones about his conceit. He can't pass a mirror without glancing into it, and his home in Ayot Saint Lawrence is chockablock with photos of himself."

Dearly though I loved her, I would have preferred sitting for Harold. His portrait of Conrad had caught the poet, intellectual, and aristocrat—a gold and blue study, the subject smoking a pipe. (I used to think that a pipe-smoking man was above reproach.)

We discussed marriage. I told Laura of my youngest brother's wife popping the question on top of the Empire State Building. She agreed that women should take the initiative. I invariably reacted to major situations, seldom chose or initiated moves. There was Paris, for instance, waiting for me to spend Christmas there, hope of persuading Conrad a slender thread. Arnold Bennett's statement, "One always has to choose between a good husband and a good artist," would have baffled me before Conrad. Passively, I suppose, I chose the latter, since Conrad had little energy left for the business of living.

We parted with affectionate hugs at King's Cross, I seeing Laura off for Newcastle to do a portrait. She had given me a different slant on matrimony, shown me that a childless careerist could be fulfilled by her art, be happy, and make her husband happy, too. I pondered our fortnight spent on a project dear to my heart, and decided to become a feminist like Laura Knight. Surely Conrad wouldn't mind a *successful* feminist.

34

MY DREAMS OF A YULETIDE in Paris were dashed, though the children's visit helped soften the disappointment. Conrad spent Christmas Eve soaking in the tub, suffering from sciatica. He had sent off *Great Circle* to Scribner's with a sardonic "About time another book goes spiraling down the drain," then applied for a Guggenheim without much hope. Cassels had turned down all his works.

To Fletcher he wrote that God looked after the sparrows, but not the Aikens. I contracted and expanded like an accordion depending on his mood. That had now sunk to a dismal low—the letdown of a Lazarus who found returning to life anything but pleasant. Jessie, herself apparently bankrupt, answered his request for a rent reduction by proposing he make over to her the trusteeship of Cousin Julia's $10,000 inheritance for the children. He replied that he had no authority even if made a trustee, and in any case wouldn't do so.

"Don't despair, darling, we're still better off than those in the States," I said. His friend Bob Morss had just returned from the States, where the gloom was so thick he was relieved to get back to England. "Everybody's wearing his tail between his legs, real estate is nowhere, and banks are glutted with gold but daren't lend," he told us. As a British representative of Ginn & Co., Bob hoped to have work for me in connection with the new Child Readers. I had also looked up a friend of Margaret's in London, an illustrator for juveniles earning £1000 a year. She promised to sound out the editor and her son-in-law, who wrote nonsense books.

All this was just soothing syrup to Conrad and about as nourishing as cotton candy. At any rate, 1933 began with a whimper, one piece of good news being FDR's inauguration, after a Democratic landslide and with a wet Congress. "Now you can go home again," I teased. Conrad was naturally pleased, related as he was to the Delano branch of the family.

I suggested starting a bookshop next door, the Workmen's Club having gone bankrupt. "Yes, why not?" he said tartly. "All we need is some capital and a 15,000 mailing list."

A remaindered copy of *Blue Voyage* that I found in Boots's Library for sixpence he inscribed for an elderly American couple who proved to be blithe spirits and a welcome addition. Arthur Houghton was a roving journalist and secretary of the English-Speaking Society. His wife, Mabel Dwight, a grande dame originally from Stockbridge, Massachusetts, had lived all over the world for thirty years and thumbed her nose at it.

Conrad warned her that we were pariahs. "How delightful," Mabel replied in her rich baritone. "But then, Rye isn't Great Britain, as some of the local gossips like to think, just because Queen Elizabeth visited here centuries ago. I hope you will both come to tea soon. I will ask the lady whom I was told was not 'gentry.' No, she wasn't a trollop, she had been a mannikin."

The Houghtons had rented The Other House, a famous haunt on Mermaid Street immortalized by Henry James. "What do these walls say to you?" Mabel asked, revolving slowly in our drawing room like a model on a pedestal. "They give off vibrations I don't like." She was a novelty, with her bizarre headgear, hyperboles, and risqué stories.

On a Friday the thirteenth I had an upsetting letter from Laura Knight. Apparently my editing was too thorough. She had decided to write the memoir without a ghost, then edit it along with me. I felt devastated, though *why* I can't imagine today. Rewriting rough drafts was standard procedure. I hadn't used shorthand for years. And Laura, attempting dictation for the first time, sometimes forgot what she had said, often reminisced when I didn't have my notebook, or wanted my undivided attention. So a great deal was lost on paper. A delicate business among friends, and I scourged myself. Conrad's "Your genius for incompetence" was no balm.

February brought Malcolm Lowry, the welcome mat out this time for a graduate with a third-class honors' degree in English tripos. He looked neater but also heavier, having switched to beer. After bailing him out of jail countless times, Lowry Senior still expected Conrad to save his prodigal son from ruin. Those monthly checks were manna. Conrad began talking of Spain in the spring. I seconded the notion eagerly. A change might curtail Malcolm's drinking and do us all a world of good.

The first to rejoice with a writer's success, Malcolm commiserated with Conrad over Jonathan Cape rejecting *Great Circle* and accepting *Ultramarine*. He respected his mentor as a genius of the highest order, and felt that Eliot owed Conrad a great debt. As for fickle fame, Conrad speculated to Fletcher (still languishing in Bedlam) about surviving Eliot, whose overrated reputation was sure to shrink, he said, while "our own is underestimated and is therefor—I knock on wood—bound to grow." However, Conrad told me that he would never become well known now, though he considered himself one of the best living writers of prose and poetry. No one read his prose because of his reputation as a poet, he said. He would never again do a novel as good as *Blue Voyage* or even *Great Circle*.

"We might as well face it, Aiken," said Fletcher, shortly before drowning himself in 1950, "we're forgotten."

I don't remember Conrad alluding to his own suicide attempt. It might never have happened. Was the burden of gratitude too onerous, or was he transmuting the experience into art? His avoidance of the subject made for still more self-consciousness. His shyness alarmed me. Playing dumb crambo one evening at the Nashes, he was stupendous as an innkeeper acting out the word *fleas*. But performing for the first time in twenty years proved such an ordeal that he threw up when we got home.

I could only play it by ear, curbing my temper, pre-testing my remarks, humoring him like a nurse a difficult patient. Since he had begged me never to leave him, I felt spiritually abandoned. Much later I discovered that Conrad had told several friends about his attempted suicide having a profound effect on him, making everything more real. He said it had brought us much closer together in a better way, that I had been marvelous, taking it all like a brick. Yet in his autobiography, *Ushant*, he expressed regrets at his "admirable experience," calling the act a double betrayal, of his philosophy of consciousness and his obligations to his ancestors and descendants, the three children and his writings being synonymous. (Harry Murray's comment was a deflating statistic: suicide had become so common as to be vulgar.)

The current gossip in Rye contradicted Conrad's optimism. Our marriage was on the rocks, according to his court jester, Ed Burra. Tongue-waggers probably were given something to chew on by my screams for help that night the previous summer. One day a voice reached me over the garden wall: "I couldn't help being amused at what Miriam told me about our neighbors." Silence, preceded by a loud "Shh!" My thoughts flew back to the time Conrad returned from London saying he had slept "innocently" with Mary Howard in her Mews flat. Surely she wouldn't risk our friendship, after declaring she would never have broken with her mad mother but for me. Or would she? I pictured myself being cut off from family and friends by three thousand miles, with no possibility of a job or financial support.

Although absence hadn't made Malcolm's heart grow fonder of Ed Burra, the surrealist painter kept up Conrad's spirits at weekly dinners with us by satirizing Rye's characters in his falsetto drawl and cockney accent. I did not join in the merriment, afraid of being the next target. I seemed, in fact, to have no more energy or willpower than a thistle. Dozing off in trains and hotel lounges had become a habit. One day, playing Mozart duets with Dicky Dixon, I made several clinkers before collapsing on the sofa. Margaret, alarmed, urged me to see her woman doctor. She still didn't know about my taking ergot.

Though Dicky irked Conrad by calling Rye a dreary hole, she kept us in gales of laughter with her ribaldry, all remarks ending in "Balls!" We had formed a little clique, Margaret, Dicky, Mabel, and I, rotating at each other's homes, hugging the fire and guzzling port, exchanging views about everything, including the white-slave traffic and royal scandals, Dicky smoking her tiny pipe. Mabel and Margaret added to my dossier about Lady Tavistock. A poor clergyman's daughter, they said, she had accepted many humiliations such as a niggardly £30 annual allowance for the sake of a future ten or twelve huge estates when the Marquis became Duke of Bedford. "*If* she can hold out until then," Mabel grunted. "He's said to be a skinflint, ironclad puritan, and anti-American." So I was not likely to see her again, *quelle dommage*!

Dicky and Margaret contributed the latest stories about Johnny (Radclyffe Hall) and Lady Troubridge, whose "womb worries" had developed into a cliffhanger. Her operation for fibroids had cost £500, Johnny engaging five specialists, a special room in a special nursing home with special nurses, so Margaret reported. "My Una's ovaries are still safe, thank God," she shouted, accosting Margaret on High Street, oblivious to pedestrians. "Not that she wants to breed, but it's nice to know. Just think, all this time she suffered in silence so that I could write *The Master*. It was a sacrifice for *The Master*. What they found in her was outrageous. Why the poor woman was rotten inside, her appendix like a dead mouse's tail, only bigger, whilst her ovaries were the size of peas." Even a first-class tart, said Margaret, would never have committed such a breach of taste.

We were digesting this tidbit one February day at Mabel's when the borough's power suddenly failed during an unprecedented snowfall of six inches. "How maddening," she cried, "and no candles in the house." My innocent "One should never be without candles in Rye" convulsed everyone, including Dicky, a good sport and always amusing about her lesbianism. "What must the post office think," she chuckled, "when they hear Vilma and me calling each other 'darling'?"

I had become quite fond of her and was therefore sad to hear they were splitting up. Vilma had found a replacement in Dover. Rye on the rocks! Who was next? At their "house cooling off" party everybody felt out of sorts, Mabel with a toothache, Margaret vexed with Conrad and Paul being at odds, Malcolm in his typical trance, while I had the curse and grieved over losing Dicky. She wouldn't remain long in Rye. I heard no criticism from her about Vilma, only exoneration. With self-mocking bravado she sang "My Love Lies Bleeding" at the piano. Superb. We came away chanting, "Doleful, Doleful!"

In March I made an appointment with Margaret's doctor in London. Conrad raised an eyebrow. "Submitting to her managing touch again?" Yes, I said, when her advice was sound. At Ashford, changing trains, I ran across E. F. Benson hobbling into the station on canes and followed by his valet with the luggage. It was a cold day and his face had a bluish tinge. During the forty-minute wait we chatted near the ladies' rest room. I was tempted to tattle on Vilma outlining a novel about Rye characters, suggesting that each of us do one either roasting him or else not mentioning him at all, which she said would enrage him. What grudge had she against the poor man? He had been so nice to me, given me a lovely lunch last autumn, again asking me to bring Conrad next time. The talk turned to George Moore, who was still ripe in his grave. Benson said, "I once went to *Parsifal* with Moore, and during the Magic Ring scene he leaned over and whispered, 'That music was composed by the organist collaborating with one of his choirboys.'" I hated myself for laughing when I hadn't got the point.

I found Dr. Graham sympathetic, brisk, and efficient. After taking my physical and psychological history, she said, "No wonder you're run down, poisoning your system for six years. Hasn't anyone told you that overdoses of ergot block the blood flow and cause gangrene besides playing havoc with your system eventually? It has driven people insane, and it can be fatal. Throw that bottle in the rubbish can!"

Her findings explained my symptoms of hallucinations and general malaise: prolapsed uterus, flabby tubes, weakened heart, anemia, nervous exhaustion. "You would probably miscarry," she told me, "but you can't afford the risk of pregnancy. Raising a child in such an emotional climate

as you describe would be disastrous. I strongly advise against conception."
Before I left her office she fitted me with a diaphragm.

Conrad was not unduly upset by her verdict. "You may be close to a
nervous breakdown," he said, "but so am I, though I don't need a doctor
to tell me so." As for Laura, I felt shriven after she told me that "the ghost"
showed in my draft and that dictating was too exhausting. "We'll work on
it together, Jerry dear."

35

ON THE FIRST OF APRIL we embarked at Tilbury in a stuporous state,
the Bay of Biscay happily smooth as glass. Fate had approved of
Spain. We were so torn about splurging on a holiday abroad that we
tossed a coin. I made three dresses in five days, we got our shots, and we
sublet the house for thirty shillings a week to Malcolm's friends, the Gerald
Noxons. Jenny promised to look after Jeake's House and Squidge.

The *Ormonde* ostensibly catered to one class, tourist, but those on E
Deck like ourselves were obviously below the salt. I no sooner sat down
to lunch, Conrad and Malcolm being in the bar, than the headwaiter
informed me that Madam was in the wrong salon and occupying the
Captain's table. Madam walked out again, crimson-faced.

We docked in Gibraltar at 7 A.M. To my jaundiced eyes, that granite
disgorgement seemed shrunken, the African coast in a blue mist. Stupefied
by the torrid heat, noise, and violent colors, we decided that one night on
the Rock was enough. Radios blared, barrel-organs ground out rhumbas,
hawkers screeched their wares, beggars with faces like dried figs clawed
our sleeves, a voluptuous danseuse clicked castanets at Russian sailors, and
British soldiers trooped down Main Street with a flourish of trumpets,
disrupting a funeral procession.

"A mad jumble of the living and the dead," Malcolm remarked, his eyes
blue as the Mediterranean. Ferrying through the Strait to Algeciras, we
passed several feluccas, the design of their swallow-shaped lateen sails
unchanged for centuries, he said. I marveled at Malcolm's good nature.
He took the vexations and discomforts in stride—three hours in a stuffy
coach to Ronda, the unmentionable plumbing in our hotel, our sleep
disturbed by drunken caballeros shouting, "Olé, Olé," while the Civil
Guard signaled the all's-well with piercing whistles. At least the food was
excellent, an eight-course dinner, ragamuffins serenading us outside grilled
windows.

We viewed the Tajo and the bullring, the natives snickering at Malcolm's
girth—a Gulliver in Lilliput sporting a ten-gallon sombrero. "Good thing

he doesn't understand Spanish," said Conrad. They were both marked men after ordering triple brandies at one bar. *Aguardiente* drinkers stared, awestruck. I hoped Malcolm would survive the barbs and arrows of Ed Burra, who was to join us in Granada.

Conrad dozed fitfully during the train ride from Ronda to Granada, a seven-hour endurance test. Malcolm read *Ulysses* and perspired in his shirt-sleeves. He had carried off the hotel key for the second time. The pair of shorts I bought for him were obviously too small, for he said he felt he was walking backwards in them.

I kept my face glued to the window, exclaiming at the wild, precipitous terrain plunging nine hundred feet to the pueblos below, where women hung their wash on giant prickly pears. The locomotive labored uphill at a snail's pace. We could have picked aloes and poppies along the way. Malcolm leaned out the window, gesticulating impatiently at the fireman, who mimicked him. Later, coasting downhill at a fair clip toward the foothills of the Sierra Nevadas, he raised his arms in triumph.

The setting sun flooded the valley with rainbows and delicate cloud shadows. These snow-capped mountains symbolized hope and heartbreak, beckoning, but then retreating the closer we approached. I stared and stared, hypnotized. What an inspiration for a tone poem by Ravel or Rimsky-Korsakov. And how puny, amid such grandeur, were mortals such as the desk clerk at the Sevilla Inglatera in Gibraltar. While I was debating whether to register as a housewife or journalist, he handed the fountain pen impatiently to Conrad. My husband pointed slyly to a previous signature of a tourist guide: "Senor Smith y veinte Senoras."

Our request for two rooms brought a wire from the Carmona pension in the Alhambra: "Reserving bath rooms." Malcolm, frequently in need of a bath, chortled at Conrad's dig, "They must have known you were coming." A scrawny, lynx-eyed youth met us in Granada—Tendé, the Carmonas' son-in-law. The horse-cab Tendé hired took us to the Hollywood Café and an earsplitting black jazz band. "We travel one thousand miles for this?" Malcolm grinned. At least there was cold beer for parched throats after the long, tedious journey. Tendé sniggered at Malcolm's capacity. Conrad dismissed him as a twirp, but I foresaw trouble.

Spain was much the same as he remembered it in 1926. The Workers' Republic had left the peasant as poor as ever, disease a constant companion. Granada seemed overrun with beggars, some one-eyed, many with infected eyes. Decay underlay natural beauty. The roses had already withered. Trudging up Alhambra Hill to the Moorish fortresses and palaces, we passed a dazzling profusion of magnolias, oleanders, and orchids. "Look at that fat belly," a paunchy Spaniard taunted, pointing at Malcolm. Conrad snapped, also in Spanish, "Look at your own."

The white stucco Villa Carmona near the Generalife appealed to my romantic soul. Grilled windows and balconies overlooked the patio—stage props for *Carmen*. Weather permitting, we ate al fresco, enclosed by flowering bushes and fruit trees, a fountain and a well. Pomegranate petals dropped into our omelet, soup, or *olla podrida*, delicious fare. All this for twelve pesetas a day. The smell of olive oil and saffron blended with musk and urine. The neighborhood swarmed with cats, dogs, chickens, goats, and donkeys, the plaintive mating cry of the donkey like a squeaky bucket drawn up from a well.

The household consisted of the imperious widowed Senora, her unmarried sister Carmen, her handsome, slipshod son Pepé, a pretty daughter, Tendé's wife, and their infant, Luisa the singing maid, and a mad, mad cook. The family doted on Conrad since he spoke Spanish and lent prestige to the pension. The roster of notables in the guestbook included Manuel de Falla, Herbert Read, Katherine Lee Bates, and John Singer Sargent. We were in good hands. Among the dozen guests was an Ohio schoolteacher, who glowed on meeting Conrad. "My pupils just love your poetry," she said. "They memorize the most difficult lines in your Preludes." He blushed with pleasure.

We strolled to the embankment the first evening for a moonlit view of Granada. It shimmered like a mammoth birthday cake, flanked by the Sierra range and sun-dried plains, whitewashed houses strung along the valleys. Conrad repeated his salute of bygone years with Martin Armstrong by tossing English pennies over the parapet three hundred feet below. They hit a monastery roof with a faint *ping*. Malcolm's coins, however, dropped soundlessly into a void. "No echoes, no answers," he sighed. "The story of my life." A premature judgment.

Siestas were a farce. Nightfall brought a hideous din—caterwauling, barking dogs, a turkey, rooster, and peacock gurgling, crowing, and shrieking respectively. Any disarrangement in the antiphonal score heightened our anxiety. The plangent cathedral bells rang out with a unique rhythm. Daytimes the Alhambra thrummed with chatter, radios, hurdy-gurdies, children singing at games, girls performing arias while making lace curtains or embroidering shawls, swains serenading under balconies, and in doorways mothers crooning lullabies, gypsies warbling *cante hondo* and soliciting via flattery: "*Muy simpático, veinte céntimos; mucho color, veinte céntimos . . .*"

I photographed tutti-frutti sunsets, caged quails fattening for the table, burros facing the wall like punished children, mourning garments (black most prevalent) ballooning on clothes lines. But shrines and gateways were usually blocked by street urchins clamoring hoarsely for "Moneys, cigarettos, jonny penny." I shouted, "*Anda, anda,*" in vain. You could travel far on three words—*anda, bueno, agua. No comprendo* was also valuable for unchaperoned women, considered fair game for roving males, blondes most desirable.

Though I was only a brunette, extravagant compliments from perfumed cavaliers became a routine thing. Trailing Conrad down the steep, crowded Guesta de Gomerez one day, I heard a fervent "*Que guapa, que hermosa*" from a young Spaniard. He assumed I was unescorted. When reprimanded, he spat on Conrad's shoes.

Meanwhile Malcolm went his solitary way. Not cooperating, Conrad complained. But easily moved to mirth, as when an American tourist inquired if Conrad spoke English, when I asked for an embrace instead of paperclips at a stationer's, or seeing a sign at the cinema that read "Children not at the breast must pay for their seats." Symbolism intrigued him—for instance an ironmonger wrapping nails for a customer in a rotogravure page depicting the Crucifixion, or a thunderstorm occurring on Holy Thursday, the first in five weeks.

Malcolm's easygoing nature encouraged Tendé to bait him. During mealtimes, guests in the patio would be alerted by a sly "*Psst, el borracho*," Tendé pointing him out. A barfly? They recoiled, the ladies clucking, "That nice, handsome young man? What a pity." While shopping in Granada one morning I saw him lurching through the streets, jostled and jeered at by young and old. To scatter them would only have doubled his humiliation. He stopped at a music shop, listened to a flamenco record, then continued his zigzag course, the Civil Guard stolidly watching him.

Conrad was losing patience with his protégé. Conventional tourism, even restored Moorish palaces, left Malcolm underwhelmed. He was bored with histories of lesbian harems and jealous homosexual attachments broken up by the husband or a eunuch. Nor could he be lured to the caves in the Albaycin by flamboyant gypsies in ruffled skirts performing fandangos, boleros, or tarantelles to Spanish tzigane music. He ducked our excursions to the Cathedral, marketplace, and charming hamlets like La Zubia.

"Why come to Spain at all?" Conrad said, exasperated. When Malcolm joined us reluctantly on a picnic in the foothills of the Sierras, his indifference was an insult to the lovely Alpine roses, wild foxglove, and bee orchids growing beside the swiftly flowing Darro. He preferred to explore his inner landscape and circle his own orbit in the many cantinas of Granada.

Whenever Luisa flicked the feather duster in Malcolm's room or made his bed, she sang her heart out and gazed at him with adoring eyes black as olives. He needed a friend badly. "Even the bedbugs avoid me," he said in a melancholy mood. "Because they're too busy devouring us," I replied. At our first complaints, Carmen raised her bovine eyes to the sign *No chinches*, and when shown the evidence, my spotted corpus, she murmured, "Must be a new kind of mosquito." Conrad snorted. "More likely an old Spanish custom." Persistent protests brought her with the Flit gun, her sighs so heartrending as she sprayed our mattress that I decided to conceal the night's ravages.

This patient, overworked drone was forever picking up after Malcolm. Conrad translated a torrent of Spanish one day. "Carmen wants to know if that pair of tired blue socks she found in the *beno* are yours. I suggest they are, and that they walked into the bathroom looking for a little water."

36

THE MENFOLK could think of little else but the season's first bullfight on Easter Sunday. Neither Malcolm nor Conrad saw anything in it to condemn. They deplored cruelty, whether it be a little girl twisting a dragonfly on a spike, a naughty urchin held by the heels over a precipice, or a donkey hobbling on fettered forelegs. The violence and bloodthirsty text and illustrations of juvenile books appalled Conrad, as did children in the cinema laughing raucously during the murder in *Fantamos*, by Paul Tejos. But the *cornada*, I was told, was a battle between evenly matched contestants. It purged the spectator of aggression besides initiating him into manhood, blunting the sensibilities and brutalizing men of war. Conrad treasured a snapshot, inscribed "*Don Ernesto Hemingvia, toreando a un cabestro castrade en Pamploma*," of a beaming aficionado posing beside a bull.

We drove to the *corrida* on a bright cool Sunday with Professor I. A. Richards and his German-born wife. The British literary critic was currently teaching semantics at Harvard. He had long wished to meet Conrad, and at once asked him whether the phrase "The nimblest of the necromancers" in a certain Prelude referred to T. S. Eliot. "Yes? I guessed as much. It's an accepted fact at Harvard." He enjoyed hearing about the Texas rancher who wrote Conrad requesting handwritten copies of all his Preludes—some sixty to date.

When Richards heard that Lowry was with us, he exchanged glances with his wife. Sitting beside Malcolm in the taxi, I sensed a moroseness. He felt *de trop*, even disliked, by his former examiner (and hero) at Saint Catharine's College. Head lowered, shoulders hunched, as if about to lunge, he had the menacing majesty of a bull, *El Toro* being Tendé's latest nickname.

The arena was packed. Ladies were advised to sit high up and near the

exit. We sat far back in the sun's glare, the Richardses and I armed with
smelling salts and dark glasses. Seats in the *sol* cost less than those in the
sombre. Tipsy soldiers and peasants behind us swayed and swore over
goatskin flasks. I pictured Malcolm as the bull out there, maddened by
picadors until it crumpled, the spinal cord cut, its death agonies hailed
with savage roars of *Olé*, *Olé*, the leading matador exhibiting the beast's
ear, then its tail.

Three boys hurdled the *barrera* at different times, executing veronicas.
They were congratulated by the matadors, spectators, and the police, who
then marched them off to jail. Such unprogrammed exhibitions might
launch a brilliant career, said Conrad, if a patron in the audience bailed
them out and sent them to a bullfighting school.

I refused to look at that butcher, the favorite matador borne trium-
phantly along the street to wild cheers and music, showered with flowers
by pretty girls. "How could you enjoy seeing horses gored and all the rest
of the ghastly display?" I asked.

"Because we're more civilized than you," said Conrad with a pitying
grin. "Do you know what I'm talking about?" He shrugged at my blank
stare. "You wouldn't hurt anyone consciously, but you've got a hell of a
lot of aggression deep down. I have too, of course, but I work it out by
identifying with gross spectacles like this."

And also by taking it out on me, I thought, ordering strong black coffee
in the grubby café and smoking strong, nasty Spanish cigarettes. Plied
with beer, prawns, and potato chips, my escorts relived the "terrific experience," the beautiful sword-and-cape dance, a supremely graceful and
dangerous moment when the matador placed the *banderilleros* and dealt
the coup de grace.

When Conrad told the Senora, "My wife couldn't take the bullfight,"
she replied that she felt the same way, as did most Spanish women. In
fact, Belmonte's wife never even saw one. I felt vindicated. Malcolm, tight
as a tick, sniggered when someone corrected Conrad's mixup of *cornada*
with *cornudo* (cuckold). The Spanish were a paradox to Mrs. Richards.
"We were stoned in Cordoba for refusing alms," she said. I couldn't understand the duality of the Spanish either—Carmen so kindhearted, Tendé
viciously baiting Malcolm. Our paying guest was on the defensive that
evening, boastful and pugnacious, something alien to his nature. He tried
to ingratiate himself with Richards, who wanted to discuss Harvard with
Conrad. I could see that Conrad was about to explode.

The two simmered down next morning, diverted by the hens cackling
in octaves. Conrad meanwhile made a sentimental discovery in the tiny
wine and sausage shop near the Carmona pension, actually a showplace
owned by the aged, half-blind Angel Barrios, once a renowned guitarist.

He showed us a framed parchment of celebrity autographs including that of Richard Strauss. The walls were covered with paintings left by artists in lieu of cash, among them two self-portraits of John Singer Sargent, reportedly worth sixty thousand pesetas each, and a watercolor of Sargent's niece, Reine Ormond. Malcolm stood transfixed when this was pointed out. "Cynthia of *Blue Voyage* here? Uncanny."

Barrios played for us upstairs in his living quarters, original flamenco melodies, the wrinkled face bent over the instrument—a Velasquez come to life. We listened, sipping *neuve reine*, a clear amber nectar spiced with herbs. It had the delicate bouquet of mead and tasted like sunshine. The men discussed Garcia Lorca, the musician-poet-playwright who perceived an affinity between deep-song and Negro spirituals, organizing the first *cante hondo* festival a decade earlier.

When Barrios heard that I also improvised, he waved me to the piano. My performance suffered after his superlative one; still, he said graciously that a rare gift should be cultivated. "Those untapped riches I mentioned years ago," Conrad reminded me significantly. I came away with an autographed copy of Barrios's piano solo, *Guijaras*. In bed I heard my first Spanish nightingale—a single liquid note repeated ad infinitum, as in a voice lesson.

My cup overflowed when I dreamt a poem which Malcolm pronounced positively Blake-ian and Conrad praised as the best thing yet. "If ever you controlled your subconscious, you might become more than a time-server," he said. My soul flowered like a night-blooming cereus.

As expected, Ed Burra's arrival had complicated life still more. The surrealist painter created a sensation—the travel-weary, shabby figure in a dusty green hat and dragging a stuffed laundry bag, his only luggage. "I took the wrong train from Barcelona and got lost," he said in his languid voice. "But then I wound up in Almeria, a spot so beautiful I wouldn't have missed it for the world."

Ed's music-hall ditties rendered in falsetto did not beguile Malcolm, who usually faded away when the pixillated rival joined Conrad. Wherever he happened to be, he left behind souvenirs—weird figures decorating paper napkins or tablecloths, or scraps of paper. Conrad finally prodded Malcolm into showing Ed the town. The two started downhill, husky, rotund Malcolm stalking ahead, Ed's slight figure lagging drearily behind. The experiment fizzled out soon enough after stares and gibes in Spanish, interpreted by Ed: "The big one is a German drunk and the skinny one is queer."

Early in May, I developed a violent gastric attack. Conrad fetched the only "English-speaking" doctor in Granada. "Your tongue plis, say ah, plis, no pain here, no pain there, hm, nothing wrong I can see, twenty pesetas plis, *buenos dias*." He never asked if I'd been drinking well water. Remembering the proverb "Look closely at money and water before you take it," Conrad decided to investigate. He caught Luisa filling the Avollanes bottles at the well. When he blistered some ears in the kitchen, the Senora flung back invectives, defending her duplicity. He came upstairs glumly advising me to stick to wine. "God only knows how long this deception's been going on." Apparently he was immune, like Malcolm, who stuck to alcohol.

In time the Senora forgave Conrad for suspecting polluted water. One word from him about the noisy rooster keeping us awake and it appeared on the table as chicken fricassee. I couldn't eat a morsel. Meanwhile my fears of a rupture between Ed and Malcolm were justified.

One day at lunch Ed caricatured him as a blimp in a sombrero. Always ready to make capital Tendé pounced on the sketch and passed it around, provoking giggles and guffaws. Malcolm snatched it, added a pipe to the mouth, tore it up and flung the pieces in Tendé's face, then turned on Ed and said with great restraint, "That was an unkind thing to do. The trouble with you is that people are too good to you." Ed shrugged. "Oh you don't know half the things they say about me."

Perhaps not. But he could kill his detractors with a crayon or paintbrush, whereas Malcolm had no such outlet. I fumed at Conrad. "Can't you muzzle Tendé? The Senora would do something if she knew about that punk making life miserable for Malcolm."

Late one night in May we sat in the patio with our drinks, tobacco smoke spiraling up to a star-studded sky, nightingales competing with owls, Ed looking like a gargoyle in the flickering candlelight. I. A. Richards was reminiscing about Harvard, Malcolm again interrupting with his drunken maunderings, Conrad holding himself in.

I could imagine the tongue-lashing Malcolm got next morning on their long walk. "Your behavior reflects anything but credit on me. You're a scandal at the pension and *persona non grata* with the police. I'm fed up with making excuses for your besotted states, apologizing for your disgusting hangovers. Hell's bells, when will you come to your senses? Your father keeps asking what the score is . . . "

Malcolm returned crimson-faced and crushed. He wasn't allowed to live in London, or go to sea again, and he dreaded being cut off from the parental purse. Conrad began to talk of cashiering him, though we could ill afford losing the monthly twenty-guinea checks. After the American dollar depreciated to fifty cents, his brokers had sold off one-hundred-dollar shares to cover themselves. He had had a hard time cashing a £30 draft at the Banco Hispano Americano. The whole dilemma cast a pall on us.

37

WE HAD BEEN HEARING RUMORS of plots to overthrow the Spanish Republic, monarchists paying "leftists" half a million pesetas to go on a six-hour strike. A demonstration by Catholic University students was quashed, the Palm Sunday procession a fiasco, Catholics afraid to step off the pavement lest they be heavily fined. Police patrolled Granada with heavy muskets, searching pedestrians for bombs and guns.

I could hardly take those slouching, cigar-smoking pumpkins in comic-opera uniforms and shovel hats seriously. But Conrad feared that Malcolm might touch off an international incident. Undesirable aliens and suspicious foreigners had been under surveillance, and Malcolm was known to the Civil Guard as *el borracho*. Emboldened by Ed's caricature, Tendé now spied on Malcolm, reporting to Conrad, for instance, "Thursday I see him in the Hollywood Café; he ask for three *aguardientes* and two senoritas."

Malcolm's drinking tapered off in the next few weeks. He bore Tendé's torments like a Spartan. But even an Englishman has his breaking point. During a period of regression one afternoon, he heard taunts of *"El toro, el toro,"* while climbing the Alhambra. Wheeling around, he saw Tendé cavorting with friends, aping his wobbly gait. He grabbed the fellow by the scruff of the neck, rammed him uphill a hundred yards or more, flung him down, yanked him up for a repeat performance, then left him in the dust.

"Where did you deposit him?" Conrad inquired sardonically when his protégé related the triumph with pardonable pride. "At the Puerta de la Justicia?"

I rejoiced. "Three cheers, that's my Malc. Justice isn't always blind."

From then on Malcolm had no more trouble with Tendé. But Fate had other entanglements in store—an exotic American girl, who arrived with her French escort. I unwittingly played Cupid by suggesting that Malcolm show Jan Gabrial the Generalife. He returned looking like a mesmerized owl, instantly smitten—"so much in love I could die."

I was glad he could relate to a *femme*, but had misgivings about a glamour girl in a large picture hat who found him "so handsome and fascinating." During her brief stay, they were inseparable, doing the town and roaming the foothills. When they fell into a brook, he on top of her, he seized the opportunity to outline the plot of *Ultramarine*. That, said I, was true love.

Their romance touched off arguments at the pension about virginity and Spanish morality, causing a flutter among such as Tendé's wife, who was forbidden to join mixed groups, speak to men, or go anywhere unescorted. The ladies mellowed toward our scalawag, waxing lyrical over his transformation. He now bathed daily, shined his shoes, borrowed my nail file, and absentmindedly wore his shirt inside out. He seemed reborn, shed radiance indiscriminately, kissing little Nina, and loving everyone (except Ed).

"All this primping and preening is positively revolting," Conrad said. His violent reaction mystified me. There were acrimonious exchanges between them after Jan left with her Frenchman. Had the relationship progressed from teacher-pupil and father-son to deadly rivals? Late one night, returning from a stroll, I heard a terrific row in the patio. Malcolm, in an alcoholic stupor, was bellowing, "And what about incestuous Susie?", a reference to *Great Circle*. He then threatened to kill Conrad, not for the first time either.

"What's all the rumpus about?" I asked. Conrad remained mute as a graven image in the silence, broken only by the *whoo-i* of owls.

Twenty years later, in *Ushant*, he supplied the answer. Hambo (Malcolm) speaking: "Well, it was . . . understood between us. . . . You had eaten your father's skeleton—why then shouldn't I eat yours? Not symbolically only, either. . . . You as much as admitted that now it was my turn—my turn to kill you. First, by taking Nita. Yes. For of course we both knew that both of us were powerfully drawn to that open wound— you first. . . . Not so? Yes—in the shadow of the Hundred Fountains, at the Alhambra, you proposed to share her, as foul a sort of voyeur's incest as any second-rate god could imagine."

The rift shortened our holiday by a week, Conrad now determined to drop Malcolm. *Adios, adios*. Spanish farewells are like Beethoven finales. Spain was lost, it's said, because the people talked too much. The Carmonas loaded us with lunch baskets, wine, and two enormous bouquets. Appropriately enough, a bomb had gone off the night before, the incident hushed up. A melancholy quartet entrained for Algeciras, Malcolm in a blue funk and suffering from an intestinal bug. Worse still, he had nothing to read for ten hours, having forgotten his two *Ulysses* volumes.

The flowers wilting in my lap represented my hopes of Spain producing a miracle. I thought about old Barrios and his wine shop, Conrad finding Sargent's portrait of his past love, the unspeakable Tendé, the regrettable Jan, Malcolm in jeopardy with everyone, Paradise Lost, about the only useful souvenir a recipe for *olla podrido*, which was to add luster to my shaky reputation as a cook.

From Algeciras, we dragged Ed along to Morocco on a whirlwind look at Ceuta and Tetuan. He sulked, we sweltered. Malcolm remained in Gibraltar to search for solace and adventure. He must have found these, for the police were downright nasty when we returned, until assured by Conrad that our *amigo* would be sailing with us.

In the morning we boarded the *Straithard*, encumbered with baskets, shawls, Spanish posters, donkey trappings, Egyptian runners. Frayed nerves and edgy tempers prevailed. Malcolm shared a cabin with "three Somerset Maugham colonels who were dying of the hiccups." His evil genie pursued him. A disenchanting letter from Jan in Lisbon kept him fastened to the desk, penning an interminable ship's log, when not in the bar. What Conrad called the first fine careless rupture marked the beginning of an ill-starred marriage.

England's green restful landscape was a reprieve, though homecomings are usually a letdown. Important mail had been lost, the house looked a mess, our Jenny had taken another job, and dental troubles compounded Malcolm's misery. The Spanish bacillus still caused ructions. So did his drinking. The thorny issue again thrashed out, he begged for Conrad's respect and permission to come again, for he loved Jeake's House. "I've been an awful nuisance, Jerry, can you ever forgive me? I do appreciate your putting up with me," he said, leaving me at a loss how to convey affection and sympathy.

The morning he left for London he couldn't find his ticket. When I offered to hunt for it, he said with a feeble smile, "Don't bother. I think I chewed it up." Later I found it near the rubbish can. Within a fortnight we had a suicidal letter. He had been taken to a nursing home for dysentery complicated by alcoholism, thence to the "pump room" to be dried out. *Ultramarine* had spawned a few piddling reviews. "If the art of writing is imitation, the author has mastered it," said the *Times*. He couldn't bear to look at his brainchild. His family meanwhile prayed for him, urging him to try writing advertising copy.

38

AFTER ALL THE *Sturm und Drang* we welcomed the children's brief visit with grateful hearts. They refreshed us like a Mozart rondo, Joan more cherubic than ever, Jane prettier, John a tease, trimming his father at chess and getting trimmed on the tennis court. He still held out for London University. Their presence cushioned the letdown of returning to familiar surroundings.

Dr. Graham had recommended bicycling to strengthen my back. I found it the ideal mode of travel and exercise for a weak spine, but couldn't coax Conrad to join me. Such a delicious sense of freedom, skimming along level stretches of Iden, Peasmarsh, and Udimore. On a happy impulse one July day I stopped at a lunch and tea sign, HUNDRED HOUSE, the house a fifteenth-century thatched gem belonging to the Farrs, Bill and Peggy.

They turned out to be a fun-loving, hard-working couple—"good old Sussex ware."

The oak-paneled tearoom, where I bumped my head on a low beam, was filled with antiques and curios—a square piano, a polished coffin stool, ship's models, choice pewter, and above an enormous fireplace a w.c. lid painted green. "Everybody goggles at our conversation piece," said Peggy, a tall, animated brunette, bringing me a cup of Lapsang Souchong. She laughed when I thanked her for not serving teabags, which reminded the British of surgical dressings. Rapport established, we found much in common—books, music, tennis, cycling, people.

One day we cycled to Brede Place, circa 1550, a stone house grim and solitary. Peggy said that Stephen Crane had lived there with his common-law wife, Mrs. Frewen, née Clara Jerome, sister of Jennie Jerome Randolph Churchill. "Moreton Frewen's family had the property for two centuries. Ghosts scared away servants, but Katherine Mansfield and J. M. Murry sublet the place around 1914, also D. H. Lawrence and Frieda. We heard that they all squabbled like cats and dogs."

Mulling over those bickering celebrities, I felt less guilty about *our* skirmishes—Conrad's and mine. I could never reconcile the tyrant with the poet who wrote *Senlin* and *Punch*. Instead of idolizing Conrad, perhaps I should have remembered his horrendous childhood. I missed every vital clue to his behavior. He said it all in *Blue Voyage*. Most of his love letters were cloying, but then a poet felt everything intensely, and he had found falling in love a revitalizing force. Rereading them shattered me. Invariably I fell under his spell.

Conrad was in London when I dined with Margaret. Relieved not to have him there with his hawkish eye on Paul, I whistled, at their request, and played Scarlatti and English folksongs at the piano. Paul said I made them both weep. Margaret then played Sussex pub chanties while he sang in a pleasant but asthmatic voice. It was a sentimental evening with no repercussions for once.

The next time Margaret came to dinner she looked pale and agitated. Paul had had all his teeth out. His doctor took a grave view of the asthma. Midway through the meal, Robert Nichols burst in, shouting "Where's Paul? Arthur Bliss is outside and in a buying mood. We're in a fearful hurry and can't stop." Margaret spoke with him in the hall, then returned, shaking her head. "He's a mass of hysteria. You can blame a dormant kidney for his bad manners."

We hadn't seen Robert or Norah for eight months. They were in Austria, and had spent Christmas in Semmering at the famous party given by Dorothy Thompson and Sinclair Lewis—reportedly a wet affair, what with ten days of rain and plenty of liquor. Robert elaborated on that affair a week later, when we were asked to cocktails. "Nonnie and I had a corking holiday," he said. "We took in the Salzburg Festival and the fabulous cafés. I got an average of three hours' sleep, and had a near romance with a blonde American actress. Unfortunately she turned pure at the last moment." Norah seemed less serene. Her eyes kept straying to her houseguest, Joss, his latest love.

The garden was a blaze of color, a French impressionist study, the sun highlighting Conrad's glasses and reddish hair, a wristwatch, tiepin, a metal shoe buckle, E. J. Moeran's yellow pullover. We met Virgilia Peterson Ross (the future Princess Sapieha), Raymond Gram Swing, the radio commentator, with his wife, Betty Gram, a feminist conspicuous in slacks and large floppy picture hat, and Major Yeats-Brown, who brought the second Mrs. Thomas Hardy, five years a widow.

Why, I wondered, did so many famous men's wives have limp handshakes? Her voice, manner, and two-piece mustard brown stockinette gave the impression that life had dealt harshly with her. Markedly self-effacing, she sat beside Conrad, listening raptly to him. I wanted to join them, if only to escape a cheeky hornet buzzing around my ginger beer. His reserve usually dampened me at social gatherings so I felt farouche, making gaffes and mixing up names. He considered me elusive, a will-o'-the-wisp, but allowed only one-tenth of himself to surface, as shy and secretive as Hardy, who allegedly put his wife's signature on his own biography.

Fragments of dialogue swirled around me. "I'm having a tubercular kidney removed, *not* my balls. . . . I told someone at the exhibit that Max Ernst was obsessed with the phallic symbol, then turned around and found him glaring at me. . . . Paul put in a whole year designing Tilly Losch's all-mirror bathroom; there's to be a steel ladder so she can admire herself from every angle and height. . . . Oh Paul and I are devoted to Chardin and Vermeer and Watteau. Their paintings are filled with serenity, and no less significant than the most heroic works of Van Gogh or Picasso. . . . You're making a great mistake in moving to London, Margaret. It's a powder keg, violent demonstrations hushed up in Hyde Park, fifty thousand Communists . . . Revolution is imminent. . . . I wager Benjamin Britten will astonish us with his music. . . . J. G. Fletcher fled the English lunatic asylum for the American lecture platform . . ."

Conrad was in fine fettle, savoring some secret delight when we left the party. "You certainly made a hit with Mrs. Hardy," I said, taking his arm. "Did she say anything interesting?" Yes, he replied, about her husband's writing habits. Then he added, "Who knows but what we might become a second Thomas Hardy and company, people flocking to Jeake's House from all over the world, making pilgrimages."

Wishart was to bring out all his works, but Conrad still planned a "foray" in the States. Malcolm Lowry, romancing Jan somewhere, wouldn't show up that summer and further checks from his father seemed dubious.

Whatever my vexations and grievances they were a small price to pay for the rich life Conrad provided. One of the greatest intellects, as J. W. N. Sullivan called him, he attracted the gifted and adventurous, the romantic and sophisticated—creative artists who expressed the beauty and wonder of life in painting, writing, and music.

Now and then a bluebird alighted on my shoulder. In Playden at the auction I found a six-octave harpsichord with a stack of music, all for £2.10. "*Mirabile dictu!*" Conrad congratulated me. It seemed an extravagance, but Dicky Dixon pronounced the 1780 Corri & Dussek a museum piece, a shrewd investment, which it proved to be. We placed it in the dining room, the only available spot. The local blacksmith made a special tuning fork for the octagonal pins, and Norah's tuner put it in shape. I polished the rosewood case to a mirrorlike glow, then with John a willing captive christened it by playing Corelli and other baroque composers.

Our performances in turn opened the door to the Old Hospital opposite—bread upon the waters. Humphrey Ellis's note asked if we cared to listen to the Bach prom concert on his Victor H.M.V. We would indeed. The interior was even more sumptuous than I had imagined. Conrad was charmed, setting foot inside for the first time. Our host stood in a tangle of wires we had tripped over, admitting plaintively he didn't understand all these atmospherics. After testing the equipment and fussing with the amplifier, the shy, absent-minded bachelor settled down to enjoy a two-hour concert with his guests. Rye's "best" were there, including the vicar. And Mr. Williams, the organist of Saint Mary's, invited me to hear a Bach recital.

The children sat demurely, hands folded, until refreshments were served. Magic-lantern slides—paintings of Elijah, Christ among the Apostles, and the Conversion of Saint Paul—wound up the evening. We thanked Mr. Ellis for the first of other similar invitations. Altogether a felicitous occasion, the conversion of a stranger to a cordial neighbor.

39

FOR GOOD LUCK, turn a penny in your pocket on hearing the first cuckoo in spring. For bad luck, have a black cat cross your path. Or an alluring, tawny-haired Irish witch. I had become superstitious. Why had Deirdre refused Radclyffe Hall's offer to buy the Old Vicarage, though I couldn't fathom Johnny considering life in a remote part of Romney Marsh with nothing to look at but sheep, moorhens, and giant willows.

I was drying my hair before the fire one chilly summer afternoon when Deirdre sashayed into Jeake's House, a pink rose big as a bath sponge tucked in the belt of her white linen dress. She had been bringing her beaux for inspection. One of them, a musician about as romantic-looking as *Blutwurst*, had wheedled her husband into buying a spinet for the cottage. An old man's darling, she had her every whim indulged, and her endless allusions to Vernon's devotion were getting on my nerves. "So amusing how Nash follows me around," she simpered. "If I leave him for five minutes he gets the wind up and goes looking for me in a frenzy. Everybody thinks I'm his daughter. Last week a colleague of his gave me a telephone message in London for 'your Daddy.' People have referred to him before as my father, but never as Daddy."

I said, "What do you bet Daddy gets no hot meals or other service?"

Conrad ticked me off for being catty. He thought Deirdre a manic-depressive, a typical Celt living in her imagination. Margaret saw through the vivacious flirt to her bohemianism, and would have shut the door on her long since. Norah also. "She made up to Robert just as she did to Conrad, and always the same refrain—'What shall I do?' The wildest of the wild Irish, a type that drives me mad. She told me she doesn't love her husband, but that he was too long a habit to give up."

Deirdre was just one more obstacle to our working schedule. That summer was a repetition of the previous one, visitors streaming to our door, guests to lunch, tea, dinner, the weekend. A facsimile of Conrad's dream of pilgrims, it struck me as more of a zoo. We should have charged admission. Fed up with extending hospitality, I turned sullen and was duly punished.

The "gentry," some of whom had put us in cold storage, now welcomed "those scandalous Americans" unabashedly. Brisk and beaming, our near neighbor caught me cleaning Conrad's jacket and smelling of petrol. "I would have called on you long before," said she, "but I was erroneously told that you were a great friend of Radclyffe Hall and Lady Troubridge."

Another day I opened the door to the local doctor's wife. "Are *you* Mrs. Aiken?" she asked, staring. I should have replied, like Dorothy Parker, "Yes, do you mind?"

Had Mr. Ellis anything to do with this surge of Christianity? Or were these respectables less nobly motivated, come to poke around the ashes of a marriage on its way to ruin? "Hello," a stranger greeted me on High Street one morning. "Have you read *Harriet*?" I tried to remember who this lady was, and who had written *Harriet*. When she mentioned Phyllis, whose sister was coming that month, a light dawned. Phyllis was Phyllis Bottome, the novelist. "And you're Mrs. Lowell of Tenterden," I said. We parted with gratified smiles.

Finesse. Sophistication. Whereas Malcolm thought I was too sophisticated to write children's stories, Conrad said I wasn't sophisticated enough. At any rate, my manuscripts kept returning like bad pennies. Journalism was my dish. The piece about hop-pickers I was then working on sold later to the *Listener*. Meanwhile, Conrad was finding a market for his Preludes. *Everyman* had asked for five, and a photo. We heard about a joke making the rounds in American literary circles: "Have you seen Conrad Aiken's latest poem in the *New Yorker*? It's called 'Prelude.'"

Great Circle had drawn mixed reviews, and Conrad entertained mixed feelings toward Marjorie Kinnan Rawlings, suspecting Scribner's of promoting her, along with other popular authors, at his expense. Her first novel, *South Moon Under*, had sold 15,000 copies. She paid us a visit while researching her next book, *The Yearling*. Breezy, humorous, and disarmingly candid, Marjorie opened up on her marital troubles. "We fight like roosters. My husband is a man I can neither live with nor escape from."

It sounded familiar. The next time Deirdre came I called Conrad from his study, then returned to my typewriter. She had been wooing me with flowers and Nellie Wallace records. After Mrs. Hilder, our new daily, left at five-thirty I fed Squidge and started dinner with a clatter of pots and pans. Deirdre ignored the hint and came into the kitchen as I prepared hors d'oeuvres, pirouetting in her new dress.

"Feel the material, Clarissa; it's real wool. Got it in Baker Street. Three guineas. Isn't it divine? Think it suits me? Nash grumbled, 'My hard-earned money, and in a month you'll be using it as a floor mop.' But he doesn't begrudge me anything. How do you like my hair bracelet? I found it in Rye, only ten bob. It matches my earrings exactly. Also my hair, see? These earrings I'm wearing are new, too. Aren't they ravishing? Black glass. I've embroidered myself the most ravishing Russian tunic with a choke collar. Worked solidly on it for two days. It really looks like two months of work. I must show it to you."

Why must you? I said under my breath. As before, Deirdre hung on until six, then with no dinner invitation from me she went to the pub with Conrad, once again setting Rye's tongues wagging. His crude beer-flinging gesture had only hardened my heart. Unfair, ungentlemanly. I would yet remove the blindfold from Dame Justice.

And so we waded through the old scenario that evening, I defending my rudeness. "She's been here so often that I feel I've done my duty. I don't wish to encourage her," I said. "Not that she needs any . . ."

"Sweet Jesus," Conrad shouted, "and you accuse *me* of jealousy?"

"Accuse? That's hardly the word. On your own admission you've been hounding me for seven years. No man has been exempt from your pathological jealousy. Carl, Forrest, Victor, Mark, and more recently Robert,

Paul—even Malcolm playing Ping-Pong with me, and suspecting Ed Burra the time you found us under the table hunting for a shilling he dropped."

"At least I'm not rude to the other person."

"Maybe," I said, "but you take it out on my hide. The last time John and I played duets, you asked if I was trying to usurp your place in the children's affections."

"Oh piffle. You're becoming intolerable."

"Yes," I said, "whenever I assert myself I'm intolerable. One law for you, another for me. I mustn't smile at men, or see friends you disapprove of, or confide in Margaret, or keep a diary. Your jealousy is always justified, so you throttle me for 'whoring.' Well I'm no longer a docile donkey you can shove around."

Instead of sitting down to dinner, he turned on his heel, grabbed his walking stick, and vanished without another word.

The long wait began. Twilight had faded before eleven, when I went to bed, though the "insomnia" pillow was no help. He hadn't returned by midnight. Was he with Paul, Robert, or in Hastings? I paced the floor, knees buckling, heart racing, periodically listening at the window or down the stairwell for his heavy tread. He would have made a poor second-story burglar. The quarterboys of Saint Mary's struck one, two, three, four, five. By six I was frantic. Something horrible must have happened.

My nerves screamed for action. Still I dreaded raising an alarm after the strangling incident. At nine I sent Mrs. Hilder with a note to Margaret, asking if she knew his whereabouts. She replied that after making several phone calls she had traced him to the Old Vicarage.

That was a shock. Taking revenge on me? Whether with Deirdre alone or Vernon was immaterial. Had he planned it all? How else did he get to Guldeford unless by Vernon's car? What excuse had he made for spending the night other than our quarrel? Deirdre now knew about our wrangling and would use that to advantage.

"I decided to teach you a lesson," Conrad said defiantly, with an uneasy grin, sauntering into Jeake's House at high noon.

"You taught me a lesson all right," I said. I wanted to kill him, bash in his face. "Taught me to *hate* you!" Upstairs, I recoiled from my reflection in the bathroom mirror.

"My God, you really know most awfully little of women with any kind of heart or soul," wrote his former mistress, Elizabeth. "What lovely things you'll write when you do; for there is in you the ability to produce beauty and truth. But no genius, not even yours, must be fed at the price of pain."

My folly and weakness are abysmal. Why must I behave in this extraordinary fashion? *Ask dad, he knows*! Ask Clara, the negro nurse! . . . Ask that detest-

able red-faced, red-headed vulgar master (tuberculous, too) who superin-
tended when I was given the water-cure, aged seventeen! . . . Ask them all.
And ask my dipsomaniac great-grandfather, my charming imaginative fib-
bing mother, my sensual analytic father, and the delirious wall-paper pattern
on my nursery wall. *Behaviour is a function of environment*. Selah! I wash my
hands of it.

Blue Voyage

I slept the afternoon through, skipped dinner, leaving Conrad to fend
for himself, and spent the evening with Margaret. "He's incapable of
loving you," she said, her dark eyes flashing. "Otherwise he would know
such cruelty would hurt you beyond repair. I've long felt his contempt for
women. No sympathy or tenderness there, no open mind. He's deeply
unhappy and intelligent enough to know he's emotionally numb." True.
Nothing could rouse him to compassion or even sympathy, whether it be
friends' emotional disturbances or some illness. Was this singular lack the
result of an indifferent mother, or the shock of her death?

"Whenever we quarrel," I said, "Squidge jumps on the table between
us, meowing his distress, like the little pussifist he is." I smiled feebly. My
jealousy of the cat, a painful memory, indicated the depth of childish
resentment. While ignoring me, Conrad would pet Squidge into a frenzy
of ecstasy, talking to him by the hour, treating him as a surrogate child
and member of the family.

Margaret's bedroom reminded me of my mother's, a sunny bower,
everything dainty and feminine—the four-poster bed, chaise longue, white
dimity curtains, Persian carpet, Egyptian and Sudanese hangings, on the
mantel bibelots, one of them a cypress carving of a dancer whose skirts
fanned out gracefully. I wouldn't be enjoying this beauty much longer.
The house had been sold and the Nashes would be moving to London in
August.

"I've laid aside a few things you might use, Clarissa," Margaret said.
"Curtains, Arabian crewel work, Father's linen surplices. They'll make
durable nightgowns . . ."

"You've been such a good friend, seeing me over the humps," I said,
wanting to weep on her shoulder. "Deirdre made me realize how possessive I am."

"Don't let her add to your problems, my dear. She's just a passing fancy.
Paul and I see your spirit struggling to free itself. No one owns anybody,
and that goes for Conrad as well. When he argued about the role of the
sexes the other night, I gathered that a man had no further use for a
woman once she surrenders her soul. Don't let him swallow you up.
You're a glutton for punishment, you know. Ingratiating wives deserve
what they get."

"Am I one really?"

"If the shoe fits . . ." She smiled. "But I was thinking of Paul's brother, also an artist. His wife spares him every conceivable worry. They've often been on the brink of starvation, but Christine would never dream of saying, 'You'd better get busy, there's just a shilling left in the cookie jar.' She accepts every ordeal, imposition, abuse, even made baby garments for his illegitimate daughter."

"A heroine like Norah."

"Exactly." Margaret sighed. "How much longer will *she* put up with Robert? While he plays ducks and drakes with her money, he keeps falling 'deeply in love.' She's not well, has acute arthritis. He's far from well himself, but I have no sympathy for a man who manipulates or exploits his wife."

I said, "The poem he wrote on Eros pleased Conrad immensely. At least he was being productive. Norah probably married him partly for his romantic nature. Oh Margaret, loving is such a gamble. I always come to rue it when my heart rules. If only I could swallow pride and talk out this whole affair with Conrad. But I've had to tread gingerly since his suicide attempt. I can't reach him any more. He believes a poet should unmask on paper, but why wear a mask with one's wife? You once said he flinches whenever you lay a hand on his sleeve. It's true, he hates to be touched."

His aloofness was like a death-ray. He had begun *Ushant*, for instance, without telling me. Any withdrawal of intimacy or admiration took me back to Mother's empty chair and Father's want of affection. "Count only on yourself," she used to say. Didn't that make a mockery of love? Conrad was no longer a moral bulwark to lean upon. Yet I would feel diminished without him. He stamped his personality on me like a cookie-cutter on dough. I even imitated his microscopic handwriting.

How had Jessie handled Conrad's jealousy? Of course she was more articulate and strong-minded than I, with the authority of a mother. I discounted rumors of Conrad locking her in the house and forcing her to break a window to take the baby out for an airing.

"Creative artists shouldn't marry," Margaret said flatly. "They don't know how to treat women. Imagine Gustav Mahler reading Kant or Hegel to Alma when she was in labor! Oxford had the right idea in the tenth century, forbidding its dons to marry. They were given food, shelter, and women, then left alone to meditate like monks. Every comfort and need fulfilled, but they worked without the worry of a husband and father."

"Unfortunately," I said, "artists have a domestic streak and long for family life. That's the hitch. Should the sexes be segregated, except for conjugal visits, like prisoners?"

What did I lack that Deirdre had? Novelty, for one thing. What had I

ceased giving Conrad or being to him? Fencing him in, allowing him no
latitude, the indignation of a wronged wife smugly assuming it couldn't
happen to me, that I was immune from his roving eye or lustful impulses.
An honest couple would have asked each other for help. "I love you and
am afraid of losing you. I need your assurances." Suppose it was too late,
one partner tired of the other and refusing to play the game? Walter
Savage Landor would have only one response: "Ah what a dusty answer
gets the soul when hot for certainties in this life."

40

FATE DANGLED A DUBIOUS CARROT under Conrad's nose early in September—the prospect of a Freudian analysis in Vienna. The master
had read *Great Circle* and kept a copy in his waiting room, according to
one of his five patients, Hilda Doolittle, the American imagist poet. She
hoped that Conrad would take her place. Analysis was too painful, and
she was lazy. "It's not a game of chess with the old man," H.D. told him
in London. "He's a mystic and a fallible humanitarian in poor health." He
promised to discuss the matter with Bryher MacPherson, her friend and
banker, whose lucid, penetrating mind he respected. Bryher's father, Sir
John Ellerman, the shipping magnate, was reputed to be the richest man
in England.

Like Jung, Adler, and Ferenczi, Freud influenced Conrad's works tre-
mendously, but Conrad shared the fear of Malcolm Lowry and others that
analysis might destroy creativity.

> Sell him to Doctor Wundt the psycho-analyst
> Whose sex-ray eyes will separate him out
> Into a handful of blank syllables,—
> Like a grammarian, whose beak can parse
> A sentence till its gaudy words mean nothing.
> *from "Changing Mind"*
> *Collected Poems*

We had been asked to H.D.'s cocktail party. After lunch with Margaret
that day at the Brice, we separated, I tearing around without accomplish-
ing anything. Succumbing to hedonism, I climbed to the "pit" at the
Tivoli to see a movie, but halfway through, suddenly realizing I would be
late to the party, I tore downstairs, took a cab to Piccadilly Circus and the
tube to Knightsbridge.

I arrived at H.D.'s top-floor walkup breathless, exhausted, perspiring,

my hair falling down, a wreck. A tall, gangling woman shrilled, "You must
be Clarissa," and pulled me into a jampacked room resounding with deafening voices. I almost passed out. The windows were shut, curtains drawn,
lamps lits. "Conrad? Here's your wife," and Hilda buttonholed him. He
seemed to be having the bends.

I felt stranded until someone handed me a drink—a petite, attractive
young woman with a boyish bob and great poise. Bryher drew me out,
Conrad listening to my lame rejoinders, aware I was talking nonsense. A
smartly groomed ash-blonde glanced at my homemade organdie frock and
said sweetly to her companion, "Well, now I realize that clothes aren't
everything." Had Conrad heard that? But why should I care? The dress
had drawn compliments in Rye.

I ducked into the bedroom, fighting my way there by stepping on toes.
While powdering my nose, looking obliquely into the compact mirror,
H.D. staggered in and shouted, with a triumphant light in her eyes, "Now
I know what you are. You're a *negative* narcissist." I blinked. Was that
good or bad? "Oh well, it's a cross I must bear," I said. Would a *positive*
narcissist clash less with Conrad? Since I would be getting a spot of
analysis, too, I had urged him to take the plunge—a rare chance to look
up my origins in Germany and France.

The proposition was still in flux when Hilda spent a night in Jeake's
House, her potbellied, broad-hipped figure looking "like a carelessly tied
bundle," to quote William Carlos Williams. How nobly she tried to like
me! Her intensity, facial tic, hysterical laugh, and nervous mannerisms
made her an unrestful guest. She talked mostly about herself. Bryher, who
had adopted Hilda's daughter by a musician, kept pressing her to get a
legal separation from Richard Aldington, who had run off with an American belle. "Then you can sue all these women who pose as his wife, sue
them for libel." But Hilda obdurately refused. "Divorce would sever the
spiritual union I feel we have together."

On the subject of Freud she was explicit. "Freud sits outside the range
of vision, smoking cigars, which are rationed because of cancer of the
mouth. Everyone's worried about his safety in Vienna, especially his daughter
Anna, who runs a boys' clinic. He's in danger of being bombed, and may
have to flee the Nazis. That would mean the end of his practice, of course.
I don't think an ailing man of seventy-seven would survive transplanting.
He's always complained of having only seven grandchildren . . ."

Conrad wondered if she was transferring from Freud to him. "For her,"
he said, "therapy seems to involve no hard work or deep probing, just
tears, dramatics, and shedding hairpins on the sofa. Psychoanalysis seems
to make some women even more egocentric. She knows no more about
me than she did before."

While awaiting further developments, we became involved in a local contretemps reminiscent of the previous year's brush with Betty May, an actress and artist's model. Malcolm's friend Hugh Sykes-Davies, a don at Cambridge, had smuggled that hot potato into Rye. Because of her fondness for alcohol, Betty May was deemed a bad character witness and advised to remain in hiding while embroiled in two libel suits, Nina Hammet the defendant in one, Aleister Crowley in the other. Currently she was writing a cookbook, a quaint switch, I thought.

Asked to cocktails, we found the fugitive sprawled barelegged on the sofa in Hugh's rented studio, skirts above her shapely knees, a trim, middle-aged woman with purple makeup around her eyes and a Russian tea-cosy on her gray frizzed hair. She kept us convulsed by singing bawdy lyrics in her husky voice. Thwarted in efforts to sit on Conrad's lap, she kissed him repeatedly, much to his discomfiture. "That's what sexual excesses lead to," he said solemnly at home. As we left, sustained by deviled eggs and creme de menthe, she threatened to come and see us. Laura Knight, when told about her, said she was amazed that Betty May was still alive after all the "snow" she had consumed while mistress of a Dutch silk merchant.

Conrad had the delicate task of asking Hugh to keep her away. Hugh was himself a genius of sorts, phenomenal at the piano keys. His life story, a Michael Arlen novel poured out in Yorkshire dialect, had kept Conrad up until 2 A.M. His grandfather, of the Sykes Sporting Goods family, invented the inlay of tennis racquet frames and had recently won £10,000 in a libel suit against a rival firm trying to steal the patent. Hugh described the majority of Cambridge University students as hell raisers and heavy drinkers, many of them bisexual. He touched a nostalgic chord in Conrad, reviving wild oats sown at Harvard. Sensitive though he was about casting aspersions on Hugh's companion, Conrad did his duty. When Hugh protested that Betty May was really quite nice when sober, Conrad asked, "When's that?" She had only to be seen at our red door for what social gains we had made in the face of ostracism to fly out the window. I asked rhetorically, "Would Jessie have admitted her?" My priggish, stuffy stance amuses me today.

By late September cash gifts and loans had evaporated. Bryher offered to stake Conrad with £100, then raised the ante to £200. After a frantic exchange of telegrams, phone calls, and special delivery letters, H.D. wired that Freud's heart attack and lung congestion prevented him from taking on any patients, at least until January *perhaps*. Meantime, he would be studying Conrad's psyche.

Feeling "deFreuded," Conrad booked passage to the States on the *Aquitania* (steerage), sailing on the twenty-ninth. A few days before, we stayed at Margaret's flat (Conrad relieved to have Paul removed from my orbit in Rye). I had a taste of high life—cocktails with H.D. at Kenneth MacPherson's flat. The previous occupant was Prince George's mistress, until Queen Mary discovered the liaison and had him hustled out. Kenneth had transformed the garage underneath into a gorgeous Italian renaissance lounge. Bryher then took us to The Ivy, a swank restaurant, the decor branded "Early Cunard" by Conrad. He had a bang-up gourmet dinner for once—oysters, partridge, rare wines, and bombé pêche melba so luscious I could have died happily eating another one. H.D. roared at my burblings and said we must have another party soon.

On the eve of Conrad's departure, one of his former tutees, Bill Nickerson, showed us his luxurious suite in the Cavendish Hotel. We met the famed proprietress, Rosa Lewis, a faded beauty, protégé of Edward VII and one-time cook for the Kaiser. A dazzling vision in pink, she glittered with jewels and her sequinned gown was like a spotlight. The walls of her salon were covered with photographs of her clientele and admirers.

"Where are you staying?" she asked. "Bloomsbury? Oh those flats are all chocolate boxes." She opened her autograph album. It contained the names of Teddy Roosevelt, Aldous Huxley, and Henry James, among others. "Harry," she said thickly, over champagne, "was always better on the sheets than between them. I wouldn't give twopence for him between them. Sometimes I feel like an afterbirth—no weeklies, no monthlies, no anything. I've had about four hours' sleep since Thursday week. Four or five times a day I'm called to the telephone and asked if I'll cash a no-account check from some bloke what's broke and says he owes me money. There goes the phone. Now you'll see." Rosa could well afford philanthropy since she owned a string of shops on Jermyn Street.

She returned with a rustle and swish of her skirts. "Didn't I tell you? A chap in some Folkestone nursing home wanted £100. He'll get £5 out of me, no more. Have some more bubbly fizz?" Her ramblings wound up with the sensible statement "I don't mind a tart so long as she's clean and does her job well."

After seeing Conrad off on the boat-train the following day I lunched with Margaret on clams and ravioli. "You must build up strength and courage while he's away," she advised. Three long months Penelope would pine for her Ulysses. We had parted amicably, unaware of storm clouds hovering over us.

The fresh flowers Mrs. Hilder put in every room lent a mortuary atmosphere. But in my forlorn state I appreciated her gestures to cheer me up. Keeping busy banished ghosts. I began "Letters from an English Village," a series subsequently sold to *Country Life*. I resumed pipe-organ lessons, a refresher course in pedaling on the three-manual organ in Saint Mary's. Mr. Williams had me cut my teeth on Mendelssohn's *Elijah* and

wanted me to spell his pianist at choir rehearsals. I transcribed notes of
the Spanish novel that Conrad was translating and had Peggy and Bill
Farr in stitches, reading aloud clichés from *La Mujer de Sal*.

Conrad's eagerly awaited letters came in a batch, despair the keynote.
Though landing in Boston with twelve dollars, he turned down the only
job offer, ghostwriting for a "shyster" lawyer at fifty dollars a week. Erich
Fromm, whom he met on shipboard, strongly advised psychoanalysis, and
Fromm's analyst, Hans Sachs, suggested contacting Bernfeld in Vienna.

Trailing Conrad on a slower ship, Ed Burra had taken French leave of
his family. His sister was dismayed when I told her where he was. Manhattan fascinated him, but he threatened to take out Jewish naturalization
papers after being "mobbed" in Harlem. His penchant for mischief worried me. He had told mutual friends in Rye that we kept complaining
about poverty though he noticed there was always plenty to drink.

To offset the ho-hum review given *Great Circle* by the *Times*, I for-
warded a fan letter to Conrad from an Oklahoma schoolteacher. "How
happy you must be to have given so much to the world," she wrote in
part. Everything was relative. Margaret told me that T. S. Eliot, then
editor of the *Criterion*, ordered a copy of *Great Circle* after hearing that it
was magnificent, then delivered a double entendre to Paul: "Each book
Aiken writes is better than the last one." When Margaret chided the editor
of *New Verse* for rejecting Conrad's poems, he said he had taken Eliot's
word that they were unsuitable. She suspected Eliot of being at the bottom of the resistance movement. Regarding his old friend as subversive, a
rival who must remain crushed, he staged a cabal, feeling it his duty as a
Catholic to stamp out atheism and nihilism—or so her thinking went. It
might also be part revenge, since Conrad once said that Eliot didn't put
anything down because he thought he was God and was afraid of falling
short of perfection. That crack, Conrad claimed, so incensed Eliot that he
produced *The Waste Land* as a tour de force.

After finding me harmless, Mr. Ellis brought jams and other delicacies,
but declined tea. I was asked again and again to musical evenings. Like a
dignified country parson in an impish mood, he mimicked Sir Henry
Wood, acknowledging the applause. John came on occasional weekends,
at nineteen old enough to enjoy risqué stories. We spent jolly hours at
Ping-Pong, tennis, and duets.

December seemed centuries away. Rereading Conrad's works, I dreamt
of him constantly. Squidge pined for him, waiting each night on the
windowsill. Evenings were the worst, made more spooky by Channel
gales. Everything reminded me of him—his pipe, walking stick, hats,
chessboard. Quarrels forgotten, happier memories rose to the surface like

cream. If I needed money, he said, I was to write and he'd do anything he could. "Be well and happy."

In mid-October, Bryher retracted her offer to finance the analysis. "She doesn't want the responsibility of making it possible or easy for Conrad," H.D. explained. I pointed out that he went to the States explicitly to raise cash. "Then his rich relatives and friends should help him," she said. They *had* kept us afloat for years, I replied, itching to scratch her eyes out. She was unmoved. "If he's really serious he'll beg, borrow, or steal the money." Well, he had begged and borrowed. There remained stealing.

41

As always when we were apart, Conrad reproached me for not writing more often. Accordingly, I dispatched diary trivia—Harold Knight turning down Lord Rothermere's invitation to South America, Laura painting the Duchess of Rutland at Haddon Hall, I meeting Rose Fyleman, children's book writer, through Mary Howard's friend Joan Coster, whose husband, the "King's Photographer of Men," was too susceptible to photograph women.

"Squidge is curled up in a fat ball on the ottoman," I wrote, "his striped tail wagging like a metronome. John has kept me company weekends while having dental work done in Rye. On Sunday we're to lunch with the Burras. Next week I'm taking him to a Shaw play in London."

I passed on the news about Malcolm Lowry. He had brought Jan to Rye, hoping for Conrad's blessing on his forthcoming marriage, their romance rekindled in London. They didn't call on me, nor did I see them in Rye. Hugh said that Malcolm planned to marry without his father's consent or knowledge. "He hopes that we'll stake him to a honeymoon in Paris, where Jan wants to live. But we won't and can't lend him any more cash," Hugh told me. "Jan isn't keeping him satisfied. She flaunts a string of rivals, drinks up his allotment, and interferes with his work. She claims being distraught about his drinking and choking spells. He's getting barmier by the hour for sure. His eccentricities reached a point where we'll have to kick him out. He's got to clean up his own messes, but we do feel Conrad should know about his predicament."

Doctors treating Malcolm for a chronic glandular infection years later marveled that he was still alive. They said the toxic effects could well have contributed to his erratic behavior.

The Farrs, I told Conrad, were fascinated by Jeake's House. Bill agreed that the arch in the dining room was probably the entrance into a smuggler's

cave. Peggy pronounced Squidge the most splendid cat ever. She made up
in part for Margaret's absence, playing mother hen on our strolls and
cycling jaunts. "You're far from fit yet, ducky, and too serious by half.
Stop fretting. Throw your bonnet over the mill. The best way to hold a
man is to keep him comfortable but guessing." Yes? No. Not Conrad. He
considered her too outspoken and independent, a dangerous element,
another feminist.

And Robert was also on probation with him. There were still some
things about last summer he didn't understand, he wrote me. He wished
to God he could believe I had had no "flurry" with Robert. Help him to.
How? All assurances were futile. As for Robert, Conrad should have seen
the poor wretch (now minus a kidney) hobbling on a cane, flanked by
Norah and his joy-girl, complaining of being forgotten by his literary
friends. When the pain grew unbearable, his psychiatrist advised him to
dwell on erotic memories.

I had managed to get through October, with the anthracite stove and
log fires, but the bathroom and bedroom in the Arctic Circle took more
stamina. Channel gales not only accentuated the spooky atmosphere but
flooded the kitchen, rain pouring down the bogie's short chimney. Rye
might be delightful in summer, said Mabel Houghton, "but wintering in
that dreary hole is not for us." I wearied of villagers explaining their cold-
shouldering by the stock phrase, "I call on so few people." Most of our
friends were in London. Why eat out my heart? I made a poor Penelope,
no spinning or weaving, the battle with loneliness lost. I dare not read
Conrad's books any more, or even mention his name.

Several friends urged me to stay in London until he returned. Among
them were the Legges, newlyweds I met through the Gerald Noxons.
After much wavering I closed Jeake's in November, boarded Squidge with
Mrs. Hilder, and took a room in Torrington Square. Living *en pension*
again in a Bloomsbury hostel reminded me of my dormitory days in
Boston. The weekly rent, £2.5, included two meals, gas fires extra.

My decision raised a rumpus, and Conrad's cable was no surprise. "Distressed at your removal to London and dislike your intimacy with the
Legges can't you stand Rye." (Not without him. How had *he* fared the
fortnight I worked on Laura's memoir?) I was being selfish and heartless,
he wrote me, drifting in search of excitement, as when considering a job
at Amherst or with William Beebe in the Galapagos Islands. Clarissa
Aiken, who was she? Had he ever known her? I gave him no sense of
continuity. He might as well be married to a meteorite.

Judging me on my past, he was correct. When my old diaries arrived
from Milwaukee, I read with loathing about a self-centered creature thirst-

ing for adventure, restless as the wind, no goals or spiritual core. Conrad had a similar nostalgic experience rereading our early letters, "rowelled" by them. He dreamt that I said I was unhappy and that he burst into tears, asking, what about *me*? He wrote that he was unhappy enough to crawl into a sewer. Every damned thing had gone wrong. "It's as if even my retreat—my house, my heart, my love, were no longer real."

I replied that I sympathized with his fear of losing Jeake's, but that no amount of caretaking on my part would prevent that.

> Why do you wish me to stay in Rye? To serve as a watchdog? I've been loyal to a place that never wanted me; I felt an intruder. Your idea of loyalty is fantastic. My first duty is to myself. I'll do anything to help you toward a life that will endure, but if you annihilate me by overriding my needs, I won't be much use to you. I cannot let you choose my friends or dictate my life. My quest for freedom is directed at work rather than pleasure. I prefer a room of my own, however uncomfortable, and often work in my coat to save gas-fire shillings. Your idea of boarding with friends is neither feasible nor economical. Besides, I've had no invitations. . . . You find my letters vapid and hasty, with long gaps and written on the fly. Because I lead a vapid life, and the hurried notes indicate that I'm always thinking of you, scribbling my thoughts at all times and places.

With that mail went an average day's schedule. His letter asking for a copy of his short story "Pure as the Driven Snow" began with "I haven't much to say," then went on for five single-spaced pages. He said he never wanted to hear sex mentioned again after the free-for-all fornication going on in his broker's apartment. In a dispute with his host and friends, he alone held out for strict monogamy, even though "broken in two by the fear that my wife was being substantially unfaithful." To solace himself, he carried in his wallet the Cape Cod snapshots of me in the nude.

Answering his suspicions:

> Yes, Paul kissed me in greeting. How often have you been kissed since leaving Rye? I might as well wear a chastity belt for all the temptations I've had. Your letters read like a phone directory. So many exposures to ex-mistresses terrify me. Why is my body so much more important to you than my soul? Where's your sense of humor, or your memory? . . . Gertrude Townsend— curator of textiles at the Museum, remember?—writes that she hasn't seen you, that your world and hers are far removed. I suggest you call on her, then pause before Kwannon, the Goddess of Mercy [advice he gave me during our courtship]. My whole heart is in your welfare, darling, don't be angry and petty. I long to have you to myself for a change after sharing you with the whole world so long.

My cable followed. "Don't lose heart Bernfeld not until March." Hilda quoted Bryher "unofficially" that Bernfeld couldn't take on any more patients at present. Would Conrad consider a female analyst? Hardly. A more rational message reached me. "Disregard all letters including today distraught with worry please cable reassurances and enjoy yourself darling love."

Write in haste, repent at leisure. The happiest times *I* enjoyed were spent in family circles—the Freemans, the Morsses, and the Opies in Oxford. Exactly as Conrad felt when visiting the Linscotts; he came away refreshed, restored.

Students at the London hostel included youths from Germany, who gathered around the piano in the lounge when I played. One evening a rosy-cheeked Nazi enlightened me about Hitler's ethnic policies. "The Jewish persecutions started because plans for attacking the Reichstag last May were found among Jews. All Jews are of course Communists. The anarchist who set the blaze will never be caught. Why do Jews inspire so much sympathy? Their pockets soon fill with money, no matter how they are treated or where they migrate. Nazi expulsion of Jewish artists has not been indiscriminate," he insisted.

Hundwursten, Einstein called the Nazis. That I gleaned from Redvers Opie, a don at Oxford, while visiting his wife Catherine, Bill Taussig's sister. Playing violin-piano sonatas with me, Redvers described meeting Einstein at Princeton, where the two "fiddled for each other's amazement." Catherine was having her second child. The domestic scene revived my longing for a baby. I gave her the blue bootees, a long hoarded purchase, thereby surrendering hope. We took walks in the woods, read *Iphigenia* evenings, and enjoyed an amateur opera.

Greatly fortified I returned to London, only to find Conrad's shattering cable: "London letter describes you as quote on the town living in boarding house surrounded by earnest male students."

Whose slandering tongue had manufacturered that rubbish? Had Paul quoted my facetious remark to Ed Burra about the German student dishing out Nazi propaganda and Ed relayed it to Conrad? That was like pouring petrol on a bonfire. I wired: "Outraged stop cabling nonsense strictly faithful moving Anerley for your peace come back," despising myself for backing down.

Diary entry: "Is this insistence on tying down to Jeake's another manifestation of anxiety for his mother, who went 'gadding about,' neglecting the children?"

A backward look distills the humor of that hysterical odyssey on a Sunday. After spilling tears in a frigid room, I began hunting for the nearest Western Union office in freezing rain. The Charing Cross post office was closed. To save bus fare I walked to Fleet Street, found that branch also closed. Directed to the nearest one in Pall Mall, I started off, still sobbing, and got lost wandering up and down the Strand. A man followed me. I crossed the street. A car swerved to avoid me, the driver cursing. Finally I reached my destination, exhausted—a speeded-up movie of a bad melodrama.

What *was* Conrad to think when he heard I was on the town? It was typical of me, gravitating toward unattached young men. He assumed the hostel was for women only—a base canard. He said I had deceived him. Actually I never gave him that impression. I had paid for all my dinners, hadn't seen anyone not mentioned in my letters, and was tempted to end this ghastly life. "What hurts most," I wrote him, "is your distrust and readiness to believe others. When you left England, I hoped we might begin a new life. That hope nourished me until your cables and letters arrived, censuring my move to London, asking me to ignore your suspicions, then sending more devastating letters and a cable which implied I was a tart. My God, can't you ever think of anyone but yourself?"

His obsession with female infidelity has been noted widely by critics, yet I don't recall him ever telling me the best-kept secret, that I was supposed to be the unfaithful wife and Harry Murray the lover in both *Great Circle* and *King Coffin*. His latest letter referred to a deliberate cooling-off in Harry.

We leapt from one provocation to another, knocking chips off each other's shoulders. Conrad picked up my remark that H.D. couldn't fathom his tenacious hold on Jeake's House. He accused me of having let her pump me about our private life, his drinking, et cetera. I *had* been indiscreet at times, blurting out gratuitous information, but what I told Hilda, I felt, was warranted while the offer of analysis was still viable. And it was Conrad, not I, who told her about his suicide attempt. He admitted that her about-face was not because of anything she had heard, but rather what Hans Sachs told her, that he should find the money among some of his rich friends.

Conrad quoting a friend as saying he loved me too well touched off more fireworks. "Is that why you taught me a lesson by absenting yourself all night?" I wrote him. "An alcoholic would naturally resent my remark about drinking turning you into a Mr. Hyde. If you realized the misery it caused me, you would agree that I've been forbearing."

After two tender letters and a stone-crusher, Conrad wired: "You consider my peace belatedly stop talking to H.D. and others close house board cat sail Boston ninth Laconia tourist returning Rye March postpone Bernfeld until October."

I had previously dreamt of going to Boston but once there losing my nerve while calling on Conrad. Dr. Graham didn't have to remind me that I was still jumpy. But my plumbing had tightened up nicely since I stopped taking ergot. She gave me a blood-builder to correct anemia.

I cabled Conrad to expect me, though hardly anticipating a second honeymoon or being welcomed among his friends. I only hoped his summons wasn't just another tactic. "Try to greet me at the dock with a smile. I need one."

42

THE *Laconia* touched Boston in mid-December 1933. Conrad looked ravaged and his greeting was icy. "I sent for you in order to discuss divorce." No smile, hug, or kiss. In bleak silence we went through customs. In bleak silence we taxied to Cambridge along snow-banked streets, our cabby no doubt wondering what was amiss. A fool I was to have left England.

He lit a cigarette, ignoring my opening gambits: "We had a rough crossing. The children send love. Squidge, too. Mr. Hale did a good job on the rock garden, but trimmed too much off the honeysuckle. I've written all the Christmas cards except those you usually do." His stony profile dried up further confidences—all the funny, sad, and exciting experiences on shipboard.

As for my encounter with the Welsh surgeon, Dr. Llewelyn (he in a body cast and on crutches, the victim of a car smashup), that would have been construed as spiritual infidelity. But oh the relief of unburdening to a stranger, pouring out an avalanche of pent-up emotions.

"Seems to me that you're little more than a sex object to your husband," said Dr. Llewelyn. "He hasn't solved his Oedipus problems. Why do you stay with him?" I said because I loved him. "You're how old—thirty-four? That gives you two or three more years. Once sex is burnt out, he'll consider you excess baggage. Leave him before he leaves you." I said I couldn't, he needed me. "Take the midnight train to New York and return to England aboard the *Laconia*. I'll be returning and will expect you." No, I said, I couldn't.

The taxi drew up at Hampden Hall, where our affair began seven years earlier. I followed Conrad into the elevator with a sense of déjà vu. He unlocked the fifth-floor apartment I once rented, dropped my suitcase, and poured himself a drink. I could have used one, too, though I hadn't yet recovered my land legs. I was about to unpack when he began a replay of his letters, blasting me for my move to London, deserting Jeake's House while he was struggling to keep alive. Something precious had come to an end, he said. I had let him down again, just when he needed special care, if not sacrifice.

True. I could have done that much for him. The uncertainties of a Freudian analysis combined with our whole future had worried me also. After Bryher withdrew her offer to underwrite him, I put out feelers in London to find another angel. Margaret and Paul scouted for Conrad, proffering an Aiken, Ltd. Corporation project. Much as he shrank from renting Jeake's, it would help toward making Vienna possible. I had advertised in *Lady* magazine and *Dalton's*.

". . . I'm simply terrified at the idea of losing Jeake's," Conrad said. "You've always taken advantage of my absence." His voice was harsh and cutting. "The minute I leave, you're off like a shot from the gun. You crave constant attention. We had the same difficulties in 1928. Your sketchy, hollow, insincere letters forced me to believe you were concealing a great deal, seeing people I didn't approve of, getting mixed up with a loose crowd of Communists like the Legges . . . "

"Now wait a minute," I broke in hotly, "you're talking kitsch. You don't even know them. How can you judge them?" (By the next decade he was on friendly terms with the Legges.) He condoned Vernon, a deep-dyed Communist, because of Deirdre, but condemned Stuart, a film documentor, for subscribing to *The Worker*. "I haven't had your temptations, living in Creighton's love nest on Beacon Hill. Nobody has 'glad-kneed' or solicited me. No strange midnight visitors slipped into my room from the fire escape. I've had no such wild parties as you described in Walter Piston's studio, couples swapping partners and vanishing into darkened bedrooms, ex-lovers trying to recapture their mistresses, a nymphomaniac stalking you, and all the rest of it . . ."

"I've seen enough drunken parties to know what happens to women who are footloose and bored," he said. "Uncle Alfred was right in telling me it was fatal to separate."

Well, who left whom? He made me dizzy, pacing back and forth. "Your concern doesn't spring from love but from the hope of catching me out. I'm all too safe with young sophisticates like the Legges," I added, longing for a cigarette but too proud to ask. "Why do *you* consort with cads and wastrels like Bill Nickerson?"

"Oh bilge," Conrad said. "*Your* morals, not *mine*, are in question. I've got troubles enough without your complicating my life. Worry about you is the final straw. A happily married woman is careful to be chaperoned in her husband's absence."

"Happily married—who, *me*?" I would have laughed but for his anguished state. "Here's something to celebrate our so happy reunion," I said, and I brought out the champagne a pathetic little Rotarian had won in a paper-dog race.

The blue eyes hardened. "Which of your gentlemen friends gave you this?" Before I could explain, he spun around, opened the window, and sent the bottle crashing below. I shuddered. Suppose it had hit someone? Oh what was the use?

I grabbed my handbag and flew downstairs to make a phone call. Would my sister-in-law sanction Dr. Llewelyn's idea of returning on the *Laconia*? The operator was ringing the number when I had a chilling presentiment. I ran upstairs, too frightened to wait for the elevator. Conrad sat at the kitchen table writing a farewell note to John. Oh my God, not another crisis! I should have known after his signal: "I'm in a state of deep depression, can't sleep or talk or hear what people say . . ."

The instant I flung my arms around him, he broke down, wracked with sobs. Head buried in his hands, he wept just as Carl had after returning from the woods with the pistol still loaded. Incessant weeping, Conrad predicted, would be his final fate. Patch up our differences. Compromise. Try again. The alternative was unthinkable.

"I'm almost ashamed to mention it," he said, making love that night, "but I fear I love you so much that I would still want you even though you had an affair."

Whatever held us together came alive. Rancor and tension subsided in his arms. Perhaps his suicide threat would still bring us closer. I couldn't picture life without him, couldn't get enough of him, wanted to see him every day or, that impossible, to hear his voice on the phone. I distrusted his love, but I would never get him out of my system.

"Our whole future may depend on what you do," he said later.

Since he needed more time to raise funds, our return to England was postponed. Many years later I learned that he had asked his brothers for the two hundred and fifty shares of First Investment Counsel Corporation stock. Rob told me, "I begged him not to touch those securities, but he said he simply had to have the money fast. So he cashed in the stock through redemption. The sad saga of his small fortune coming and going— a complete wipeout, including the $2,500 loan from Kempton."

Kemp had embittered Conrad by suggesting that his writing wasn't work, that he had better give it up for real work, as though literary creation were not the most exhausting and thankless job, a poorly paid career fraught with anxiety. What grieved him, Conrad said, "was having the classic example of the philistine toward art crop up so close to home."

He greeted 1934 with a wry "Happy New Year, if you can find one!" We arrived late for dinner at the Brimmer Street home of Professor Samuel

Eliot Morison, the historian. Liquor flowed on every occasion. Repeal was the magic word on everyone's lips after a fifteen-year drought.

Another evening at a friend's apartment we heard John Cowper Powys expound his pet theory of trees and boulders possessing souls. After a lengthy discourse the British mystic, spying Conrad in the corner of the room, boomed, "Don't you agree, Aiken?" Everyone hung on the answer. He opened a bleary eye and said, "No," with deflating effect.

We renewed contact with the world, Conrad a controversial figure, *Blue Voyage* having lost him his tutorial job while *Great Circle* provoked a minor furor. Paul Nash said his name would be mud among Rye's pious fuddyduds. Over here the novel was being parodied as the "Harvard Square *Hamlet*."

Divorce was in the air that spring. Several couples we knew were splitting up, Maurice for the second time. "Good husbands are as scarce as good jobs," I wrote my sister Gertrude, who had finally become engaged, at twenty-five, to her future husband. "Do let it take this time." I felt guilty not visiting the family; having the flu was no excuse. She said my letter was the most sisterly one in a long time. The perfect housekeeper, she put me to shame looking after Father and doing more than her share of drudgery.

A staid married couple, Conrad and I raised no eyebrows at Sanders Theatre concerts, lectures in Emerson Hall, or browsing in the Widener, where his uncle was still librarian. Social affairs generated high spirits and released the coquette in me. That in turn activated the puritan in Conrad. With one to two close friends he scintillated; otherwise he crept into his shell, a captive audience at parties and acutely self-conscious. I remember exasperating him at the Robert Hillyers' in Cambridge, "flirting outrageously with the Harvard faculty," he claimed, his tolerance decreasing with his alcoholic intake. As we headed toward Brattle Street he booted me—my first and only kick in the rear—and from a gentleman. My startled indignation would have struck him as comical had he been sober.

I couldn't return the gesture tit-for-tat when he flirted with our host's blonde lady friend at the Longwood indoor tennis matches in Chestnut Hill. Conrad paid her such marked attention that I finally got up in pique and said I was leaving. "Oh must you go, darling?" he asked blandly.

"We can't love without possessiveness," he once told me. "We must rediscover the virtue of jealousy." Neither one needed any prompting.

Decades afterward I won the friendship of the beautiful blonde poet. We laughed at my possessiveness. She told me there were rumors in those days that Conrad was on the loose. One evening after being plied with liquor in his friend's apartment, she woke up and found him sitting on the bed, stroking her brow.

By May he had scraped together $1,800 and begun *Landscape West of Eden*. When we sailed back to England—our cabin directly over the propeller—I was pregnant for the second time, and assailed by qualms. What of Dr. Graham's warnings?

Part Four

43

IT WAS A HAPPIER HOMECOMING this time. We saw Rye through a rainbow—red-tiled houses higgledy-piggledy, gulls flying from the church spire as the gilded quarter-boys struck the hour, Mermaid Street cobbles sprouting new grass, the Virginia ivy blanketing Jeake's House up to the chimney, the brass knocker shining on the scarlet door.

Mrs. Hilder greeted us with an ingratiating smile and a bandaged hand. It had become infected after a neighbor's sick cat scratched her. She had taken good care of the house and Squidge. He twisted and circled in ecstasy. "What idiot said that cats don't like people?" Conrad remarked, picking him up and stroking him.

Unpacking upstairs, I laid aside some discards for Mrs. Hilder. She tried on a yellow straw hat, remonstrating, "Oh that's much too nice for the likes of me, Mrs. Aiken. Besides, where would I get a chance to wear it?" Her eyes lit up at my good news. "Oh that's wonderful, dear, just wonderful, I'm so happy for you."

My heart light as thistledown, I went into the garden. Mr. and Mrs. Starling were making housekeeping plans in the pear tree. Conrad stood by the rope swing on the lower terrace, smoking and listening to the caterwauling over the wall. "I suppose the most exquisite lyrics sound like that to God," he said.

"Are you giving birth to a poem?" I leaned against him. "Put your arms around me before they won't meet, and say something nice."

He tossed away his cigarette, twiddled an eyebrow, and said sheepishly, "Oh to be oviperous, now that spring is here."

I counted on his strong paternal feelings. He liked the idea of an off-spring, provided we could afford another mouth to feed. The infant's squalls would probably drive him crazy. I glanced up at Jane's room, the future nursery. Would the children tolerate another half-brother or sister? Jessie's son by Martin was now three. Had she welcomed it as joyfully?

Friends reacted variously to my news. Norah rejoiced, saying wistfully, "I'd like so much to have a child." But Peggy Farr, like Margaret, had misgivings. As for Deirdre, I could imagine her reaction: Breeding was obscene and selfish, Conrad would lose interest in me. With his need of being mothered and fear of surrendering to a female, that was a distinct possibility.

Keeping my appointment with Dr. Graham I felt abashed. "Yes, you're three months' pregnant," she said, displeased after examining me. "Where was your diaphragm?" Forgotten in the heat of passion, I said. "Don't scold me." She ruled out tennis and bicycling among other precautions. "Normally, having a first child at thirty-five carries little risk, but you probably won't carry this one to term."

My euphoria shaken, I shopped for infants' wear all the same, before lunching with Margaret in her Saint Pancras flat. She gave me salmon patties and a stern lecture, reviewing all the reasons against having a child, primarily the possibility of inherited mental defects. "I can't see you raising one in such precarious circumstances, Clarissa, and it's not fair or realistic expecting a baby to salvage a marriage."

I had been ambivalent about the whole thing until I needed a child to bring us together—the worst of all reasons. Conrad was enough responsibility for any woman, Margaret said. "I hate to dim those stars in your eyes, my dear, but there are worse things than being childless."

She shook her head when I asked if she missed Rye. "Paul and I adore London. It has everything our hearts desire."

Back in Rye, my domestic seizures increased. I experimented with hazel hen and widgeon, Indian curries, sweetbreads in Béchamel sauce. I pampered Conrad with calf's brains and mushroom caps in sherry-flavored cream. I knitted baby clothes, started an orange pullover, laid out dress patterns. With my child in mind as a future pupil, I guided Squidge's paws over the keys, picking out the thematic intervals of Scarlatti's *Cat Fugue*.

I must have forgotten Dr. Graham's warnings when I talked Peggy into bicycling. Whizzing through the ancient Landgate, she shouted, "Remember, keep to the left, ducky, and mind the lorries."

It was a glorious blue-gold day, the air balmy and with a tang of the sea. We skimmed along Romney Marsh, surprising a heron, flushing crows and gulls. At a tollgate we paid a farthing, a custom dating to A.D. 900, when Rye and Winchelsea were islands—a quaint tradition, like getting a row of pins in lieu of a farthing change at the draper's.

Later, maneuvering our bicycles on the saffron shingle along the Channel, I stopped to gather bedstraw, bugloss, and trefoil, and Peggy said, amused, "You can't just leave wild flowers alone, can you?" I grinned. "The vandal in me." We sat below the dunes, eating egg and cucumber sandwiches.

I got home fagged and in a sweat after pedaling miles and miles, pushing the bicycle up a steep hill. Mrs. Hilder, shelling peas, said Conrad had gone to the movies in Hastings. Squidge meowed for food and got underfoot. "You're a nuisance," I scolded, filling his saucer, then cut up liver and lights, wincing at the bloody mess as usual.

While taking a bath I began to hemorrhage. Oh God. Now what? Wrapped in my robe, I went downstairs and called Mrs. Hilder. She turned pale and cried, "Hurry and put your feet up, dear," settling me in the garden wicker chair. "I'll bring the hot-water bottle and fetch the doctor."

And so I lost my baby. As with the abortion, I was three months pregnant. My ambivalence in ignoring the doctor's precautions while longing for a child was commonplace enough—a subconscious impulse to abort partly from fear of a mentally defective child, partly from fear of childbirth (Mother's close brush with death, I a breech case).

I'm sure Conrad expressed sympathy, though I don't recall any special tenderness. Perhaps he felt secretly relieved. Anyhow, I read into his restraint a feeling that I had forfeited my last chance of womanhood, postponing responsibility to remain a child and play games, like Nora in Ibsen's *Doll House*.

The trauma of my miscarriage ran deep, persisting for years. From then on, I could never quite free myself from Conrad's influence. Infants and children haunted my dreams. An empty crib stood between our twin beds. Babies were snatched from my arms. I pushed empty prams uphill, shopped repeatedly for maternity gowns (all of them too small in the middle). I climbed through windows, strayed into homes uninvited at Christmas, was tried and convicted of infanticide. Guilt had me by the throat.

Music provided solace as always, and making music transcended listening to it. Playing chamber music with the Sewards, Peggy Farr's neighbors at Starvecrow, filled a vacuum, despite a tiresome host.

Financial problems buzzed around us like flies around carrion. Conrad really couldn't have afforded a child. Taxes gobbled up half the advance for *Great Circle*, the book admired by Freud and reviewed by Aldous Huxley as "a remarkable novel written with perfect taste and an astonishing verbal felicity." The occasional $80 check as London correspondent for the *New Yorker* was in jeopardy, the editors reluctant to pay Conrad's hotel expenses. He feared getting the sack after the Wimbledon tennis matches were over.

We were working on *La Mujer de Sal* one August afternoon when he flung the volume across the room, exploding, "I'm sick of this puking thing! That I should have to be doing hack work, at forty-five, and going on from this to reporting tennis by cable . . ." I suggested, imprudently, that he had a lot to be thankful for. "Yes, haven't I?" he said, glaring through his black-rimmed glasses. "My works are all best-sellers, I have a famous reputation all over the world, the critics sing my praises, I've got plenty of money, and a devoted family surrounding me, not to mention perfect health. Fuck *you* and your pollyanna platitudes."

I picked up the offending volume and left the room, hurt but empathizing. If published, the novel translated would yield only a pittance of the net royalties. His moodiness was warranted. He was living so close to madness, all his energy going into creating poems out of suffering—like the mythological bird feeding on its own flesh—and exposing his viscera to an indifferent public. "He is one of the few great poets of our time," said Malcolm Cowley, "and he has received less attention than dozens of little poets . . ."

When my profile of Fletcher appeared in the Boston *Transcript*, I was relieved that the poet was in the States beyond reach and unable to contaminate Conrad with his gloom. By October 1934 he was in no position to afford analysis with Bernfeld or anyone else. (Freud was then a British exile, safe from the horror of the Nazis but not that of a cancerous mouth.)

The bone-chilling winter found Conrad afflicted with sciatica and catarrh, I with low back pain, at times bent over like a croquet hoop. Conrad implied I was malingering. I took his lectures lying down, and one day while stretched out on the couch complained about the Virginia ivy loosening the bricks, causing dampness to seep into the house. "It's ruinous for an arthritic, if not for your ailments," I said. "If Jessie never said anything, she couldn't have had arthritis."

"Oh bilge," Conrad said. "How can a few loose bricks or stones make that much difference? It's just your imagination."

"Is it only imagination that the counterpane on our bed is soaking wet in the morning? I'm only saying the creeper contributes to the dampness. Didn't I hear your doctor advise you to have the vine cut down?"

"I won't have that ivy touched, you understand?" He stood glowering at me. "You'll regret it if you disobey me. Nothing must be altered."

His obsession with Jeake's House continued to baffle me. But I needed treatment at once. Margaret pleaded with me to see a bone-setter in London. Mr. Rabey had performed miracles with war casualties. "Your health is more important than Conrad's prejudices," she added, when I said he wouldn't like the idea. "You must get help."

Since he refused to remove the ivy, I removed myself to London, entering Rabey's nursing home. Never before had I been so "deared" as in that cozy, congenial ward. "Will you have a haddock for breakfast, dear? . . .Did you have a good night, dear? . . . Is that position comfy, dear? . . . " A cancer patient my age showed me her shroud, a white china-silk nightgown embroidered with a blue dove of peace, white silk stockings, and a cake of Yardley's lavender soap. "If you come prepared," she said, "nothing happens."

Free from pain at the end of a fortnight, I felt so marvelous walking upright once more that I began speculating about adopting a child. Mr. Rabey agreed with the local doctor that the ivy had best be eliminated. That bolstered my resolve. To argue with Conrad further was useless. Accordingly, the next time he was in London I had the nurseryman cut down part of the creeper.

The expected storm turned into a hurricane. "How dare you countermand my orders? The children will never forgive you. They loved that ivy. Typical treachery, confronting me with a fait accompli." He raged when I reminded him of leasing Jeake's without consulting me. "Stick to the subject, damn you, with your *tu quoque* . . . Oh what's the use, I'm through talking to a stone wall."

I was ignored, given the silent treatment—or, as the English say, sent to Coventry. But it had its advantages. I got things off my chest, filibustering to my silent partner, and imitated him by holding monologues with the cat. "Did you swipe my scissors, Squidge, or did a pixie steal them?" A cough or sneeze had the impact of a thunderclap in the eerie stillness. Faint sounds were amplified—the hiss of a burning log, the death-watch beetles calling their mates in beams and walls. When I practiced on the organ at Saint Mary's the steeple clock ticked "Doom, doom, Doom, doom," the long brass pendulum swinging above the choir like a sword of Damocles. Playing with the diapasons full out one day, I brought the vicar bustling in to ask if I were trying to raise the dead. No, only the living.

Christmas was bleak, even with the children sharing part of it. John had passed his scholarship exams and would continue at London University College, much to Conrad's disappointment as a Harvard alumnus. Difficulties with both John and Jane dampened the holiday cheer. Conrad was out of tune with everybody, withdrawing from me and disliking himself increasingly—a fertile season to begin *King Coffin*, a novel about a cuckolded husband bent on killing a stranger at random, then taking his own life on finding the victim's wife having a stillborn baby. "We're all murderers at heart," he once said. I remembered Margaret Nash telling me (exaggerating?) that he had thrown Jane as a bawling baby out of the window.

The day Conrad took me out of Coventry he said, "You look just like a mud turtle." No doubt. Wives should wear masks. A cynic's acid test of marriage is whether you can sit across from the same face at breakfast for five years without wanting to smash it.

I now dreaded the cycle of creativity but would not go to extremes to avoid friction. Docility only inflamed Conrad the more. Each scene dimmed the glow of romance. He was trapped; the man had fallen in love, the poet found marriage intolerable.

> It's the endless repetition of what should very seldom be repeated. . . . By god, no matter how much you love a woman, the time comes when you don't want to sleep with her. For a while, anyway. Or at any rate one wants holidays. But how are you going to manage it. You can't say to your wife, Darling, I'm fed up with you—I know your body too well—the toes, the knees, the flanks, the moles, the hollows under the clavicles, the median line, the asymmetrical arrangement of your breasts, the pelvis, the pink patch of eczema on your side, your perfumes and undergarments and brushes and combs, your toilet habits, every one, the faint bubble of caught breath with which you fall asleep—but just the same I love you, will always love you. If only you'll be tactful and not too exacting about this. Don't ask questions, darling, whatever you do. Don't say a word. Sing cheerfully as you go about the house, greet me with the happiness of the lark when I come home, be busy, have lots of things to do, put no pressure upon me, don't betray by so much as the flicker of an eyelash that you're aware of the fact that I've abandoned you (but not geographically)—and who knows, one fine night . . . who knows? Everything might suddenly become beautiful and strange once more. You would be a stranger to me, and I to you; we would commit a joyful infidelity with each other; each of us would be new. Hell's delight, that's only the beginning of it. The fringe.
>
> *Great Circle*

Now and then a miracle came to pass. Conrad always knew what I was thinking, or so he claimed, and what I would say or do. Lacking such telepathy myself, I was taken pleasantly by surprise when he told me I was beautiful. Immediately I *felt* beautiful, rushing across the room and smothering him with kisses.

Making love that night, he said, "I can always be reached by affection." Well, who can't? We exchanged pledges as ephemeral as soap bubbles. Was it a good or bad sign that Deirdre's visits had tapered off? I could forgive him anything but infidelity.

44

THE SPRING of 1935 was the coldest in a century. Winter's ironclad grip seemed endless. We shivered intermittently until June, and welcomed the arrival of summer.

We had sublet Jeake's House to a Lady Beasley, thankful to be joining Harold and Laura Knight at the Malvern theatre festival in August. It was to be a holiday. It would also, I hoped, be the occasion for a glimpse of—perhaps an introduction to—G. B. Shaw, my idol. Laura had promised to try to arrange a meeting with the semirecluse, but warned that he was a terrible tease and could be very rude. "Go away, no I have no message for America," he roared, giving an American newshen the brushoff. "Read my plays and you have the story of my life." Doing so only whetted my appetite.

Before leaving for Malvern, Conrad and I took a breather from worry, making the rounds of art galleries and museums in London, saw a movie or two, and dined with Malcolm's friend John Davenport. He promised to con away the Preludes from Dent's (who kept them almost a year) and submit *Time in the Rock* to Heinemann's. Except for the monocle, Davenport resembled Malcolm strikingly—lusty, robust, dynamic. Malcolm was still living in Manhattan squalor, and had himself admitted to Bellevue, a ten-day "cure" to be documented in *Lunar Caustic* and *Under the Volcano*.

The long trip to Worcestershire by bus was exhausting. After we reached Malvern a taxi took us through suburbia past high hedges enclosing ugly stone houses to the Kinnersley, a small inn with a superb view of the Cotswolds. The only male guest, Conrad chafed, a restive captive without proper facilities like a shaving mirror. He was also plagued by an abscessed tooth that had bothered him for two months while reporting Wimbledon. From the first morning, when he said he'd have whatever was the *pièce de résistance*, the coy, beady-eyed madam addressed him as "Your Lordship." We planned to stay there a week working on the translation of *La Mujer de Sal*, before making the two-mile transfer to Great Malvern.

We welcomed the move and were happy as grigs to see the Knights. They had sold some paintings and looked fit and tanned. Laura's blue eyes glimmered. "We'll have a royal binge." The memoir was going well, she said; she had a publisher, and she and I would work on it together in London. Harold found lodgings for us at The Three Arches, a picturesque ruin which Conrad renamed The Fallen Arches after the food deteriorated. At any rate, Conrad was handy to The Unicorn, the favorite pub among the theatre players.

Malvern nestled in the Wych Valley, burgeoning with tourists, mountain climbers, and playgoers. Sir Barry Jackson, impresario and founder of the festival, produced a four-week repertory season primarily Shavian—a profitable circus to the natives, who queued up at the theatre to ogle and mimic Shaw's fans. We saw four plays, by no means his best. "If he ate a good thick raw steak once in a while," Conrad suggested, "and had a good thick raw affair with some barmaid, he might inject a little blood into his plays." Harold demurred. "What about *Saint Joan*, written at sixty-seven? Shaw's not the first playwright to make you think, but he gives you a chaser with the bitter medicine. God knows, Ibsen never handed his audience any laughs."

Hear, hear, I said, trotting out some Shavian witticisms.

Laura often lunched with the Shaws. She had sold Shaw a watercolor depicting a concert audience, a fatuous face in one corner, inspired by a remark made to Harold Samuel, the pianist, "I *love* Bach, he's so soothing." Her portrait of him, exhibited at the Royal Academy the previous year, looked like a cross between God and a malicious satyr, said Sir Cedric Hardwicke.

Deck-chair loungers lining terraces and balconies at Malvern watched in vain for the lean, angular figure in the gray Norfolk jacket. At seventy-nine, Shaw no longer took morning strolls, much less climbed the Worcester Beacon for a view of the Black Mountains in Wales, which we four did do. The Shaws had been ill, Laura explained, and were still mourning their protégé T. E. Lawrence, killed in May on the motorbike they had given him.

When at last she pinned Shaw down for tea, I had the dithers. He had snubbed an American socialite who offered him passage to the States if he would dine with her. What chance had I? What could a naive provincial say to an intellectual giant who disliked Americans? And couldn't bear being interrupted?

Long before four-thirty I stood watch at the Mt. Pleasant Hotel, clutching my camera. Harold paced the garden room, Laura smoked Kensitas and commiserated with Conrad, whose infected tooth (and no doubt the occasion itself) had him miserable. "There they come," I whispered, galvanizing attention on the sedate couple trudging up the steep incline past the mulberry tree, Charlotte in a dark blue coat and straw hat, "a ladylike person at whom nobody would ever look twice," to quote her husband, he armed with an umbrella, an older Shaw, but still looking like an overgrown schoolboy in knickerbockers.

Laura introduced us. He gave Conrad a piercing glance and me a fleeting one, then dropped into a chair, fanning himself with his panama, "Whew, it's time Malvern had funiculars," he said in a light baritone with an Irish lilt. "After all, they're artistic enough in themselves." His white hair and beard looked freshly laundered and his face had a peculiar pink pallor except for the rosy, drooping line of the cheek. I had overheard a bus passenger say that his nose wasn't so red this year, but there was still some red in his beard.

Harold shared the sofa with Charlotte. What inner turmoil that stolid figure concealed, I mused, living in the great man's shadow. They brightened when the tea tray came, with sandwiches, milk, and an apple for the master. He broke it in two and drank his milk like a man.

"Whenever I'm told something has been especially prepared for me, I notice everybody helps himself first," Shaw complained. He reached for a cucumber sandwich, frowning at Laura's cigarette, ash dropping on her yellow frock as she poured tea. What was to be the climax of my long pursuit began and ended with a nonstop monologue brooking no interruptions.

"I seem to be losing my memory—can't remember a person five minutes after meeting him. One of these days I'll see Charlotte in the street and ask who she is. I'm certainly becoming more solitary, but as I grow older I find I have no great need of people."

"Mr. Shaw," I began timidly as he munched another sandwich, "your plays . . ."

"Some people can't bear to be alone. That's what's wrong with actors. They're afraid to be by themselves, with nothing to do daytimes. And if they have, there's no energy left at night for their performances. I had an actress who refused to stay in bed until noon, refused to be pampered. Instead she went about doing social-service work, and do you know her charm began to vanish as her performance fell off. Actors are such spoofs," he said with a mock grimace. "It takes a playwright to impress character on them. They've really got no personality . . ."

On and on he droned, Harold's grizzled head, Laura's flaxen one, and Conrad's russet one gradually sinking. The sun also. Slipping behind the hills, it turned the crimson sofa to drab red, fading the bright blue walls of the orangery. I tried to catch Conrad's eye, hoping for verbal fireworks, but the poor wretch was nursing his swollen cheek.

". . . and the critics dissatisfied with *Fanny's First Play* were those I had omitted to caricature in the epilogue. It's quite true," Shaw continued, "you can caricature a man on the stage so precisely that his identity is unmistakable, and he will feel flattered. But if you're writing an autobiography, in England at any rate, you can be malicious only to a certain extent, calling somebody a pig or swine or old goat. But if you say his check's no good, or that he keeps two domestic establishments, you're hauled into court. Now, an autobiography is a dull book unless you're malicious, and unless you disclose yourself subtly it's like a bad photograph."

He finished his milk, glanced at his gold watch, whistled, got to his feet, murmuring, "It's six o'clock, my dear, we must go," and did so, picking up his hat and umbrella.

Dear God, was this all there was, after my years of hopes and exertions? Not even an autograph? I aimed my Leica at the trio, as Laura accompanied her guests part way, Shaw striding between the two ladies and dwarfing them.

Later, at The Unicorn, in need of a bracer, we drained pewter mugs of golden ale, I wailing my disenchantment. "Those cold, impersonal blue eyes, that icy, detached manner—does he ever communicate?"

With close friends, yes, said Harold. "Don't be too hard on him. The Shaw you saw today isn't the real one. He's had a bad year. Did you expect him to embrace you the way Laura does everybody?"

"No," I said, with a meaningful look at Conrad, "only to be aware of me." My paragon a paradox, I removed his halo, only to replace it after learning more about him. His public image, he told T. E. Lawrence, was his greatest work of fiction.

Robert Payne, who knew the couple well, told me years later that he found Shaw to be as wonderful as Charlotte was tiresome. So that starry-eyed, infatuated schoolgirl hadn't been so far off after all in pronouncing GBS that rarity, a humane genius.

45

MALVERN, our last excursion together, acted as a tonic. We could never repay the Knights for their lavish hospitality. Dined and wined every evening, Haig & Haig and Liebfraumilch flowing along with amusing anecdotes, we met fabulous people, some of whom were to prove fruitful contacts for Conrad.

But our financial situation was no better. I had sent off begging letters without his knowledge. One went to Bob Linscott, another to the incipient American Academy of Poets, raising funds for life endowments. I suggested they transfer Conrad's name from the list of sponsors to that of supplicants. "If the Academy materializes, would you be interested in guaranteeing my husband an income of say £500 for a period of five years in return for royalties until the advance is paid off?" A proposal he had submitted to other individuals. "Despite the strains and stresses of the Depression years," I wrote, "he produced two novels, a volume of short stories, four volumes of verse, and sundry criticism. We have now exhausted all our resources at a time when he is ill and in urgent need of help."

September brought his dental ordeal, the second molar extracted, and he was in "the goddamnedest agony" when the ethyl chloride wore off. The dentist had sprayed it, not daring to inject. I bought Conrad some rye. It had seen me through a similar emergency. On that occasion he berated me for "wallowing in self-pity and making a big fuss over nothing."

The tables turned, I commiserated with him. He insisted that the wrong tooth had been pulled. "My resistance is lowering with age," he told John, who was present. "I'll probably have to have all my teeth out, and then I'll blow out my brains." Ed Burra failed to defuse the atmosphere by suggesting that he might be cutting new ones. My tactless remark was no help either. "You might bear pain better if you had it more often."

"Have *you* had an ear infection or a fractured skull or two tail operations?" No, I said, just dental complications, arthritis, an abortion, and a miscarriage.

Mrs. Hilder danced attendance on Conrad all afternoon, running to High Street several times for the right flavor of ice cream, then down to the fishmonger in the Strand for ice. By six o'clock he had finished the whiskey and was ranting like one delirious. He wanted dinner at six-thirty, then after watching me clean a widgeon, a favorite of his, ran down our neighbors to John, who sat in the garden swing acutely embarrassed, having heard them stir next door.

At the table Conrad sampled the wild pigeon and spat out a mouthful. "Are you *insane*, serving food with sharp bones to a patient with a mouth wound?" I apologized. He demanded an omelet. I made one. He threw it up.

John retired early. I sat upstairs reading Chekhov, my heart thumping, one ear cocked on Conrad's movements. His rapid mood alterations kept me off guard. I couldn't adjust fast enough, never knew what to expect next. Presently he came lurching into the drawing room. "I *hate* you," he said. "One of these days I'm going to slit your throat. But first I have an important truth to reveal." What was it? I asked, removing my reading glasses. "I'll tell you when I'm bloody ready. But perhaps it's *too* important to tell." I didn't have to guess, having found blonde hairpins on the sofa. His inquisitions had ceased; his frequent absences and evasions told me plainly I was being eased out of his life. Our marriage was unraveling like the orange pullover I never finished.

How fine the line between angel and devil. When I stopped feeding his genius I dropped out of step with him. I mourned the Conrad others knew. "'E's a real kind, thoughtful gentleman what would go out of the way to be kind; not many like 'im, sir," the pubkeeper's wife told Malcolm Lowry.

I developed the jitters. Easily rattled and increasingly forgetful, I mixed up envelopes, sending a check to my errant young brother in Milwaukee and an admonishing letter to the local cleaners. Both were returned with large question marks.

Mrs. Hilder had been getting on Conrad's nerves. He said her jeremiads reminded him of the Wailing Wall women in Honegger's *Judith*. He wanted her sacked. I procrastinated, while irked by her habit of slipping home for "just five minutes." She was a good-hearted woman and dependable. Delivering the verdict I felt a brute, as with Mrs. Kipp, and wept too, seeing tears drop into the parsley she chopped.

Olive, my next daily, was a pretty brunette with an ambition to fold napkins into bishops' mitres. After serving as parlor maid to Lady Bountiful on the hill, Jeake's was a comedown for her. Her ladyship's relationship with Edward VII, father of George V, was one of those well-kept secrets in gossipy Rye, where every tidbit was avidly passed on. A threadbare one involved a skeptical old steward, new on the job, who failed to recognize His Majesty at the gate. "Aye," he said waggishly, winking at the august visitor, "I understand a king comes through here every day."

"Grannikins" to her family, she was quite temperamental, Olive confided. The housekeeper told her that in sixty years of service she had seen her ladyship occupy his lordship's bedroom only twice "and then during tempests."

Music was the only bond between me and Lady Bountiful, a soloist at Saint Mary's Church. Thanks to Mr. Williams, I had a job as organist at the twelfth-century Norman church in Icklesham, five miles from Rye. All my hopes were pinned on making good. After the service, I would browse in the little churchyard, jotting down epitaphs for Conrad.

I had secretly written Dr. Taylor in Cambridge to inquire about child adoption. He held out little hope, quoting a *New Yorker* cartoon captioned, "My dear, you know there's the *worst* shortage of illegitimate children now!" A colleague of his had a thousand applications and failed to see a suitable infant in six months. More to the point, Dr. Taylor was inclined to agree with two British physicians who advised me against applying further. A history of mental illness on both sides was definitely unfavorable.

Conrad was in better spirits as he bent an elbow with Walter Piston, who paid us a brief visit. They played chess and Ping-Pong, engaged in witty conversation and genial banter.

We gave our guest a plausible performance of compatibility, lest some of our friends in the States hear about a marriage on the rocks. After he had gone, the oppressive climate thickened with our sparring matches. By December we were sleeping in separate rooms, Conrad affronted when his snores or alcoholic harangues drove me into the guest room. I packed my bag several times and started to leave. Each time something pulled me back. Unhappy wives stick it out, fearing abandonment, change, and the unknown, or because of financial-emotional dependence. My feelings paralleled Dorothy Thompson's exactly: "Whenever I separate from Hal it is as though I came out of a delirium into sanity, out of a maelstrom into a quiet place. And yet my heart goes rushing for him as he careens his way outward."

Leave him, I would tell myself. No, no, he'd be there all alone. Don't fret, he'd find company fast enough. Don't take his guff to heart, Peggy Farr advised. "All intellectuals downgrade women. And for the love of God, stop being a doormat. Where's your spunk? Give him a little of his own back. He'll respect you for it."

The attacks went on, outbursts of violence, fluctuations and irrational conduct I couldn't handle, but challenging nevertheless. "Better to be stung by a nettle than pricked by a rose," an English proverb admonishes. One night when Conrad tried to goad me into fighting (as he often had Malcolm) I sat sewing silently. He threw a book at me, then said tartly as I stood up, "I notice you walk out whenever I have something interesting to say. I *am* interesting, if you but knew it."

That was a clue I missed. The pathos of his statement stopped me at the door. "You're fascinating. But you're also cruel, and you don't love me," I said. "With so much power you could afford to be kinder."

"Putting a pistol to my head again, Madame Ovary?" His pun on Flaubert's heroine had cropped up more often lately. "Demanding love just like Jessie? You should know by now that's fatal."

Love is cruelty. Love is hate. Love is a desire to revenge yourself. It's a bloody great butcher's cleaver. . . . Its will is destruction: it tears out the heart of the beloved, in order that its own heart may break. Love is murder. It's a suicide pact, and all for what? All for death. . . . Our little domestic death. It's a ballet. See them go to bed together—listen to them murmuring adoration— hear them whisper and kiss—O God, all that silken sinuousity and hypocrisy and ecstasy . . . and all of it a thin masque to cover the raw red tomb-face of primordial hatred. Skull purring at skull, death's-head kissing death's-head, the caress a strangle, consummation a swordthrust. It's killed me: I'm dead. I've eaten my father's skeleton and I'm dead. I shall never love again, any more than I'll ever be able to stop loving. Christ, what a fix we're in. Help- less. Burn off our hands. Drink ourselves into permanent unconsciousness . . . In the spring the young libido lightly turns to thoughts of lust. Pressure of the seminal vesicles . . .

Great Circle

What rebuttal was there? He had all the answers, disarming his oppo- nent. When my sister-in-law wrote me that at times she hated my brother with frightening violence, I understood all too well. Love needs mutual respect to survive, but hate begets hate. It took me a long time to discover how much Conrad distrusted and hated women while lusting after them. "The deadly female thing," he capsuled the theme of *Conversation*, a later novel, "working itself into the superior position and drawing the male to

bed, even persuading him that he was the one who thought of it, by
gosh." A Don Juan persecuted by the flirtations of his wife, the eternal
Lorelei trapping man.

46

O N THE FIRST SUNDAY in January I started for Icklesham, leaving
Conrad at the breakfast table tracing the Aiken genealogy for his
children. The Raleigh wobbled perilously, buffeted by a nor'easter. I had
to push it uphill past Winchelsea, a jewel-like Channel glittering in the
brilliant sunshine. My thoughts were on the previous Sabbath, when I
mixed up the order of the service, playing the *Gloria* after the *Te Deum*.
No woolgathering today, I told myself sternly. Keep your mind on the
job. The rector was already disillusioned. I had to make good, excel at
something to win back Conrad's faith in me.

The congregation sat huddled in the cold, damp pews of Saint Nicholas.
Shivering at the pipe-organ, I pulled out the requisite stops. The first two
hymns went well, but in the third I lost count and began another verse
while the *Amen* was being sung. The rector was sorry but he felt obliged
to find another organist. I took my five shillings, mumbling regrets, straddled
my bicycle, and started home, scattering tears to the four winds.

Conrad was still at the breakfast table, now reading a Quaker ancestor's
letter aloud to the three J's. I hesitated to interrupt him, then asked him
to step into the kitchen and close the door.

"I'm not surprised," he said when I told him what had happened. "With
your chronic incompetence and carelessness, you're bound to mess up
everything."

I stared at him in disbelief, shocked by his rebuff. "You don't realize
what this job meant to me," I said. "I wanted so much to succeed, to feel
like somebody, and make friends . . ."

"Then why don't you organize your life? Why do you keep failing in
everything you try? You should be earning at least $500 a month, consid-
ering your talents." Conrad was seething with impatience. "Now pull
yourself together, for Christ sake. Making a big scene over a five-shilling
job, especially with the children here . . ." His voice cut like a knife.

I began preparing dinner, thankful that Olive didn't come Sundays. The
round of beef in the oven, I tackled the Yorkshire pudding. Squidge kept
circling me, in a frenzy for his liver and lights. I set his dish on the floor,
straightening up so suddenly that I rammed my left eye against the sink
edge. My cries of alarm brought Jane. She called Conrad. He applied cold
compresses while John ran for the doctor. Jane and Joan hovered nearby,

expressing concern as I leaned against the cupboard, holding the compress to a bleeding eye.

The doctor said, "You were fortunate. A fraction of an inch lower and you would have lost that eye."

Conrad saw him to the door, then glanced at the bandage and said caustically, "I almost believe you don't *want* to see."

Perhaps so. I had a classic case of accident proneness, breaking the record in clumsiness, stumbling, falling, bruising, and scalding my arms. Another form of self-hatred, like Conrad's ferocious animosity?

My eye looked less like a poached egg by the time I resumed work on Laura's memoir. In Saint John's Wood I brooded over our misfortunes and conjugal strife. Our tiffs became so violent at times that I had to close the windows. As a rule I pulled my punches, fearing to break Conrad's spectacles while giving him ample cause for anger. I still carry a scarred upper lip, souvenir of a scuffle with him after my rudeness to a pretty acquaintance. His caressing voice and tender glances were so at odds with his treatment of me. I couldn't see the central fact, as did discerning friends who loved him uncritically, recognizing a passionately driven individual cruelest to himself. I still judged him by ordinary standards.

In February it was Conrad's turn to lose his job, as foreign correspondent for the *New Yorker*. His London Letter on the death of the King caused a rumpus that upset the editors. George V had died at Sandringham on January 20 and his oldest son, the Prince of Wales, had begun his brief reign as Edward VIII.

It was not to be a good year. Word came that my oldest brother had been committed in New England. Margaret had long worried about Joe's aberrations. The news revived fears of ending my days a melancholic, like my father's sister. Was my family correct in saying that all my troubles stemmed from having deserted God?

Malcolm Lowry came early in the summer, a wretched, disoriented mortal, in disfavor with Conrad, *his* marriage also on the rocks. They had interminable arguments about Jan, Malcolm driving Conrad to fury by his "mooning and fretting over that hardboiled little bitch." Meals were eaten in strained silence, angry dialogues echoed through the house. Their "beautiful friendship" had worn threadbare.

I again nursed hope for our sick marriage when I heard that Joan would be spending the summer with us. The young should have shamed us into behaving like adults. Conrad leased the workmen's club next door, intending to install a printing press, but after conferring with Ed Burra, Paul Nash, and the Knights he decided to open an art gallery for a summer exhibit, rounding up about twenty well-known artists in Rye and elsewhere. I was to act as treasurer and receptionist for this project.

I felt greatly restored and more sanguine after returning from a bicycle tour through Normandy with Catherine Opie. Among my souvenirs was a limerick I wrote which drew guffaws from Malcolm and a tepid smile from Conrad.

> On a rainy day in St. Lo,
> An old lady had need to go,
> So she squatted, alert,
> To perform under her skirt,
> Her umbrella above instead of below.

Olive's successor, May, helped me with the spring cleaning. She was a ray of sunshine, the nearest thing to matchless Jenny, with the charm of an old-fashioned valentine. One morning while weeding out garments, I remembered the hectic rush to the laundry to retrieve Conrad's wallet. Now, searching the jacket pockets of his tweeds, I found not money but a letter. It was signed "Elizabeth." His sister? His former mistress in Oxford?

Neither, as I learned, skimming over the sentences with growing panic. ". . . My love is for you. . . . I will come this evening at eight. . . . I could copy your name from a cheque that faces me each week, but would like your hand . . ." The red-haired bank clerk? My heart began fibrillating. Was it carelessness, or had he left the letter where he knew I might find it? How long had this been going on? Was that his secret, "too important" to tell?

I heard the grandfather clock below strike eleven. The front door slammed after a tempestuous outcry from Malcolm. I folded the evidence. Tear it up and say nothing? Face the inevitable, since our marriage was finished anyway? No, I couldn't ignore this. The time had come for a showdown.

Downstairs I closed the kitchen door on May, then called Conrad into the front hall.

"What's up?" He came carrying a martini.

I confronted him with my discovery. He brazenly denied it. "You must be off your rocker." I read a few phrases aloud: ". . . you know, dear, dear Conrad, I do see something of your miserable life, and it's unfair . . ."

His face flushed. "It's all true," he said. He stood under the green witch's ball looking grotesquely flattened out. "I told her how unhappy I was with you and that I couldn't communicate any more."

"Your hypocrisy floors me," I said. "How does one communicate with a block of granite?" With sad wonder I recalled phrases in his letters upholding chastity between lovers and married couples. "Everything nice you ever said to me was a lie. Just stringing me along. I'm expected to condone your affairs, but not look at another man. I'm to stay put wherever you leave me, then come running when you whistle. It's all right for you to read my diaries, but when I read your letters, Oh Lord, what pious reproaches."

"What's the use of arguing? You just don't understand me," Conrad said, "never have, and never will. We're psychologically bad for each other."

"Ten years ago you said we were made for each other. Four years ago you begged me never to leave you no matter what . . ." I tucked the letter in my blouse, trying to stop trembling. "You always did insist on running this marriage, and now you've run it into the ground."

"Oh Jesus," he said, "the fact is I'd have kicked you out long ago but for sheer inertia."

"In that case, I'll save you the effort." With a sense of drowning in icy water, I started upstairs.

My bag packed, I returned to the front hall, got into my coat, opened the door, and was halfway up Mermaid Street when he called me. Back I trotted like a dog summoned by its master.

"I may have flirtations, but I'll never fall in love again," he said stiffly. "I'm too old. Divorce would break up my life."

What about *my* life? The sting of rejection made me reckless. "You once said a woman could share a man but a man could never share a woman. Well, I'll never share you with another woman."

He shrugged and left the house.

> And that grin, the grin of the unfaithful,
> the secret grin of self-congratulation
> facing the mirror at midnight, when all has gone well,
> when the returning footstep has not been heard,
> nor the errand guessed, nor the change of heart perceived,
> nor the eye's secret discovered, nor the rank perfume
> smelled on hand or mouth
>
>   that grin like a flower
> which opens voluptuously amid poisons and darkness
> at the mere sight of itself as if to say
> courage you have done it let now bravado
> match in its brazenness the mercurial deception
> go forth and kiss the cheek of her you have deceived
>
> you too have known this and failed to be ashamed
> have brazened it out and grinned at your own grin
> holding the candle nearer that you might see
> the essential horror.
>
>   *Time in the Rock*

This time there would be no reconciliation, as in Cambridge where our love was reignited. The waste of psychic energy, being cast off like someone with a pestilential disease, after giving yourself body and soul to building a stable marriage. That a single human being out of billions should mean everything in the world was a terrifying thought, the more so in an alien setting. Jeake's House was never home to me. "He'll break your heart just as he did Jessie's." Beatrice's prediction rang in my ears. And Dr. Llewelyn's. The captive adjusting to the captor through uncharted years of *diablerie* and madness had grown to love her chains. Please be cruel to me, I can't bear kindness. A great love warranted great sacrifices, he told my sister-in-law. Well, I wasn't indestructible or a tower of strength, like Frieda Lawrence or Aldous Huxley's wife.

After sending May off to the cleaners with Conrad's suits, I stood in the kitchen, turning the gas jets on and off. Alone I couldn't carry it off. Malcolm, a fellow-victim, might agree to a pact. Had he returned? I couldn't remember. In a daze I went through the house, calling him. No answer. The impulse faded as he remained absent that day. Enough melodramatics. Stop sniveling and *do* something. The door's ajar. Conrad opened it for you.

47

I SHALL ALWAYS bless the art exhibit—a breather and respite that hot summer of 1936. It left me less time to brood. I sat next door near the entrance at a table heaped with sixpenny catalogues, keeping a sharp eye out for artful dodgers. "Do we pay now or later?" Now. "A bit slow, aren't you?" A bit rude, aren't you?

Officiating at the private viewing, E. F. Benson, then mayor of Rye, asked with a twinkle if Paul Nash's watercolor, *Skeleton*, was supposed to be surrealist. I said glibly, "No, it's quite conventional compared to those in his London exhibits." I had bought a coq-feather cloche for the occasion but forgot to invite the Rye Art Club. Although I assured the president that it was an unintentional oversight, nothing invidious, she said huffily, "I suppose it was really because you didn't want us."

Day after day I sat knitting and listening to giggles, shrieks, groans, and curses. Ed Burra's surrealism provoked the most acrid comments. "Revolting . . . look at that limb in *Two Women*, like a sausage . . ." "Any child could have done better . . ."

"What do you mix your paints with?" one irate female asked. "Spit," Ed replied, leering. "That's just what those daubs look like," she said, sotto voce, turning her back on him.

Mrs. Burra took umbrage at the gallery director for refusing to put her son's sixth painting in the balcony, a Laura Knight watercolor preempting it. (To allay suspicion of American profiteering, the shilling catalogue cover carried a Laura Knight reproduction.) As Ed's mother struck off Laura's name, her husband announced loud and clear, "I really detest some of her work," then smirked, saying blandly to me, "I hope you haven't been listening, Mrs. Aiken."

"No, Judge Burra," I said, perjuring my soul, "I've been busy adding up the cash."

Joan, who had come for the summer, reported a retired Indian colonel at a tea party boasting of having outwitted "the lady cashier." He had the grace to blush when he learned I was her stepmother.

Joan had come by the noonday bus from Sutton, arriving at tea time. I never realized how much she missed a sitdown meal at that hour—such a polite little girl. She reminded me of my self-effacing sister. I know she was lonely without Jane and John. She spent her mornings at a local school, her first one, since Jessie taught her at home until she was ten. Afternoons hung heavy on her hands. Sometimes we took the tiny tram across the marsh to the Camber Sands, bathing when the tide wasn't out of sight, or we would fish for mackerel, up to our middle with nets if the seines were being dragged in, after which came the hot two-mile walk back to Rye.

A mutual friend revealed Jessie's true feelings toward me: "She couldn't bring herself to utter your name over the phone." I understood that perfectly (in fact, I later felt the same way about Conrad's third wife, Mary Hoover). At any rate, Jessie sent me a warm, appreciative note later that summer. For Joan's sake, and Malcolm's, Conrad and I agreed on a temporary truce, though a precocious ten-year-old would of course sense the tension. Hearing voices raised in anger was frightening, something unknown in her stepfather's house. In later years Joan said that she was greatly upset by my furious hysterical expostulations and Conrad's soft-voiced but deadly rejoinders.

John's refusal to go to America with Conrad in mid-August touched off a terrific row. When I asked whether I could go in his place, Conrad said curtly, "It's nothing to do with me. If you can get the house ready in time—but there's Joan, and the art show. I can't really afford it, I'm already borrowing heavily."

"And I'm dead beat. I've earned a change," I said.

"Selfish and unrealistic as usual. Can't you get it through your thick head that there's a war looming and it's John's last chance to escape conscription? I might still persuade him to take out papers in the States.

You're not a male of military age, twenty-two. You could get back to America easily if war was declared. He couldn't leave England at all."

I felt *he* was being unrealistic in hoping that John would switch to Harvard from the time he started University College of London, in 1932, leaving behind his family, friends, and business prospects as a chemist. Resentments festered, sapping our vitality; hearts and minds were closed.

"Oh God, why is life so difficult?" My outcry, while pedaling to Peasmarsh one Sunday, startled a crow, its "Caw, caw" mocking me. As usual I was leaning on others, bound for the Farrs to let off steam. I simply had to talk to somebody, and Peggy could bail me out of the blues, although this time matters had gone beyond that stage.

"What's wrong, Clarissa?" she asked, over tea and crumpets.

I wound up my recital of woes to her and Bill with a lament. "Why did I have to find that accursed letter? I felt so cheap showing it to him."

"The truth would have come out sooner or later," Peggy said, vigorously. "It's time you stopped crawling to Conrad. You must know by now that a poet pumps the vitality and will-to-live out of everyone he touches. I remember when I first learned that musicians were nothing like the music they played, that artists were not as fine as the pictures they painted, and that writers of every type fell far below the standard of things they wrote. It was such a relief that Bill was a hardworking chap who practiced the ethics he upheld."

Ah yes, the disparity between the artist and the *Mensch*! Conrad a frightened poet with waning powers? Possibly. "Suppose I meet this Elizabeth in the street," I said. "Do I cut her or give her a sweet smile? And suppose she's pregnant?"

"That's Conrad's problem," said Bill, lighting his pipe. "You've got enough to handle." He shrugged when I reminded him that Conrad had suffered too much too early. "There are many kind, decent, humane people who have suffered in childhood. They don't all make life unbearable for us."

"Chins up, ducky." Peggy filled my teacup. "What happens happens, and it's punishment enough. Don't be chivvied into doing anything reckless. You've been through the wringer and aren't fit for much now, but you're important, have a great deal to give. Whatever you decide about Conrad, we'll support you. Meantime why not nip out and buy yourself some glamorous clothes? You'll be amazed at the difference in your morale. Cheerio," she added as I left, "now remember, no more *crawling*."

Bicycling back to Rye I felt less stranded. What was the use of hanging on to a sick love? Sex had tapered off with friction and boredom. I no longer fed Conrad's genius. I had turned into an avenging angel. He felt threatened in his masculine pride. And yet I couldn't or wouldn't believe that he was through with me.

The week before he sailed was chaos. The translation of the Spanish novel had to be finished, we expected three paying guests that weekend, and I was busy next door. As I told the Farrs, I felt bad leaving Joan on her own so much, but my time was not my own. Except for spending a few nights in London with Margaret, I had a full schedule. It wasn't cricket expecting May to do the housework and the cooking, I pointed out to Conrad. Then, hitting a raw nerve, I said, "If John or you would help occasionally . . . but, like you, he only shows up at mealtime."

"You'd better keep your opinions of the children to yourself or you can get out right now," he said. "Your jealousy of John has damaged my feelings for you more than you'll ever know." While I blinked at that neat twist, he added, "You succeeded in preventing him from going to the States and I'll never forgive you for that."

"What are you talking about? John decided for himself," I said. "Even if I had wanted to influence him, I couldn't have. He told you repeatedly that he chose London University. I remember asking Grayson McCouch not to interfere in your relationship."

"I'm talking about *now*." The basilisk stare shook me in spite of my indignation. "Taking John's side against me was the meanest and lowest thing you've yet done. You've become a regular virago. I'm damned sick of it."

"I'm no virago *or* your scullery maid," I said, and with that I slapped his face, astonishing us both. "And don't start analyzing me again, peeling off layer after layer until there's nothing left of me. You make it impossible to be decent."

"A hell of a way you have of showing your devotion." He turned crimson. "You're putting more distance between us with every word."

The morning I accompanied Conrad to the boat-train I thought of Peggy's advice, wishing I *could* crawl. Walking on chilblained feet was like treading on live coals. The cardboard wedged in my sandals had become dislodged, and Conrad winced as a passerby snickered to his friend, "Must be something new in footgear." We had slept like two stone effigies in our hideous Bloomsbury hotel. The room conveyed something of the macabre atmosphere in his short story "Mr. Arcularis."

At least I hadn't alienated John. "What's this about being hateful to me, Jerry?" he replied, when I asked forgiveness. "You know very well the boot's on the other foot. I could kick myself, remembering certain days . . ."

"All aboard!" The guard's bellow resounded through the cavernous Waterloo Station. With a hasty kiss and a constrained "I'll write you," Conrad got into his compartment. Doors slammed, the locomotive pulled out with its inimical high shriek and gathered speed. *Clickety-clack, clickety-clack, he'll never come back, he'll never come back . . .*

48

IN RYE AGAIN, I found an invitation from Hilda Ziesser, a former *au pair*, to spend a few weeks at her parents' pension in Bavaria. It was a rare opportunity to see the country of my origins, to trace my ancestry, and perhaps a voyage of self-discovery might yet save our marriage. Surely Conrad wouldn't mind.

After our clashes, the conciliatory tone of his letters seemed a bit odd. On the *Europa* he had as usual scraped up an acquaintance with an attractive girl, found Redvers Opie on board, and learned that the ship's barber kept a fine supply of "French letters." He had seen his protégé in Manhattan, a thinner, better-balanced Malcolm Lowry. Malcolm's wife, Jan, was working nearby on a newspaper. They intended trying their hand at film scripts in Hollywood. After that, Mexico. Conrad was negotiating with Scribner's for a two-year advance of $4,000 on his autobiography, *Ushant*.

A note from Jessie thanked me for Joan's summer visit and for coping with an ink-stained frock. The bottle had leaked after I packed her things— my fault.

Dear Mrs. Aiken:
   It was kind of you to bother when you must have had dozens of things to do. Half the ink came out easily, due to your thoughtfulness in keeping the spots moist. So 1000 thanks for looking after her so well.

Dear Jerry,
   I arrived safely and without being sick! The Big Scene about the ink was nothing worth telling really . . . I hope Squidge hasn't eaten the kitten yet.
                                                                          Love,
                                                                          Joan

The art show closed and I decided to accept Hilda's offer. After emptying my piggy bank I booked passage to Germany, cabled Conrad, then wrote him the itinerary, asking for our joint passport. Travel was my doctor's prescription in part for nervous exhaustion. "Nervous exhaustion my foot," he shot back. With war imminent, the idea was insane. If I needed a change, why not Malvern? Gallivanting around the world whenever he went away on business demonstrated once more that I could manage for myself, and maybe this was once too often. Unless I gave my solemn word of honor that I would never again abandon my duties to Jeake's House out of whim and spite, he wrote, he would divorce me at once.

On what grounds? I preferred the risk to eating humble pie. If I couldn't please him, I could at least please myself. "Have a good fling," Peggy Farr said enthusiastically. May, my trusty daily, would board Squidge and keep an eye on the house.

Along the way I tried to forget our problems, shaking off dejection and brushing up on German, my *Kindersprache* so airily renounced thirty-odd years earlier. Breaking my journey in Cologne and again in Heidelberg for a day's sightseeing, I found everyone friendly, the danger to tourists nil. A few swastikas were visible, *"Heil Hitler"* commonplace and Jew-baiting blatant in graffiti—*"Juden Nicht Willkommen!"* The Nazi motto, "Strength Through Joy," seemed more positive than the one I was raised on, "Through sorrow, joy," and I couldn't believe that those wholesome looking, smiling German children were being trained to kill.

My ancestral search seemed doomed. I hunted for my maternal grand-mother in Trier on the Moselle instead of going to Châlons-sur-Marne, seventy-five miles from Paris—misinformed from the start. I should have checked with my aunts in Chicago before going off half-shod. However, the trip through central Germany all but compensated me, especially the *gemütlich* atmosphere in trains.

I remember a family scene in one coach, the father in shirtsleeves fan-ning his tanned, shaven head, his Frau's tongue going lickety-split, her periodic *"Nicht wahr"* startling me like a hat-pin jab. One passenger—a middle-aged man, appropriately enough—read Heine's poems, whisking me back to the third grade where we learned *The Lorelei* in German. That legendary siren lurking among the rocks on the Rhine halfway between Bingen and Coblenz enticed sailors and fishermen to their destruction while she brushed her hair with a golden comb. Little did I know that, on growing up, I would be tagged as Lorelei Two in Conrad's lexicon.

In Munich the *Dienstmann* threw my bag through an open window to ensure a seat. En route to Bad Reichenhall the locomotive labored steadily uphill, passing diminutive stations painted bisque with blue shutters, life imitating musical-comedy art, scarlet geraniums and white petunias in window boxes. At each station a toy-sized guard held up a white flag on a stick. I waved, tempted to blow kisses.

Bad Reichenhall was a paradise of lakes and mountains; Conrad and Paul should have come along, for it contained a famous spa for treating catarrh and asthma. A comely girl in dirndl and apron ran gracefully along the train, waving and gesturing forward. "So happy to see you again, Clarissa!" she exclaimed, her dark eyes shining, the same lovable, exuber-ant Hilda I remembered so fondly. Her bear hug knocked off my hat. She laughed when I said, *"Ich hab Heimweh."* If only time reversed itself.

Chattering like schoolgirls on vacation, we started off in a pony cart to her parents' pension, a rococo frescoed dwelling with numerous balconies. It stood close to the Austrian border. Hilda joked with the border guards about the yellow onions the peasants hung on the barbed wire to dry. Her handsome parents put me at ease immediately. Strongly anti-Nazi, their traditional "*Grüss Gott*" prevailed over "*Heil Hitler.*"

These wholesome, God-fearing people made me realize how far I had strayed from my beginnings. The mountain air was so fresh and clear, I spent most of the time outdoors. Under a shade tree bordering the Weisbach, a brook sparkling with white pebbles, I read Conrad's ominous decrees and answered them, tears blistering the note paper. Despite my determination to put him out of mind pro tem, every sensation I had referred back to him—his charm, genius, flashing anger, the consummate poet wasted on me, the intellectual I feared, the romantic I disappointed, the puritan I affronted.

Hilda divined an undercurrent of anxiety and melancholy, though she knew nothing about our troubles. She put herself out to distract me. In fair weather we bicycled, knapsacks on backs, my little Leica and diary recording the scenery. We climbed the foothills of the Bavarian Alps, rode up the *Predigstuhl*, visited the *Statsopfer* and Mozart's birthplace in Salzburg, and sampled the cafés Robert Nichols raved about.

One day we made the hour-long climb to Hitler's stucco chalet at Berchtesgaden. Cars and motorcycles roared by, an endless procession, Hermann Goering waving from his Mercedes-Benz and being cheered wildly. Nothing about that fenced-in complex indicated an impenetrable fort with bomb-and-gas-proof cellars, or anti-aircraft guns fixed in nearby mountain slopes. "Keep moving," the Schutzstaffel barked from sentry boxes, as crowds milled around, cameras and field-glasses trained on the Berghof. I saw faces that conjured up pilgrims at Lourdes expecting miracles.

My three-week holiday was cut short by a letter from Conrad implying that his return was contingent on mine. So I cabled that I was leaving in a few days and would stay with Laura. The Knights had just returned from Malvern. I was eager to read Laura's published memoir, *Oil Paint and Grease Paint*, since I'd had a small part in creating it.

We exchanged summer experiences in London, while Laura nursed me through a bout of the flu, grieving meantime about our marital rift. "Tell Conrad not to be such a blooming idiot," she said, sighing. "You might as well have stayed in Bavaria." Instead of Conrad, I found another cabled ultimatum: "Your reply critically unsatisfactory unless you profoundly realize and regret irresponsibility situation hopeless."

He had threatened divorce before. We would weather this squall, too. But I scuttled that hope when his next letter told me that he was living in Charlestown, Greater Boston, and that his landlady, an artist named Mary Hoover, was painting his portrait. He had turned down a $3,000 job on the Boston *Herald* book page, expecting to earn more by writing a guide-book for the Federal Writers' Project. He proposed that I close Jeake's House, join him in New York in early November, and go with him to Savannah, his birthplace and the scene of his parents' tragedy.

I might have said yes to all this if I hadn't found a backlog of abusive, threatening letters in Rye (such poor timing on Cupid's part), which caused a growing suspicion that Mary Hoover was more than his landlady.

49

RYE SEEMED BLEAK and barren after Bavaria, Jeake's House partly stripped of the Virginia ivy (my doing). I missed the autumn coloring in a town void of trees. Before reading Conrad's letters, I struggled with the bogie in a dank, arctic kitchen. The anthracite stove was going full blast in the dining room when I sat at the typewriter to answer his charges of being irresponsible, spiteful, extravagant, et cetera. It was all my fault, he said; later he reversed himself, telling Laura that I wasn't to blame, it was simply that our natures were incompatible. I was to pay a price for that Bavarian binge, but I never regretted what was to be my second and last glimpse of Europe.

"My dear husband (if you know the meaning of the word)," I wrote. "Set down your glass to read a letter long overdue.

For ten years you registered disapproval of me, being as hateful to me as you were loving to the children. The arrogant tone of your cables and letters suggested I was your servant, and had taken a lover. A fool I was for not doing just that, as two good friends of yours recommended. Irresponsible? Let the record speak. I've had the entire care of this eleven-room house for six years, with a man but not a helpmate around. It was NOT spite or seeking revenge that sent me to Germany. I had long dreamt of doing so. Yours was the revenge in spoiling my vacation, trumping up war scares, family visitors, psychological harm and other bugaboos to deter me. You go completely crackers over separations . . .

Extravagance? Every penny of that trip I earned by my freelance work. You asked how I could have blown £130 in two months. I enclose a list of household expenditures. The Lady Almoner at Guy's Hospital was incredulous when told I couldn't afford 3/6 diathermy treatments for my spine. In December I go into the "charity ward." I've seen you through some pretty rough spots. As long as you were ill, you tolerated me; now that I'm unwell, we are "psychologically bad for each other." How can you, surrounded by love and admiration, be so petty and cruel to any human being?

If this is the letter you've been goading me into writing, as grounds for divorce, let me know. Should you consider a fresh start, I'll do my best to cooperate. In any case, I suggest that you get things off your chest before we meet. I can't take any more scenes, and so would appreciate your refraining from the usual dramatics and saying hurtful things, such as that I prevented John from going to America. The enormity of my "unforgivable" sin hasn't damaged John's friendship with me. In fact, we're thinking of sharing a flat in Hammersmith . . .

John's reactions surprised me not a little. He wrote:

If Cahoun is only trying to get you over to the States to discuss divorce, he's making his biggest mistake, because he won't get any one else in a hurry who'll be as good an influence on him, let alone as good a cook! So go only if you feel a divorce would benefit *you* (and I'm not sure it wouldn't, in the long run). I don't see why he might want you over there (forgive me), unless he knows he's going to remain there, or merely wants to chastise you at short range for darting off to Germany. Well, none of this boils down to anything. Perhaps the balance is slightly in favor of staying here (and I'm not merely trying to justify the fact that I'd very much like to have you stay here). He ought to define his attitude instead of making you play this harrowing guessing-game. And what do *you* want to do, and what do *you* want to come of it, Jerry? Because whatever you decide, don't let it be too much in his favour and not nearly enough in yours.

What I would have liked, of course, was to have the Conrad I once knew. Although Joan named me, decades later, as the wife who made him happiest, Rob said, "You had the worst of him. I told the three J's that you got the short end of the stick. You were the one he chewed on."

As word spread that I was holding the fort alone, more of Rye's "gentry" capitulated. Fragile, elderly Lady Tupper asked me to tea with the disarming remark, "I feel I've known you a long time." And Humphrey Ellis crossed the street to bring me a jar of red currant jam. An acquaintance of Margaret's urged me not to break up the home. "Christian Science failing, why not have an affair?" Peggy Farr advised me to insist on alimony and to make carbons of all my letters.

Conrad's response stressed the too-little-too-late theme. No use clinging to the children, he said, after complaining for years about dismal Rye and Jeake's House and after depriving him of the feeling of having a home to fall back on. Still, he admired much of my letter of denigration, inaccurate though it was—above all, the sensible idea that "maybe a divorce was the best way out for both of us." (Full Belly says to Empty Belly: "Be of good cheer." Easier to consider divorce from a love nest than from a house that had never wanted me.) But before he asked for a divorce, he said, "I want to be as sure as I can possibly be that you are going to be secure and self-sufficient and not too damned unhappy. I don't dare face the responsibility of asking for my freedom if it's going to leave you terribly and perhaps fatally at a loss—and something of that kind, owing alas to your genius for inaccuracy and incompetence and so on, I very much fear."

Therefore he advised me to return to the States, where we could "discuss the thing in all its ramifications" and where I would be in a familiar environment among friends who would help me. He hoped that we would manage the thing wisely. "And I want to add that I'm dreadfully sorry for all the hard things I've said and done, but also that I don't feel truly guilty about them—the real trouble has lain in a deep psychological disagreement between us, and that, I fear, there is no mending."

I agreed that reconciliation attempts were useless, considering the report I had heard of his having an affair with Mary Hoover. "They are obviously lovers, very much in the public eye," said Catherine Opie, returning from the States. "This eliminates one more reason for my crossing," I wrote him. "Don't worry about the fatal consequences of divorce on me. Thanks to your long neglect, the change will be comparatively painless. . . . I will manage somehow despite my 'incompetence.' But until you decide whether you intend bringing a third bride here, I suggest you cable authority to sell the furniture and objets d'art. Meanwhile, please send cash. I'm very low . . ."

Waiting for his answer, I couldn't settle down to anything. Article writing was a farce. The piano and harpsichord remained untouched, lest the floodgates open. My bravado gradually collapsed as December approached.

The Nicholses' marriage had also foundered. Rye on the rocks! I hardly knew which one to feel sorrier for, Norah, thin and haggard, or Robert, again hospitalized. "I'll be thinking of you, Clarissa, and most anxious to hear how you get on. Count on me if you want anything." Gentle Norah. She would soon be moving to Aldeborough, Suffolk, later to be honored by Benjamin Britten writing his opera *Peter Grimes* in her cottage.

The Nashes were still together, Paul gravely ill. "I'm very concerned for your future," said Margaret, when I saw her in London. "I wish I could have done more for you. You loved Conrad dearly and helped him very much when he needed you most. You should never have had so rough a time. Try not to be hurt or bitter or sink into despair."

The days went by with monotonous sameness, shortened somewhat by efforts to keep dry and warm. Continual warnings came over the BBC of low-pressure systems from the Hebrides, but no bulletins about the royal scandal until early December, when it appeared that a crisis was near and that the King might have to choose between the throne and Wallis Simpson. On the third of December she fled to the south of France.

I had in the meantime entered Guy's Hospital in London for more treatments, but was back in Rye by the time Conrad's cable of the fifth arrived, ending a fortnight's suspense. He had dispatched the cable from Savannah. "Yes," it read, "though your welfare still my primary concern I do want to marry Mary but will borrow funds come to England immediately to discuss arrangements if you prefer nevertheless still think your coming here better."

As our neighbors handed me the mail, curious eyes probed when I unfolded the yellow slip. "Anything wrong?" I shook my head, forcing a smile, asked the Mortons to phone May to come the next day, thanked them, and picked up Squidge and fled.

That evening a Channel gale transformed Rye into an Edgar Allan Poe nightmare. Rain slashed the windows and flooded the kitchen, the wind howled down the bogie chimney, and lights began to flicker. I scurried from one room to another, trying unsuccessfully to weatherproof windows and doors, then mopped the kitchen floor, started a fire in the drawing room, and ran a hot bath.

The copper geyser hissed and gurgled, steam peeling the Spanish posters further off the wall and obscuring the mirror, which was just as well. I couldn't bear to see my face. As I mulled over Conrad's cable, a tight inner knot was forming. How easy it would be to slash my wrists. The notion made my heart thump. *Was* bloodletting as painless as freezing to death? Blot out the thought. I pictured Jessie during *her* Gethsemane. She had survived, though Martin was there to comfort her.

I went back in the drawing room where the fire was burning. Squidge jumped on my lap. How often had I taken out my anger at Conrad by pushing his pet out of the way. Why had I hung on so long? I wondered. I know now that it was for a variety of reasons including pride, compassion, and masochism. Divorce was unthinkable even for a lapsed Catholic, especially one marrying a divorced man. I wanted to help make up for the loss of his children. He believed I could heal him. I was challenged by those who bet on an early smash-up. Above all, I loved him.

The difficulties of loving! Happiness might be four feet on a fender, I reflected, glancing at Conrad's empty chair opposite, but better two feet than perpetual friction. Huddled by the fire, I smoked one cigarette after another, wishing I could drink myself into a stupor, like Malcolm. How had other wives fared, living here over the past three centuries?

The windows rattled eerily. I waited out the storm by the fire, too scared to venture upstairs. Tomorrow I would take inventory and organize things. So many unfinished projects—the orange sweater, stories to revise, books to read, music to learn, my diary gathering dust. John would have to be notified that I was returning to the States, however reluctantly. A work permit was unlikely in England, and I couldn't bank on free-lance writing to support me.

When the gale subsided I doused the embers, swallowed some aspirins, brushed and braided my hair, added water to the chemical pack, and scuttled upstairs, teeth chattering, praying to be spared another *Angst* dream.

My prayers were unanswered. Next morning, my scalp prickling, I ran downstairs pell-mell to the front hall. Thank God, Harold's portrait of Conrad was still intact, untouched. I breathed a sigh of relief, so vivid was my nightmare of slashing it to ribbons with the carving knife.

50

TRUNKS, CRATES, CARTONS. The front hall looked like a warehouse after a cyclone. For five frenzied days I trudged up and down stairs, a sleepwalker unable to sort out things. "Will you be taking this, mum? Should I store that, mum?" May's soft voice and doe-like eyes would be haunting me. Seven years before, Jessie had cleared out everything. But because Conrad's plans were so vague I couldn't decide what to take, or leave, beyond my clothes, books, music, our correspondence, and negotiable items.

Laura had bought the harpsichord for triple what it cost me. That covered my passage on the *Queen Mary* third-class. For tideover cash, I hoped to sell some Japanese prints and the Chinese kakemono in Boston. As curator of textiles at the Museum, Gertrude Townsend might find a buyer. "Stay with me until you get your bearings," she had cabled—a timely poultice. I sent the forwarding address to my London solicitors.

Farewell notes went off to Humphrey Ellis and other friendly neighbors. I said goodbye to Squidge in the garden. May promised to find a good home for him. I had given her my Raleigh. The expressman came as I ate my breakfast kipper, then the taxi. She helped stow the luggage, and we embraced. I said I would miss her sadly but hoped she would find a nice household. "Don't fret, mum," she replied with a forlorn smile, hands clasped over her apron, "I will take care of everything, and write you."

Window curtains were hastily pushed back as the cab rattled over the cobbles. Their patience rewarded at last, those neighbors probably recalled Jessie's exodus with the children. On the train to London I tried to concentrate on a whodunit, but my mind was a pinwheel. *Tout casse, tout lasse, tout passe*. December 11, 1936, an unforgettable day—the King's abdication. And mine.

"The King, lady?" news vendors clamored at Charing Cross. I glanced at a headline: "The King's Today's Move." Edward had declared his intention of marrying Wallis Simpson. The man who had spent his life training to be King was giving up the throne. The initial ripple of dismay swelled and churned into a national crisis. Fellow-passengers on shipboard vilified the "American divorcée." As a compatriot, I felt guilt by association.

We gathered in the lounge to hear the former King's farewell speech over the amplifier. An awesome hush marked the historic precedent, the first voluntary abdication of a British monarch. ". . . I have found it impossible to carry the heavy burden of responsibility and to discharge my duties as King, as I wish to do, without the help and support of the woman I love . . ." There were moist eyes, including mine. That "dying fall" in his voice, so like Conrad's, drove me out on deck.

At the rail I stared at the water, black as my despair. Jump, coward. Funking it again, as when Malcolm couldn't be found in the house last June? A suicide pact would have embarrassed him. Well, now he was in Mexico with Jan, *his* marriage also in shreds.

Shivering with the cold, and panic-stricken, I waited for the deck to clear. No one would notice a passenger overboard, and all my troubles would be ended. No more failures to explain or apologize for, no "I-told-you-so's" from my detractors.

Suddenly a microphone voice startled me. "Mrs. Conrad Aiken, please come to the purser's office! Mrs. Conrad Aiken . . ." Minutes later I was handed a special delivery letter, several addresses crossed out. From Conrad? My heart leapt, then sank as I read the signature in my cabin. It was from Robert Nichols.

Dear Clarissa:

I tried to get in touch with you again, but though Stevie Smith gave me your London address, she didn't give me your phone number. I was glad to see you again though grieved to find you looking so distressed. I am the more surprised at Conrad's divagations, since he was always so jealous of you, tho' the Lord knows you gave him no cause—nothing but love and gratitude. You had kept your wonderful integrity. There were never more honest eyes than yours, and I am sure you have nothing to reproach yourself with. . . . For that is what destroys us, as I know to my cost. I who permitted the bitter disillusions of my existence and the evil of circumstances and oppressions of long illness to make me impatient with my lot and thus forfeit the companionship of a person so noble as Nonnie. I have paid for it, and the worst . . . is the knowledge that Nonnie paid for it. . . . But my burden is lighter than yours, since I have nothing to forgive. . . . I do not know how you feel about Conrad. It would be natural even in so fine a nature as yours to feel rancour. But it doesn't help. *Only forgiveness helps*. . . .

I know you have pondered a certain way out. Abandon all such thoughts. Indulgence in them . . . only weakens one, and the act itself only discourages others from their attempts to try and make something of what must be borne on their own pilgrimage.

And surely, dear Clarissa, the fact that you have nothing to reproach yourself with should be a cause of strength. . . . Maybe there is no justice in the universe, but if none our hapless plight is not vindicated by suicide since . . . whatever is unjust will not free the reproach of the victim's death. Well, bless you, dear little Clarissa. I will think of you often. Write me, who am your friend, Robert Nichols.

I will. And bless *you* for your providential letter. The friend whom Conrad considered mad as a hatter restored my sanity, shook me out of a morbid impulse. I would take inventory and get acquainted with myself.

My memory is a blank from the docking of the *Queen Mary* in New York to my arrival in Boston. A letter from Ed Burra awaited me in Gertrude's apartment. "I hear Conrad is expecting a happy event," he wrote. "It doesn't surprise me as I'm starting to get numb at the extremities owing to shocks over a long space of time & alcohol poisoning." If Ed's reading of the rumored "happy event" was the right one, it never came to pass, thereby spoiling Conrad's surprise for Rye's vigilantes. He had written Ed, "It would be fun to reappear a few years hence complete with the third Mrs. Aiken, by gosh—and perhaps a child or two. *That* would give them something to talk about . . ."

I went through the usual stages of "liberation," from bitterness to re-orientation of sorts. Initial negotiations had broken down. I suggested to Conrad that he get the divorce he so often threatened me with. "Cite mental cruelty." Rancor ran like sap in the spring. I wasted precious time dwelling on his *diablerie* instead of dredging up my faults. Easy for him to pen a magnanimous valedictory: "Now that it's all over, I like to remember the brighter side, the many good things you did for me; I had much happiness with you, loved you very much, and will always love you in many ways . . ."

I declined Mary's offer of a mattress while furnishing my modest flat on Beacon Hill. It smacked of collusion, besides connoting a lost mate. Conrad rightly said that cutting him in Harvard Square was plain silly. No doubt I felt myself the aggrieved partner, just as he did himself, but a friendly exterior was only civilized. He said Jessie hadn't behaved too well either. Did she also "fall out of step" with him? I wouldn't stoop to the stereotype about having squandered my best years on him, but I wasn't above fuming at being unloaded like excess baggage after saving his life.

"You have got to learn that you can't go about the world disregarding your husband's feelings. If love doesn't teach you that, maybe misfortune will," he once warned me. Apparently I hadn't yet met my quota of misfortune. For one dispossessed, forgiveness was the rub. His inconsistencies stymied me. In 1926 he told a friend, "The lady is a miracle, the only person since reaching adultery that I want desperately to marry." By 1936, "Mary was just the sort of woman I could fall in love with," and he had done so while he was angry and despaired of me.

My attorney advised striking Conrad off as a total loss. "You're much better off without him. He's bust and always will be. [Wrong guess: prosperity rewarded his efforts in later decades.] We had a peculiar conference that ended in friendly fashion. You say his charm will always save the day for him. I failed to see that charm, but he *was* worried about you."

Bob Linscott confirmed that. "He's frightfully knocked out, unable to think or work. He'll never be happy or at peace unless he knows you've made another life. His prospects are slim. Don't count on them."

I didn't. Before going to work at a summer job in the Catskills I began taking voice lessons, hoping for a radio job after broadcasting George VI's coronation over WRUL in May 1937. Divorce proceedings had been postponed by my attorney to give Conrad time to earn something. But his Mexican divorce scotched that. "We offered you all the money we had, and you refused it. So now we're spending it in Mexico, where we'll get married," he wrote me.

My father died in April of that year. I did not attend the funeral, unable to face the ordeal of a prodigal and neglectful daughter making amends. Guilt multiplied.

Conrad and Mary were already settled in Jeake's House by the end of the summer. This caused some matrimonial embarrassment, as my British solicitor noted, since the Mexican divorce was not legal in England. I could either file nonsupport papers in Boston, getting a judgment for an attachment in England, or else prefer charges of bigamy there. But what use was a captive spouse? I couldn't imagine walking into Jeake's House to claim my errant husband. A mutual friend who cut him in Rye was enlightened by five pages of "highly inflammable material" about me and my "poison-pen letters."

My divorce became final in 1938. In court, friends testified to his intimacy with Mary Hoover, an artist twenty years his junior. I was awarded $500 alimony. Within thirty minutes or so, our union had legally expired. I felt absolutely nothing—nothing until an Aiken fan damned me for "smearing a great poet's reputation by charging him with adultery."

51

THE FORMALITIES OVER WITH, what would I do with my freedom? For nearly ten years I went around in a fog, wasting time and postage on "hate" manuscripts, stories with downbeat themes and tragic endings, and usually about wronged women. "You're buried prematurely," friends lamented. How disinter a living corpse? Jane wrote me:

> If only I could have twisted some happiness out of your letter. I'll have to manage my way to America one day, if you aren't considering a return to England, and say what it is so difficult to write. I never even tried to tell you how very, very nice you made those visits to Rye and how grateful we are. No use saying how sorry I am that it had to end. Things always seem to be ending. I hope you have some happy memories and begin another life that leaves you not too much room for ghosts.

I couldn't get along *with* Conrad, now let's see whether I could manage without him. It took more than a new hat to restore my morale and start anew. After boasting of my competence, I *had* to make good. Establishing credit remained a big hurdle. "Who vouches for you?" No one. During my six years abroad, friends had scattered and my sister-in-law was over-burdened. "Sorry, madam . . ." I wore hand-me-downs, or else made my clothes. Frugality was no stranger. Even so, my struggles were minimal compared to the hardships of Depression victims. I never went hungry.

Divorcing a celebrity was doubly shattering. I could no longer bask in the reflected glory of a "complete man-of-letters," winner of several prizes. Conrad kept cropping up in print, interviewed and photographed with his third wife—publicity lacking during my tenure. They were much better off financially, too, with a summer home on Cape Cod, and his birth-place in Savannah converted into an art center.

Friends asked if I missed him. Of course. After ten years together, I would have missed the Abominable Snowman.

"I hope you get your Martin." John's wish for me never materialized. Perhaps his father spoiled me for other men. I remained single, my marriage "unfinished" until Conrad's death in 1973. However, I did not pine for him in "lonely chastity," but took lovers. I had two marriage proposals, one from a brilliant scientist and neurasthenic, which I refused, another from an Austrian sculptor, which I accepted out of sheer gratitude. I couldn't believe anyone would really want to marry me. Nor did he wish to, as it turned out. Posing as a starving artist, he relieved me of most of my savings, to raise funds for his girl friends' abortions.

Meanwhile, a treasured friend restored my *amour-propre*—William E. Borah, whom I met in 1939 while doing publicity at Poland Spring, Maine.

The isolationist senator from Idaho, then seventy-four, offered me balm.

He died the following January, the year I moved to Manhattan. He was often in my thoughts, as when I watched the United Nations building, from my fifth-floor walk-up, replacing the old slaughterhouses along First Avenue. What would he have said about "The Great Debating Society," as cynics called it?

During the war I combined free-lance writing with jobs in Washington, D.C., such as secretary's secretary to Jean Monnet, future "Father of the Common Market," at the British Supply Commission.

By 1948 identity problems and writer's blocks catapulted me into that procrustean bed, a Freudian analysis at New York's Mental Hygiene Clinic. Diary entries document weekly sessions at twenty-five cents a throw. I waited my turn among drug addicts, prostitutes getting VD shots, blind veterans, and bewildered old people. The nurse beckons. "Mrs. Aikens?" Aiken. Once plural, now singular. "Sit down, what's new, any dreams?" Dr. R's soothing baritone spurred me on to furnishing reams of dreams.

But these weren't enough clues. Everything had to be ventilated: internal conflicts, shameful thoughts, resentments—I didn't want to know what was wrong with me. Dr. R suggested I come to his office, where he could try sodium amytal. Patients paid $10 an hour and up. Since I was earning only $65 a week rewriting pulp features for Dell, I elected bimonthly visits of a half hour for a limited period.

Tears were shed, but few neuroses. Foul play by my subconsicous sabotaged the first trial with sodium amytal. By way of a posthypnotic suggestion, I kissed Dr. R's hand, pretending to have "gone under." He knew I was shamming. Why hadn't I told him the truth? The old placating instinct? Coquetting instead of probing? He was merely trying to measure my responses to suggestions, and at what level of consciousness. Deep resistance demanded more than 7½ grains, the maximum dose allowed in an office without hospital facilities.

He used to humor me by holding my hand after using sodium amytal. One day, asked to associate with the word *love*, I remained mute and horizontal for a costly half hour, grimly preserving my dignity. Once back at my typewriter I let loose with all the gutter words I knew. At the next session Dr. R scanned the list, asking why I hadn't come right out with it. I shrugged. A lady doesn't.

Later that day I wept copiously, free-associating into the mirror, afraid I'd never stop. "Isn't it a lovely face?" No, hateful. "You haven't asked to hold my hand," he said, implying that a man was of secondary importance to a narcissist. I could only love one who fed my romantic dreams, only recognize people as extensions of myself.

Apparently I had cooperated in life but not participated. I indulged in self-disparagement with no intention of changing. Actually, I wanted to be a woman, forming my own opinions, shedding influences that equated sex with sin. But Conrad's persistent "Face your mistakes" only put my back up. What about *his* faults? We both wore hair shirts, too inhibited to work out our sexual problems. Having fallen in love with romantic images, we made excessive demands on each other, expected compensation for childhood deprivations. Disillusioned, we piled up resentments.

Conrad was never really mine. I only borrowed him. Jessie had far more of a lien on him—she was a model wife and mother. True or not, I still question his taste in quoting Aunt Edith's prediction in *Ushant* ("Aunt Sibyl" in the book) that he would suffer terribly by losing the children for a "fly-by-night *ignis fatuus*." What he dignified by the name of love was an unfortunate infatuation which everybody but he himself admitted. His parting words had left me bemused: "If only you had given me a chance; you were the only woman for me. It's all your fault, and you know it."

Unfortunately, there's no training school for poets' wives. I learned too late that my real rivals were not women but the daemon—what Thomas Wolfe called "life's monstrous and utterly relentless enemy, and the best friend that mankind ever had." Dylan Thomas's wife, also deaf to poetry, was savagely jealous of such a powerful rival. His fans were "thieves of my love" to Caitlin. He attracted women most likely to be destroyed by him.

I would doubtless have lasted longer had I tried harder to relate to Conrad's poetry and been *replenished* by it. I would have sympathized with his "horrendous vision" had he confided his parents' tragedy at the outset. He knew far more about me than I did about him, and his family history contained the more vital statistics. His secrecy shortchanged me. The one clue he gave me in an early letter I overlooked: "If I offend you, forgive me; if I hurt you, remember that I love you; if I disappoint you, allow for me; if I fail you, don't abandon me."

I compared my experiences with those of other artists' wives and found the American male author to be a chauvinist magnified a thousandfold. His pleasures were taken mostly with male friends, his mate regarded as a sex object more often than not, and excluded from his intellectual life. Conrad, suppressing self-expression, attacked my diary. "He eats me," Malcolm Lowry complained, while devitalizing his own intimates. (The rift between the two ended in a break around 1954, I believe, *Ushant* partly to blame. Malcolm urged his second wife, Margerie, not to read the book, so deeply hurt was he by references to himself as Hambo.)

Hemingway referred to women as if they were a favorite breed of cattle. "You can always trade one healthy woman in on another," he wrote in a letter. "But start with a sick woman and see where you get. . . . If you leave a woman, though, you probably ought to shoot her."

We become sitting ducks by telling how it really was. Hemingway once threatened to kill Max Perkins if Scribner's published anything about him by any of his four wives. Caitlin Thomas's painful *Leftover Life to Kill* differed strikingly from Agnes Boulton's soft-pedaled memoir, *Part of a Long Story*. Even so, O'Neill's second wife was allegedly divorced for having said that O'Neill wanted a wife, mistress, mother, and valet.

What ordinary mortals can't swallow about artists is the ravaging of others. But the daemon will continue to destroy with impunity. Art, after all, is born of a colossal ego re-creating the world in its image. "A creative person has little power over his own life," said Jung. "Those pay dearly who have the creative fire." So do those who are closest to them.

Joan Aiken once said of her father, "He had an adverse effect on all three wives, although he would always be loved." Conrad's irascibility was logical. He had three strikes against him—he was a sensualist born of Puritan stock, he was traumatized at a crucial age, and he was a poet shackled by his daemon. With no parents to emulate, he turned misogynist, perpetuating his father's hatred and distrust of females. Unable to avenge himself on his mother, her fidelity in question, he made puppets of his women and humiliated them. He *couldn't* have confided in me. Not until I saw the link between sexual potency and creativity could I comprehend his jealous rages so deplored by his friends. Faithful to one mistress, his art, he did what any artist of integrity must do. Fearing impotence, he sought self-renewal in yet another love.

The notion that I could have healed Conrad was wishful thinking on his part and *hubris* on mine. Nothing could have shocked him out of that childhood numbness. He described just such a boy in his greatest short story, "Silent Snow, Secret Snow." During the sixties he learned that the family doctor in Savannah had been a drug addict, deaf to Anna Aiken's dilemma. Caught in a trap, she told one of the nursemaids shortly before being murdered that her husband had counted the sheets of stationery on her desk, checking to see whether she sent letters to the North. Behind the carping, cruel man I sometimes knew was the orphan "possessed" by his parents' murder-suicide, no more villain than his father.

52

M Y REMORSEFUL FRIEND Robert Nichols had the answer. Only forgiveness helps. *Tout comprendre, tout pardonner*. But along with Conrad I had to forgive *myself*—the appeaser, the clinging vine, the self-centered creature who once lapped up favorable mention of herself but howled like a wolf at unflattering ones, and resented the "scenes" Conrad created to give him a feeling of realism.

Many years passed before I learned to be my own good woman, developing confidence and belief in myself by reaching out to others. Insight came on leaden feet, serenity lagging behind. Guilt attached to the wrong things emerged as anxiety, bolstering a sense of unworthiness. "If I am not for myself, who will be for me?" Rabbi Hillel put it in a nutshell centuries ago. "If I am for myself alone, what am I?"

That my achievements fell far short of my potential was hardly surprising. After all, I had driven with the brakes on for most of my life.

"You survived and kept your identity," a friend remarked. "Don't belittle that. Going it alone in this world isn't easy." True. But I meant to enjoy life, too—and succeeded, according to a Boston psychiatrist whose wife played duets with me. He cut me down to size at a party. "You are very gifted, an artist, you play gratis and by ear, but you don't know where to draw the line between trained and untrained talent. What I like about you is your good humor. You have a nice ready wit and lots of sparkle. You're damned attractive, and the exotic in you attracts the exotic in me. Instead of talking about hedonism, you practice it. I admire that."

Just suppose that by some miracle Conrad had accepted my pleasure-loving nature. Life would have been a gift for him, instead of a burden. The impulse and capacity were there. "Laugh three times a day," he prescribed for Maurice Firuski as an anodyne. Allowed more latitude and treated as an equal, I might have nourished his ego and served his creature comforts beyond the line of duty. Instead of being punished for being "the *anima* type," I might have synchronized with that "lusty young fellow doubling as a Puritan and moralist," who "shuffled off women," and identified his wives as Lorelei One, Two, Three, while writing with relish about bawds, sybarites, and libertines. His dual personality intrigued critics—the ribaldry and repressed sexuality, the voyeurism, misogyny and the double standard. The high percentage of faithless wives in his novels and short stories would probably have gained more credence and weight had he divorced me for falling in love with another man.

As a mentor, Conrad was always available, his self-discipline and integrity admirable. By age eighty "America's most underrated writer" had published fifty titles: thirty-five volumes of poetry, five novels, a memoir, and several collections of short stories, essays, and criticism. Decades after we broke up I started reading his works and tributes, reminders winnowed out of my consciousness. I began to see what he was all about—his aspirations, motives, commitments, and the poet's dilemmas. Much of what he wrote came out of our relationship, but I wasn't ready to grasp it earlier. Now I feel a sense of discovery; many of his poems are illuminated by this latent understanding.

I had followed his career with interest, but had no contact with him until 1960. One morning in Manhattan on business I caught sight of a familiar figure in brown corduroy jacket and gray flannels striding along Fifth Avenue. Could it be Conrad? After twenty years I wasn't sure. Regardless, I ran after him, pocketing pride, heart thumping, calling him and attracting stares—the first time I ever ran after any man.

He spun around with a startled "Hello," then made an adroit recovery, asking what I was doing in New York. Promoting my book *Junket to Japan*, I said. The blue eyes flickered. We exchanged polite nothings against the roar of traffic. Why didn't he ask me to coffee somewhere? He had grown heavier and quite bald. "Enjoying poor health," he said wryly, when I remarked how well and tanned he looked. "I've had two heart attacks, walking pneumonia, and other ailments. But *you* haven't changed."

Had he intended that as a compliment? What did it matter? He was arranging passage to England, "and poor Mary is getting the Cape Cod house ready for sublet." Would I care to have him bring her to my apartment someday? I would be delighted, I said. The amenities over, we smiled, shook hands, and went our separate ways, he with that purposeful air of authority I once thought so captivating, I with mixed feelings, missing a chance to say the obvious—that living with a poet who touched so many lives had enriched my own life immeasurably. Still the enigma, I mused. It was my last glimpse of him.

Time does heal. I have no magic formula for growing old gracefully except perhaps to live in China, where the elderly are held in high esteem. While I miss the love and affection we all crave—the knowledge that we are important to someone—I manage to fare reasonably well. For a congenital "leaner" it's a salutary change, one's life-pattern becoming a game of solitaire. George Eliot reminds us that "the realm of silence is large enough beyond the grave." But everything in balance. Solitude isn't necessarily isolation. It depends on your outlook and inlook. Silence is indispensable in many areas of living, rests as important in a musical score as notes. I'm thankful for my piano and the writing. Every day begins and ends with music, and the curiosity of a teen-age journalist hasn't diminished with the years. There's not nearly enough time to do all I plan before the Grim Reaper beckons.

We all wish to be remembered for something. In the opinion of critics and familiars like John Aiken, Conrad did much of his best work during my tenure. He wished at one time to be remembered mostly for *Blue*

Voyage, *Ushant*, and the short stories "Silent Snow, Secret Snow" and "Mr. Arcularis." That is my only bid for immortality, nebulous though it be.

I would be happy to leave just a flower or a melody as proof of my existence on earth. In the meantime I'm learning contentment from my cat, Mouser.

Index